T0321320

The Lives
of
Lake Ontario

McGill-Queen's Rural, Wildland, and Resource Studies Series

Series editors: Colin A.M. Duncan, James Murton, and R.W. Sandwell

The Rural, Wildland, and Resource Studies Series includes monographs, thematically unified edited collections, and rare out-of-print classics. It is inspired by Canadian Papers in Rural History, Donald H. Akenson's influential occasional papers series, and seeks to catalyze reconsideration of communities and places lying beyond city limits, outside centres of urban political and cultural power, and located at past and present sites of resource procurement and environmental change. Scholarly and popular interest in the environment, climate change, food, and a seemingly deepening divide between city and country is drawing non-urban places back into the mainstream. The series seeks to present the best environmentally contextualized research on topics such as agriculture, cottage living, fishing, the gathering of wild foods, mining, power generation, and rural commerce, within and beyond Canada's borders.

The Lives
of
Lake Ontario

An Environmental History

༒

DANIEL MACFARLANE

McGill-Queen's University Press
Montreal & Kingston • London • Chicago

ISBN 978-0-2280-2223-7 (cloth)
ISBN 978-0-2280-2224-4 (ePDF)
ISBN 978-0-2280-2304-3 (ePUB)

Legal deposit third quarter 2024
Bibliothèque nationale du Québec

Printed in Canada on acid-free paper that is 100% ancient forest free
(100% post-consumer recycled), processed chlorine free

This book has been published with the help of a grant from the
Canadian Federation for the Humanities and Social Sciences,
through the Awards to Scholarly Publications Program, using funds
provided by the Social Sciences and Humanities Research Council
of Canada.

We acknowledge the support of the Canada Council for the Arts.
Nous remercions le Conseil des arts du Canada de son soutien.

McGill-Queen's University Press in Montreal is on land which
long served as a site of meeting and exchange amongst Indigenous
Peoples, including the Haudenosaunee and Anishinabeg nations.
In Kingston it is situated on the territory of the Haudenosaunee and
Anishinaabek. We acknowledge and thank the diverse Indigenous
Peoples whose footsteps have marked these territories on which
peoples of the world now gather.

Library and Archives Canada Cataloguing in Publication

Title: The lives of Lake Ontario : an environmental history / Daniel
    Macfarlane.
Names: Macfarlane, Daniel, 1979- author.
Series: McGill-Queen's rural, wildland, and resource studies series ;
    17.
Description: Series statement: McGill-Queen's rural, wildland, and
    resource studies series ; 17 | Includes bibliographical references
    and index.
Identifiers: Canadiana (print) 20240314026 | Canadiana (ebook)
    20240314115 | ISBN 9780228022237 (cloth) | ISBN 9780228022244
    (ePDF) | ISBN 9780228023043 (ePUB)
Subjects: LCSH: Ontario, Lake (N.Y. and Ont.)—Environmental
    conditions. | LCSH: Ontario, Lake (N.Y. and Ont.)—History.
Classification: LCC FC3095.O57 M33 2024 | DDC 971.3/5—dc23

This book was designed and typeset by studio oneonone in
Minion 11/14

Contents

Figures

Acknowledgments

This book began as a combined effort between myself and Colin Duncan. Though Colin ultimately decided to step away from co-writing the book after his retirement, he shaped the end result in many ways. Some of his thoughts and ideas can still be found in the following pages, and he allowed me to draw on his knowledge in the form of interviews. He then read and commented on many aspects of the evolving manuscript. Moreover, one of the most enjoyable parts of creating this book was the time I spent at Colin and Ruth's place in Kingston, which included sailing on the lake with Colin.

I interviewed or conducted correspondence with several other people: Henry Regier, Mark Mattson, Shawn Micallef, and Steve Bertman. Henry and Mark also read drafts of the whole manuscript, while Will Knight, Lynne Heasley, Michael Twiss, and Rob Englebert read certain chapters. My deep appreciation to all of these folks, as their collective insights made this a better book. Any mistakes of fact or interpretation of course remain my own.

A sabbatical leave and an SFSA award from my institution, Western Michigan University (WMU), gave me the time and resources to write this book. I have been lucky to have many excellent colleagues and students at WMU in my home department, the School of Environment, Geography, and Sustainability (SEGS), especially my colleague Lynne Heasley, who has been a great friend, supporter, and collaborator.

Even though COVID prevented me from taking full advantage of the opportunity, I thank Jennifer Read and the Graham Sustainability Institute at the University of Michigan for a visiting fellow position during my sabbatical. I also want to acknowledge the many colleagues and friends from other organizations that I am lucky to be part of: the Network in Canadian History and Environment (NICHE), the International Water History Association, the American Society for Environmental History, the Canadian Historical Association, and the Bill Graham Centre for Contemporary International History. I remain grateful for the ongoing support from former doctoral and postdoctoral supervisors: Serge Durflinger, Norman Hillmer, and Nancy Langston. Just as I was completing this book, my first academic mentor, John Courtney, passed away; I likely would have not pursued a career in academia without him.

Parts of chapter 8 of this book were previously published as "Plan 2014: The Historical Evolution of Lake Ontario–St. Lawrence River Regulation," *Canadian Water Resources Journal/Revue canadienne des ressources hydriques* 43, no. 4 (2018): 416–31. That article was co-written with Murray Clamen, with whom I also co-edited a book on the International Joint Commission (IJC), and I thank him and the journal for permission to reuse some of our collaborative material.

I made use of many different archives and libraries for this book. I want to express my admiration for the archivists, librarians, and staff members at the Hydro-Electric Power Commission of Ontario, the IJC, the Library and Archives Canada, the Archives of Ontario, the New York State Archives, and the US National Archives and Records Administration II. This book is in many ways the logical progression of several of my prior book projects, and indeed draws upon them in spots; I therefore want to thank all those who assisted me with the research I conducted for previous books on Niagara Falls, the St Lawrence Seaway and Power Project, and the IJC.

This was my second opportunity to write a book with McGill-Queen's University Press. I deeply thank editors Kyla Madden and Kathleen Fraser, who were both a pleasure to work with, as were Lesley Trites and the rest of the MQUP staff. I need to extend my gratitude to the copy-editor, Correy Baldwin, for improving the text. Jason Glatz of WMU again made a number of custom maps. I thank the editors (Ruth Sandwell, Colin Duncan, and Jamie Murton) of the McGill-Queen's Rural, Wildland, and Resource Studies Series for including my book in the series as well as for their feedback. The blind peer reviews arranged by the press also provided fair and constructive feedback.

My mother, Becky Macfarlane, continues to be very supportive in many different ways. Her adventurous spirit is an inspiration and it was a pleasure to be able to share some of our family excursions to Lake Ontario with her. My father, Bill Macfarlane, did not live to see this book, but his eastern Ontario roots are likely a big part of why I became so interested in the water history of this part of the continent back in graduate school. My in-laws, Bob and Vivian Thomson in Ottawa, provided a base from which I could frequently visit Lake Ontario (not to mention child care during some of those trips). Many other family members and friends have supported my work, whether directly or indirectly.

Above all, the most indispensable support has come from my wife, Jen, and our kids, Elizabeth and Lucas. I'm fortunate that I get to write books like this for a living, but I'm especially fortunate that I have them. Creating this book provided a convenient excuse for family trips to Lake Ontario, where we made memories that I'll always cherish.

The Lives
of
Lake Ontario

Figure 0.1
View of Lake Ontario from downtown Toronto. This picture is looking
east over the Toronto Port Lands and the Leslie Street Spit.

Introduction

On a summer stay in one of the many tall towers on Toronto's waterfront, I watched Lake Ontario change shades as the clouds rolled in. Steely grey with whitecaps as the storm approached, a roiling black when the squall struck, and variegated shades along a spectrum of azure and cyan after the sun re-emerged. At times like these, entranced by this resplendent waterbody, it is hard not to feel like it is *my* lake. Later, I came across a diary entry from the writer Anna Brownell Jameson, drafted almost two centuries earlier, that reflects much the same experience and sentiment, though unaided by a perch aloft a condo tower: "This beautiful Lake Ontario! – my lake – for I begin to be in love with it, and look on it as mine! – it changed its hues every moment, the shades of purple and green fleeting over it, now dark, now lustrous, now pale … every now and then a streak of silver light dividing the shades of green: magnificent, tumultuous clouds came rolling round the horizon."[1]

For anyone who has seen Lake Ontario from an aerial or elevated view – say the CN Tower or the Burlington Skyway – it is hard not to be struck by the water. H_2O as far as the eye can see. Folks new to the Great Lakes sometimes ask if there is a tide, or taste it to see if it is saltwater; in their defence, these "sweetwater seas" look like the ocean, the horizon a meeting of water and sky. Despite the ocean-like appearance, this is assuredly freshwater – "no salt and no sharks," as the bumper stickers say. Even though American water narratives disproportionately stress the scarcity of the wet stuff on account of the arid west, a dearth of water is hard to imagine when looking across any of the Great Lakes. Lake Ontario alone has more surface freshwater than all the US Southwest put together.

Whether Lake Ontario is viewed from a Toronto tower, an Oswego fort, a boat offshore of Kingston, or a cottage by Rochester, it is a view of abundance.[2] This liquid lavishness has fostered economic, cultural, and political systems built on expectations of abundance and growth. And this water wealth is more than partly responsible for the amity that has characterized the last two centuries of the Canada–United States relationship, promoting cooperation rather than the conflict that tends to result from scarcity. The border separating Canada from the United States, and Ontario from New York State, is out there in Lake Ontario, somewhere, equally invisible from up close or far away. To the water and the biotic life within, as well as the precipitation and climate above it, the border is imperceptible. That border, nevertheless, matters when it comes to Lake Ontario's environmental history.

From on high, Lake Ontario appears pristine. Get closer, and things look different: polluted water, fluctuating levels, impoverished biodiversity, imperilled habitat. Around a quarter of Canada's population, as well as its major financial and industrial sectors, now resides in the Lake Ontario watershed. Consequently, over time Lake Ontario has become seen as a working lake, a quotidian place to be used for utilitarian purposes like cooling power plants, dumping garbage, and flushing sewage. A side effect of abundance is that the resource can be taken for granted. Familiarity may not always breed contempt, but it can result in something just as destructive: indifference. Negligence, disdain, avarice, hubris – all have contributed to the abuse of Lake Ontario.[3]

The word "Ontario" may be derived from Kaniatarí:io or Oniatarí:io, Iroquoian terms that can be translated as "lake of shining waters" or "beautiful lake," though there remains debate about this etymology. Lake Ontario's surface is around 245 feet (76 metres) above mean sea level. This makes it the lowest of the five Great Lakes – and by an appreciable margin, as the water surfaces of the other Great Lakes, including Erie, are more than twice as many feet above sea level. To get from Lake Ontario to the level of the upper lakes, one has to climb over 300 vertical feet, no small task if you need to move a boat, let alone any cargo. Lake Ontario is also the lowest in the sense that it is the first of the Great Lakes encountered when moving up the St Lawrence from the Atlantic. This orientation explains how Lake Superior received its name: not from its obvious grandeur and size, which many might assume, but from the French word "supérieur" for upper, or highest, lake in the Great Lakes chain. Lake Ontario is the "lowest" of the Great Lakes in another way still: the extent to which it has been brought low by human degradation.

Lake Ontario seems, anecdotally speaking, the least appreciated out of all the Great Lakes.

The Lives of Lake Ontario is a transborder environmental and water history of the easternmost of the Great Lakes. I focus on how human societies and this inland sea have mutually altered and shaped each other. As the book's title suggests, Lake Ontario supports many different forms of life, human and more-than-human. It has been integral to the political, economic, industrial, and cultural lives of different societies: Indigenous nations, settler Euro-Americans, modern North American countries. People see the lake in multiple, often contradictory, ways: supplier of sustenance, quencher of thirst, receptacle of waste, font of industry, means of transportation, place of recreation, repository of identity, and so on. Because it has been so altered over time by both human and nonhuman forces, Lake Ontario itself has had, figuratively speaking, a number of different lives.

Environmental historians have not written a lot about the Great Lakes relative to their importance and magnitude: the Laurentian Great Lakes hold about 21 per cent of the world's surface freshwater, account for more than 90 per cent of North America's surface freshwater, and are home to almost 40 million people; if the Great Lakes basin was a single country it would constitute the third-largest economy in the world.[4] Few authors have taken Lake Ontario as their direct focus, though a variety of books, mostly for a popular audience, have been penned about boats, navigation, and lighthouses on this Great Lake.[5] The lake is mentioned in the oral histories of the Indigenous societies that developed around it, though perhaps not as much as one might guess given its geographical prominence.[6]

Using Lake Ontario as an organizing principle generates insights into the history of the lake and the surrounding area that are overlooked by other local, regional, or national orientations. Though the lowest Great Lake obviously shares some similarities with its upstream compatriots, it also has fundamental physical differences. For example, Lake Ontario's position as the furthest downstream means that it is the recipient of the cumulative pollution of its brethren. The Niagara River acts as a syringe mainlining pollutants from the many industries on its banks as well as the rest of the Great Lakes, joining the copious amounts of toxics, nutrients, and microplastics that spill into Lake Ontario from its own shores. But the lake's downstream position also means it has the most direct hydrological connection with the Atlantic Ocean; this, along with quirks of geological and glacial history, including the

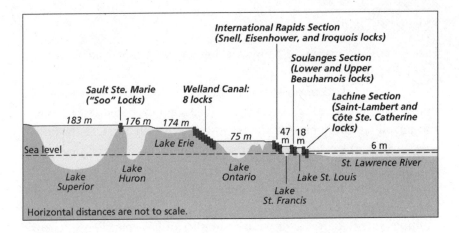

Figure 0.2
Profile of Great Lakes–St Lawrence system. Note that Lake Huron and Lake Michigan are essentially two basins of the same lake, so for simplicity the latter is not portrayed here.

aquatic obstacle presented by Niagara Falls, resulted in the species composition of Lake Ontario being historically and biologically unique compared to the other lakes. Geophysical differences in turn instigated alternative paths of human use and development that set Lake Ontario apart from the other Great Lakes.

There are plenty of ways to know Lake Ontario from both qualitative and quantitative perspectives. I have tried hard to know it both ways. In addition to frequenting its shores as often as possible and in many different locations, I have endeavoured to experience the lake from many different vantage points: kayak, paddleboard, catamaran, sailboat, speedboat, ferry, airplane, helicopter, drone, etc. I also studied it exhaustively from an academic perspective. In this book, I employ archival sources, printed primary sources, scientific studies, and interviews. I consulted archival records from the multiple political jurisdictions touching the lake: the national archives of both countries, the provincial and state archives records of Ontario and New York, and municipal- and county-level records and histories. I also draw heavily on the work of scientists, limnologists, and ecologists who study specialized aspects of Lake Ontario, particularly in forums such as the *Journal of Great Lakes Research*. Some of the other important sources of information about the changing ecological health of Lake Ontario have been the reports and records of the International Joint Commission.

Scientifically and technically, we know a lot about Lake Ontario's properties. Yet, much of the lake remains a mystery, hidden beneath the surface. This body of water can be liquid therapy or a source of transmuting inspiration

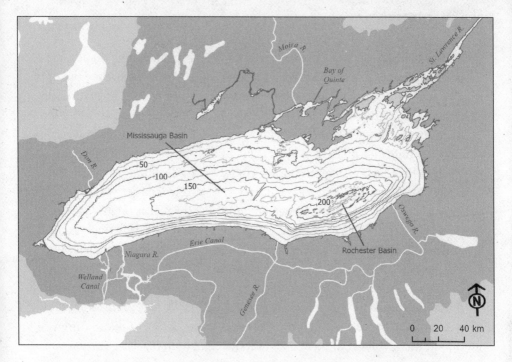

Figure 0.3
Physical features of Lake Ontario, including depth (in metres). The dark grey indicates the lake's watershed. Figure 7.4 in this book shows the full extent of Lake Ontario's watershed.

for those in, on, or beside it. For some, this lake is an old friend, replete with the types of mood swings we normally ascribe to people: calm stillness, undulating beauty, raging temper. However, despite so many people living close by, most of its watershed denizens seem reluctant to show love or admiration for Lake Ontario in the ways they do for other nearby waterbodies such as the Muskokas, the Finger Lakes, the Kawarthas, or the upper Great Lakes. Lake Ontario became seen as a commodity to be exploited, to be sacrificed for economic growth. Of course, that blindness is also a problem of perspective; traditional Indigenous ways of knowing the lake, for example, conceptualize its waters differently, as more of a relationship than a mere resource.

GEOGRAPHY AND FEATURES

In terms of the measurables, Lake Ontario is the fourteenth-largest lake in the world by surface area and the eleventh largest in volume. It has a surface area of 18,960 km² (7,340 miles²), an average depth of 86 metres (283 feet), and a maximum depth of 244 metres (802 feet). When including islands, the lake's shoreline is 1,146 kilometres (712 miles), the smallest shoreline out of all the Great Lakes. At 1,640 kilometres squared it is the second-smallest Great Lake by volume. Yet it has the highest ratio of watershed area to lake surface area of any Great Lake. The water from the four upstream Great Lakes accounts for more than 80 per cent of the inflow into Ontario via the Niagara River. The remaining water comes from precipitation, which accounts for approximately 7 per cent, and the 650-odd tributaries.

I can put some of those numbers in terms that the reader might more intuitively grasp. The lake is longest east to west, but it is wide enough in the north–south direction that you cannot see from shore to shore – that is, unless you are at the narrower western end, where you can discern the top of the tallest downtown Toronto buildings on a clear day from the opposite shore (the tourist towers of Niagara Falls, as well as the mist plume from the waterfall, are in turn visible from the observation deck of the CN Tower). Google Maps will tell you that it takes about eight hours to drive around the whole lake, provided you are going at freeway speed and excepting the time it takes to cross the international border. Incidentally, the fastest time to swim across Lake Ontario was just a shade under fifteen hours (since teenager Marilyn Bell made the first recorded cross-lake swim in the 1950s, from Niagara-on-the-Lake to Toronto, almost seventy others have repeated her marathon crossing).[7] The maximum depth of Lake Ontario is a little less than half the height of the CN Tower's 1,815 feet, and it has a retention period of about six or seven years. That means it theoretically takes more than half a decade for all the water to cycle out – the lake has a general counter-clockwise flow from the mouth of the Niagara River – though things do not actually work that neatly.

The normal variation in Lake Ontario's level over the course of a year is about two feet. The high usually occurs in June and the low in December, though those minimums and maximums have been time-shifting on account of a changing climate. Over the last century and a half, the difference between the years with the lowest and highest levels is about seven feet, a range with implications for shore infrastructure and ecological processes alike. The highest recorded levels were in 2019. Yet two years later Lake Ontario was back down considerably. This rapid seesawing of levels is unprecedented – it usually takes well over a decade to reach high and low disparities – and mostly attributable to climate change.

Lake Ontario is considered an oligotrophic waterbody, meaning that it has abundant oxygen in the deeper parts but relatively low nutrients. Anthropogenic actions have definitely altered the lake's nutrient and oxygen levels; in fact, Lake Ontario is the most polluted of the Great Lakes. The lake once had almost 100 species of native fish, but overfishing and human-caused changes to water quality have altered, probably irrevocably, the species composition. Though it had the first major commercial fishery in the Great Lakes, Lake Ontario now hosts the smallest commercial fishery out of these five lakes.

The Niagara and St Lawrence are the two principal rivers flowing in and out of Lake Ontario. I have written books about both of these rivers, which led me, both literally and figuratively, to Lake Ontario. The thirty-six-mile-long Niagara, connecting Lake Erie to Lake Ontario, is the border between New York State and Ontario, and the second-biggest river in each after the St Lawrence, the upper part of which is also the international border. One of the fastest rivers on the continent, the Niagara River drops 326 feet in total, the better part of that in an eight-mile span; about half of that drop is at Niagara Falls proper. At the famed waterfall, the volume of the Niagara River averages a bit more than 200,000 cubic feet per second. Almost all of the water in Lake Ontario leaves through its distributary, the St Lawrence River.[8] The St Lawrence is the second-largest river by volume in North America, and at just under 750 miles the third-longest river on the continent. This river directs nearly two hundred billion gallons of water daily in an almost straight line northeast from Lake Ontario to the floodplains surrounding Montreal, and then on to the Atlantic. At Cornwall, where the St Lawrence ceases to be the international border, the river's volume is 218,000 cubic feet per second (cfs), but it is almost 600,000 cfs at its ocean mouth.

Both the St Lawrence and Niagara presented significant navigational impediments: the waterfall and rapids in the latter, circumvented by the Erie and Welland Canals, and the rapids in the upper stretch of the former, initially avoided by canals and then submerged and channelized in the 1950s by the St Lawrence Seaway and Power Project. These massive hydroelectric and navigation works have impacted Lake Ontario appreciably. But there are also many smaller hydro power stations in the lake's tributaries and elsewhere in its watershed. Just as pre-twentieth-century mills and mill dams prevented fish passage, created copious amounts of sawdust that suffocated aquatic life, and affected water flows, even small hydro stations can cumulatively have noticeable effects. It is worth noting that Lake Ontario hosts the most energy production infrastructure out of any of the Great Lakes once we take into account hydro power facilities, fossil fuel storage and distribution, and the various types of thermoelectric power plants that dot the lakeshore.

The Oswego River, Lake Ontario's biggest tributary after the Niagara River, starts north of Syracuse where the Seneca and Oneida Rivers meet. The former drains most of the Finger Lakes, which are also in the Lake Ontario watershed. East of the Oswego, the Chaumont, Black, and Salmon Rivers flow into Lake Ontario. The Genesee River, the next-largest American tributary after the Oswego, begins in Pennsylvania and runs 158 miles north through New York State; it has two picturesque sets of lower, middle, and upper falls in Letchworth State Park and Rochester. On the northern rim of Lake Ontario, noteworthy tributaries, all of which generally flow in a north to south direction, include the Credit, Humber, and Don in the Toronto region and the Trent, Moira, Ganaraska, and Cataraqui Rivers to the east.

Lake Ontario moderates the local weather, creating a temperate climate. The summers are hot and humid; the winters are cold and snowy. But the weather is not always uniform throughout the lake. On a recent early September day, it was 18°C in Toronto and Kingston, while Niagara Falls and Syracuse recorded highs near 30°C. Lake Ontario acts as a heat sink, absorbing heat when the air is warm and releasing it when the air is cold. Urban areas such as Toronto also create heat islands, influencing local microclimates. In summer, the lake is influenced by warm and humid air from the Gulf of Mexico, whereas in winter it is chilled by Arctic and Pacific air masses. Lake Ontario waters have a seasonally dependent pattern of both horizontal and vertical thermal stratification – horizontal stratification means nearshore waters warm faster, while vertical stratification refers to the lower and upper parts of the deep lake having different temperatures. From about June until November a warm layer of water floats on a cooler and denser layer. Granted, this stratification is often more mixed than the above description suggests, as the boundaries between layers of water temperatures can be dynamic. Moreover, much of the water entering from tributaries may leave the lake without fully mixing in, with implications for water temperatures and pollutant dispersal.

A fresh lake breeze can quickly kick up waves that challenge light boats. Almost all summer long, the harbour in Kingston experiences by noon an onshore lake breeze nearing fifteen knots. This stiff chop is refracted around the irregularly shaped east end of the lake and the head of the St Lawrence.

By November, when the water has cooled down, the waves in Lake Ontario just keep building. The result in the open lake is then not chop but big regular waves. Wind-powered shipping on the Great Lakes would have been affected not so very differently from recreational sailors nowadays. Autumn typically sees gales, including remnants of Caribbean hurricane systems every few years. Some of these have been considerable. Hurricane Hazel infamously rearranged many physical aspects of the Toronto region in the 1950s. In November 1988, Hurricane Hugo brought wind speeds of eighty knots, an almost unheard of velocity away from the ocean.

In the winter it is very rare for ice to cover much of the lake far offshore. But by late January, ice often fills in all the eastern bays as well as the Hamilton end of the lake. If pushed up against a shore by a gale when six inches thick, ice floes can reshape coastal features, building mounds of broken nearshore ice from below. It is because of the relentless succession of wind systems, and the lake's depth, that Lake Ontario hardly ever freezes across. The waves simply do not allow it. As a consequence, all year long west and northwest winds scoop up moisture over their long fetch, which they deposit on the hills of Upstate New York as rain in summer and snow in winter. The south side of the lake is one of the most famous snow belts in the United States. Oswego regularly sees total snowfall accumulations more than twice what descends on Kingston fifty miles north; Rochester often doubles Toronto's average annual snowfall. When the temperature fluctuates around freezing, the winds bring anything from snow through ice pellets to sleet to freezing rain, what the local forecasters cheerfully refer to as "a wintry mix."

Lake Ontario's winds and precipitation inexorably affect farming and growing operations near shore.[9] After the winter ice has been swept away, onshore winds can inhibit vegetation growth by several weeks compared to inland sites. Since autumn winds are unusually warm, the growing season in lakeshore areas such as Prince Edward County, while not always so very different from further inland, is frame-shifted later in time. Many advantages have been derived from this anomaly for growing grains and raising fruit, such as the grapes that supply the local wine industry.[10] Several counties on the New York side, benefitting from the moisture and moderated climate bestowed by the lake, have historically also been major fruit producers.

For its size, Lake Ontario has remarkably little in the way of severely hostile coastlines. Mariners in distress on a lee shore could often expect themselves to survive if their ship was pushed landward and destroyed, for the cliffs are mostly soft. There are perhaps 100 shipwrecks at the bottom of the lake.[11] In the eastern part of the lake a saucer-shaped declivity, more than half a mile wide and about sixty feet deep, appears to be the result of a meteor. Closely framing the impact zone is a ring of shallows, the Charity Shoals; a very high proportion of Lake Ontario's shipwrecks occurred here.[12] Though the lake overall has relatively few shoals and islands for its size, they abound at the far northeast corner, easy to run into on a dark night or in dense fog. In the last fifty years, most of these islands ceased to be inhabited – unlike the larger ones close to shore and with ferry service, such as Amherst and Wolfe – but they were farmed and fished from for a good hundred years previously. The name Schoolhouse Bay on Main Duck Island speaks to past habitation. Today, large ships pass upbound to its north and downbound to its south, keeping their distance from each other. The crews are no doubt glad to see that the large automated lighthouse is still operational even on a moonlit summer night.

On the south brim of the lake, east of Sodus Bay, New York, erosion has created "earthen spires" at Chimney Bluffs that are attractive but so fragile that climbing these landforms is off limits to park visitors (see figure 0.4). Many millennia of endless wave action have fashioned large sand dunes at the western edge of the Prince Edward Peninsula. Much of the central part of the north shore of Lake Ontario has sand cliffs but not low dunes or spits backed by lagoons as on the southern and eastern shores.

Lake Ontario is shared by two subnational political jurisdictions, Ontario and New York State, with the surface area of the lake split almost evenly between the two. The Lake Ontario watershed is home to about eleven million people (nine million Ontarians and two million New Yorkers), a figure that has grown by 40 per cent in the last two decades. Lake Ontario was the first of the five lakes heavily settled by Europeans, and it now has the largest lakeside population of any of the transborder Great Lakes (only Lake Michigan, entirely in the United States, has a larger population close to the water).[13] If population growth continues to follow projections, Lake Ontario will be the most populated Great Lake within a few decades. Most of the residents in the watershed are concentrated in the Golden Horseshoe that runs from Niagara-on-the-Lake to Oshawa, encompassing St Catharines, Hamilton, Burlington, Mississauga, Toronto, Scarborough, Pickering, and other communities. In fact, there are more Canadians living in the Lake Ontario watershed than in the rest of the Great Lakes combined.

Running further east from the Greater Toronto Area (GTA) conurbation, you encounter Port Hope and Cobourg, then communities in the Bay of

Figure 0.4
Chimney Bluffs State Park. These earthen spires are located just east of Sodus Bay, New York.

Quinte area like Trenton, Belleville, and Picton, and then Kingston. Moving to the US side, Watertown, Oswego, and Rochester are the largest cities on or near the lake. Granted, the latter is by far the biggest of these three: the City of Rochester is home to about 210,000 people, while the wider Rochester metropolitan area has a population of over 1 million people. Some of Rochester's suburbs, including those touching Lake Ontario such as Greece and Irondequoit, are technically independent and classified as towns even though they each have populations between 50,000 and 100,000. Also within the lake's southern watershed is Syracuse, as well as the Niagara–Buffalo region astride the lake's main tributary.

Kingston, Toronto, and Oswego developed right on the water. Many well-known Lake Ontario cities – Rochester, St Catharines, Watertown, Oshawa, etc. – are proximate to the lake but are not centred directly *on* the lake. The lake provides drinking water for close to 10 million people and is the receptacle for the effluent of an equivalent number. Because Lake Ontario experienced such a high degree of urbanization and development in the twentieth

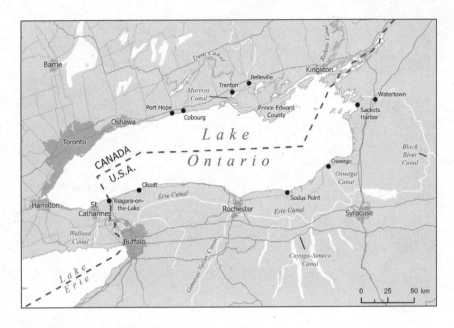

Figure 0.5
Human features of Lake Ontario. The dark grey indicates larger urban areas.
Note also the various canals indicated on this map.

century, around the western end people prioritized its waters and waterfront for industry and economic activities. Still, since only that part of the lake is highly developed, most of the basin, particularly the American portion, is characterized by rural landscapes; urban districts, roads, and associated infrastructure comprise less than 10 per cent of the basin's total land area. The watershed has two Canadian national parks, three US national parks, numerous wildlife sanctuaries, and dozens of state, provincial, and municipal parks.

ARGUMENTS AND APPROACHES

Lake Ontario and its resources both enabled and constrained the various societies that surrounded it. Indigenous communities, primarily Haudenosaunee and Anishinaabe, occupied the Lake Ontario watershed going back countless generations. The Lake Ontario environment shaped their cultures and politics, and was a factor in their relations with European newcomers. The lake was both a motivation for, and a means to achieve, the Euro-American project of politically controlling the area. The basin became divided into settler states, with Lake Ontario altered by a burgeoning array of human activities unleashed by population and economic growth. Governmental attempts to control the lake, and access to its amenities, privileged some interests over others. This means that the history of Lake Ontario is not only a history of regulating a waterbody but also one of regulating human activities.

I argue that Lake Ontario became the most politically and economically important Great Lake, at least from a Canadian perspective. The Lake Ontario–St Lawrence system tied together the territories that initially formed the country of Canada while also furnishing a fluid connection to the imperial centre, Britain. Lake Ontario, along with the two principal rivers that flow in and out of it, forms the Canadian heartland, and in many ways the lake directed the resource exploitation and economic trajectories of Canada and Ontario. All of Canada's historical capitals, and those of the two biggest provinces, Ontario and Quebec, are intimately connected to the Lake Ontario–St Lawrence system. Canada's largest city and urban conglomeration, Toronto and the GTA, grew into the contemporary industrial and financial hub of the country because of Lake Ontario. Similarly, the Province of Ontario derives not only its name but much of its economic and political clout from the lake.

Lake Ontario served as both a bridge and a barrier between Canada and the United States, facilitating interactions and transborder integration in some ways, while impeding them in others. Though Lake Ontario was central to the evolution of the Canadian nation-state, it was much more peripheral to the national imaginary of the United States. Likewise, the Province of Ontario identifies more strongly with Lake Ontario than does the State of New York. Even though it is the Great Lake that looms largest in the Canadian consciousness, by the twentieth century Lake Ontario became seen mostly as a passive backdrop or a resource to be appropriated, rather than a dynamic waterscape supporting essential relationships between the natural world and the human enterprise.

For Ontarians, it was more sins of commission, whereas with New Yorkers it was more those of omission: the former crowded around the lake but abused it, whereas the latter mostly stayed away. This disregard for Lake Ontario is symbolized by its portrayal – or, rather, its lack thereof – in artistic representations. The Hudson River School painted many waterbodies and natural features of Upstate New York, but apparently did not depict Lake Ontario. Canada's Group of Seven, centred in Toronto, also deemed the lake unworthy of artistic rendering and instead left its shores and sojourned

north on painting excursions. Ontarians too went north for their water and
wilderness recreation: Georgian Bay, the Muskokas, the Kawarthas, Algonquin Park. When downstate New Yorkers headed upstate, the destinations
included Niagara Falls, the Adirondacks, the Thousand Islands, the Hudson
Valley, the Finger Lakes, the Catskills – but generally not Lake Ontario.

Lake Ontario is the Great Lake most affected by human-built control
works, which include dams and water regulation infrastructures in its major
tributary and distributary. *The Lives of Lake Ontario* will demonstrate that
the lake's water levels, water quality, and biological diversity changed dramatically over the past few centuries, especially since the mid-twentieth century. New environmental regulations in the second half of the century
achieved only mixed results. Lake Ontario became the most degraded of the
five Great Lakes. Limited improvement in lake conditions in recent decades,
and the ongoing emergence of new and unforeseen problems, point to a recurring theme in this book: Lake Ontario's remarkable resilience juxtaposed
with its apparent vulnerability.

In *The Lives of Lake Ontario*, I seek to cover the different aspects of Lake
Ontario's environmental and human history: fish and biodiversity; pollution
and water quality; water quantity and levels; energy, canals, and dams; urban
development and built infrastructure; shipping and navigation; cultural and
recreational uses; and human adaptation to climate change. The first chapter
establishes the geological and evolutionary history of Lake Ontario, then explores how Indigenous peoples related to Lake Ontario before, during, and
after initial contact with Europeans. The second chapter covers the colonizing efforts and ecological impacts of Euro-American settlers. Subsequent
chapters delve into mobility and transportation, urban growth and expansion, and the connected environmental consequences. I then focus on the
twentieth century. For the remainder of the book, the chapters proceed more
thematically: water control infrastructure, particularly dams and canals;
modern changes to fisheries, biodiversity, and invasive species; pollution and
water quality; hydropolitics and the evolving efforts to regulate lake levels,
which continue up to the present. The conclusion combines a discussion about
the current state of Lake Ontario with my thoughts on its past and future.

CHAPTER 1

Glaciers and Empires

It goes without saying that Lake Ontario is identified with its water – but something has to hold the water in place. A lake can be defined as water more or less contained by some rock and soil shaped as a large declivity. Put another way, it is a topographical depression in the landscape that holds water. The actual water molecules in a lake cycle in and out – via groundwater, tributaries, outflows, evaporation, and precipitation – but the lake retains its identity inasmuch as the "container" arrangement remains in place. But even the contours of that container are not permanently fixed; because lakes are on land, they necessarily move with it. Studying Lake Ontario over deep time means we are examining something that has not stayed entirely still, since its location, size, and shape changed over millennia. And those changes are more than merely two-dimensional: the Earth's crust moves up and down as well as sideways on account of factors such as glaciers and plate tectonics.

This chapter first offers a selective natural history that covers, in broad sketches, the geological, evolutionary, and ecological history of the lake we now call "Ontario." The point is to establish that the structure, shape, physical properties, and species of Lake Ontario changed many times, contingent as they were on natural forces that go back eons. Moreover, all of those would profoundly affect how human societies related to and used this waterbody. After all, underpinning my approach as an environmental historian is the conviction that nature is a historical actor on both very long and very short time scales. Following this natural history, I turn to the early human inhabitants of the lake, continuing into the period of contact between them and those newly arriving from across the sea.

LOCATING THE LAKE

Lake Ontario itself is not old, geologically speaking – preceded by a number of glacial lakes, the current version, with the same outlet and basic dimensions as today, has been around some 11,000 years. How long ago did the earliest liquid predecessor to Lake Ontario form? We do not know. What we do know is that the hard rock formation that underlies Lake Ontario was in existence five hundred million years ago. It has been drilled into and assessed from many angles. The extremely old structures underlying the very possibility of Lake Ontario's eventual formation as a sedimentary rock-lined basin of water were thousands of miles away from where they are today when the components of the shales and limestones started to be deposited in a shallow sea, well south of the equator, around four hundred million years ago. Plate tectonic complications lay behind and accompanied the polar ice sheets that more than once moved down the continent, scraping forward and melting in retreat. They changed the height and size of nascent Lake Ontario countless times because they changed the large-scale regional geology within which the lake's structure lies.

Because of softer sedimentary rocks that eroded, the southern edge of Lake Ontario now has a sharper drop-off to deep water than the northern. At the lake's northeast corner lies the visible sedimentary slabs of Prince Edward County. Just east of it, Lake Ontario is all but closed off by a sort of geologically continuous sill composed of shallows and islands, including Main Duck and Galloo. Downstream of that sill lies Kingston, the "limestone city." The more gently sloping northern edges of the lake basin are composed of unconsolidated glacial till: irregular, discontinuous deposits of gravels, sands, and clays with occasional large, roundish boulders left by glacial melt. The eastern end of the lake also hosts many alvars, rock barrens that develop on flat limestone or dolostone bedrock where soils are very shallow.

Three underwater ridges cross the lake bottom in a northeast/southwest orientation. Two trend from the Prince Edward Peninsula, but one lies much further west, north of where the Niagara River enters the lake. The greatest depth in the whole basin is found at the eastern end. When the glaciation was last heavy, only some twelve millennia ago, the Earth's crust sank far enough that the whole northeast basin of the lake was below sea level and the lake drained to the southeast through what is now Oswego. Half a millennium after that, the Duck-Galloo sill reoriented the lake's outlet some ninety degrees to the north, where it now resides. But the sill had less water to impound behind itself. This was because the eastbound meltwater from upstream took to flowing down what we now call the Ottawa River, completely bypassing Lakes Erie and Ontario.

One consequence of glaciers compressing land by several hundred feet was that, for an extended period, Lake Ontario was infiltrated by saltwater. The Champlain Sea stretched to the lake's doorstep. Because of isostatic, or glacial, rebound that has been slowly occurring since the ice departed, the lake's east end is moving slightly upward relative to the west end. This effect is still raising the Duck-Galloo sill a foot per century even as the whole southern shore is gradually sinking. Lake Ontario is thus still growing due to global causes distant in time and place. That slow growth has been more than counteracted, however, by the human infilling of wetlands, extensions of shorelines, the hardening of the lake's margins, and the artificial compression of the range of lake levels. The result is that Lake Ontario's surface extent is most likely slightly smaller now than in centuries past.

While Lake Ontario may not be very old, the landmass in the middle of which it lies, North America, is old (albeit unevenly so), and is the proximate source for the vast majority of life forms found in, on, and near the lake. Nonhuman forces had caused dramatic changes to North America, and subsequent anthropogenic disruptions would prove consequential as well. What humans did throughout the Great Lakes cannot be usefully compared to what transpired elsewhere on Earth except by reference to what happened on the continental scale, which helps explain some of the local peculiarities. Northern North America in particular became a "new world" many times over. No other continent waited so long for a human presence, and several things befell North America before and after their first successful arrival that did not happen to any other continent. Tim Flannery aptly described the whole of North American ecology as an "eternal frontier."[1] The phrase could reasonably be applied to the Great Lakes as a set, especially its lowest member.

For over a hundred million years, life forms on the landmasses of the Americas evolved in isolation from those on the Australian, African, and Europe-Asia landmasses. The North American continent received a shock some sixty-five million years ago that reset the ecological and evolutionary clock: a gigantic meteor hit in what is now southern Mexico. It left a zone of extinction of nearly all non-microbial species that widened as it reached up to the sub-Arctic. North America then underwent what we could call recolonization by a subset of its previous complement of plants and animals, all following whatever trajectories they could.

A mere ten million years or so after the gargantuan meteor hit the Yucatan, the entire planet received another colossal shock as a massive release of greenhouse gases from the seafloor led to a rapid warming of the global climate, with consequences that lasted for scores of millennia. During that exceptionally warm time, many species, plant and animal, crossed from the east end of the Eurasian continent and thoroughly redisturbed the ecology of North America. By five million years ago, Antarctica had taken up so much of the planet's water into landbound ice that giant grasslands formed elsewhere, replacing forests unable to cope with the drought. A mere three million years ago, the isthmus joining North and South America had formed, further complicating the ecological situation. By two million years ago, an enormous series, by no means yet finished, of mass glaciations – followed by deglaciations – came from the north. Going not much further than the southern edges of the Great Lakes region, these glaciers rearranged over and over again – maybe twenty times – the Lake Ontario area.

The life forms that first called ancestral Lake Ontario home were thus, from a global comparative perspective, newcomers. Likely some microbes had been able to persist through the lengthy catalogue of changes listed above. But the visible species that humans have deliberately interacted with were just the latest in whole sets of arrivals at those parts of the continent's ecology that were finally within the particular coordinates of latitude and longitude they currently occupy. Ecological adaptation can only take as long as the available intervals. Considering the whole range of types of disruptions and the short intervals between many of them, it could be argued that the local ecology in the Lake Ontario region is amongst the most disturbed anywhere over a long time scale.[2]

Lake Ontario's evolutionary history is short, relatively speaking, but plenty complex. When the great ice sheets were starting to shrink, inland fish could only have spread along the glacial southern edges and they had to be species tolerant of constantly cold freshwater. As I noted earlier, the land rebounded upward after the ice, and nascent Lake Ontario's water eventually became warmer and salt free. Some saltwater species remained, salmon for example, adapting to the freshwater setting. The lake's changed drainage, from southwards to northwards, forced it to recruit species from different coastal latitudes. The geological fact of the Niagara Escarpment and the resulting waterfall, which barred water-borne species from moving up the aquatic chain, further explains why this sweetwater sea had a unique mix of fish types compared to the rest of the Great Lakes.

I will not attempt to present a complete inventory of Lake Ontario fish here. But I should indicate something of the range of types, emphasizing those species that will be most relevant to the lake's contemporary environmental history. Interestingly, some fish types have been classed in very small subgroups simply because they are very ancient, having first evolved half a billion years ago. We start our shortlist with these evolutionary seniors, not with types that resided the longest in Lake Ontario. Some ancient fish types, such as the huge but toothless sturgeon (which can be 200 pounds in weight and eight feet in length when 150 years old), are classed as vertebrates because they have a skull, even though they are not bony but mostly cartilaginous. Certain fish species found in Lake Ontario, such as the very hardy and predatory bowfin and the longnose gar, go back 200 million years. Eels, semi-bony fish, live much of the early part of their sometimes long lives far offshore in subpopulations all over the globe. Their lifecycle is fascinating. Born in the Sargasso Sea near Bermuda, eels migrate up the St Lawrence to Lake Ontario and its tributaries; they mysteriously return to their natal waters to spawn decades later.

Many species from one of the two biggest groupings of bony fish in the world, the carps and minnows (also deemed chubs, shad, shiners, and dace), abound in Lake Ontario. They are freshwater specialists with excellent hearing and jaws but no teeth, in that respect like the sucker types who are freshwater bottom dwellers, and also not unlike the various kinds of snub-nosed fish commonly called catfish if they have whisker-like appendages. One genus of elongated predatory fish only found in the northern hemisphere and widely caught for human consumption includes pike, pickerel, and muskellunge, the latter attaining lengths up to six feet. Related to them are the small mud minnows, highly tolerant of cold, and the rainbow smelt, which were not native to this watery centre of the continent. Lake Ontario alone of the Great Lakes was naturally home to the large predatory Atlantic salmon (though now if you catch a salmon there it is likely of the introduced Pacific variety). It also has native lake trout as well as brown trout, a Eurasian native introduced in the late nineteenth century.

Among the big global category of fish with spineless fins, Lake Ontario boasts a freshwater cod, the burbot. It also has one of the sculpins and some of the aptly named sticklebacks. The other large grouping of bony fish, the perciformes, tend to be quite spiny, and Lake Ontario has had a good share of them: various bass, sunfish, black crappies, and freshwater drum. True freshwater perches found in Lake Ontario include darters and the biggest representative, the tasty walleye. The perciformes also include invasive gobies, as numerous worldwide as the carps but very small in size.

Whereas fish can only move through water, there is an extensive range of life forms that through flight can cover great distances: birds, bats, insects, etc. An ecological difficulty facing those which live in the air is its temperature range, vastly wider than that of water. Air temperature at Lake Ontario can be anywhere between plus 35°C to minus 35°C, depending on the time of year. However, on most days it falls far from those extremes, with an overall average air temperature of about 10°C. Many kinds of birds simply remove themselves for the cold months. Lake Ontario is home to more than 100 species of songbird, and more than 300 wild bird species have been recorded, since the lake is an important migratory stop. The great blue heron, kingfisher, osprey, mute swan, and merganser are some of the larger and most recognizable birds in the area.

In terms of trees, this area is composed of Great Lakes–St Lawrence forest with historical patches of Carolinian forest. Several kinds of trees came to abound on the sedimentary rock shores of Lake Ontario: drooping willows and, only slightly further from the water's edge, poplars, cedars, and pines. The sheltered willows remaining on the north shore of Waupoos Island are perhaps the largest trees anywhere in central North America.

Many plant species at this latitude enter a relatively dormant phase in winter, as do most insects and some mammals, amphibians, and reptiles. The northern watersnake can be found cruising parts of Lake Ontario. Most of the lake's deep water never budges from a few degrees above freezing, whereas the shallower surface waters can attain 20°C and maintain it for a month or two, except when strong wind and wave systems turn it over. These ploughings of the surface greatly alter the nutrient dynamics because algae need light and can relatively suddenly exhaust the local food supply in their layer.

Shorebirds on sand eat small crustaceans, insects, and plants. Piping plovers, known for their distinctive calls while nesting in the sand, disappeared from Lake Ontario in the 1980s. Some breeding pairs have returned to the eastern end of the lake in the twenty-first century, though their status as an endangered species has engendered tense environmental politics over efforts to protect their habitats and dredging projects to benefit boaters. For the lake's internal ecology, the most important birds may be the piscivores. Some birds, namely ospreys, dive for fish from high above the water. Cormorants make long lateral dives in search of fish. They have trouble drying their huge wings and spend a lot of time standing on rocky shoals and trees on small islands, killing foliage with their guano. Other avian inhabitants, such as great blue herons, ungainly looking in flight and audibly creaking, catch fish while standing solitary in shallows. The common loon, not actually that common in Lake Ontario outside of the migration season, floats low on the lake's surface, making lengthy dives in search of fish. Other web-footed birds, such as swans, geese, and ducks, also eat fish and insects, as well as water plants in shallows or on the shore.

Lake Ontario's geological, glacial, and evolutionary history dictated the contours and nature of the lake, which profoundly structured and directed the choices available to subsequent human societies. Natural forces combined to position Lake Ontario as the first in a chain of large lakes connected to the Atlantic Ocean, but notably freshwater rather than saltwater, determining the territory that fell within its watershed as well as how and where water flowed in and out. The Niagara River became the primary tributary, while the St Lawrence River, rather than the other routes that had previously been distributaries, emerged as the means by which water exited. Geological and glacial machinations left both rivers, and many other tributaries, studded with waterfalls and rapids. While these presented significant obstacles to navigation, they also offered important energy opportunities; all of this would both limit and enable the economic, social, and political choices available to the societies that came to occupy the area, including where they located their major communities. So too would another product of this deep past, the flora and fauna specific to the Lake Ontario ecosystem, be a determinative factor in human history.

ORIGINAL INHABITANTS

Not long after the lake filled up with liquid molecules pouring into its post-glacial container, *Homo sapiens* entered the area. They probably originally hailed from the Europe-Asia landmass. Recent archaeological studies suggest that humans were already in North and South America thousands of years before the opening of the ice-free land bridge across the Bering Strait about 13,000 years ago. Some scholars believe Indigenous Peoples arrived on the west coast of the Americas 17,000 to 20,000 years ago, while a recent study contends they have been in the western hemisphere for more than 60,000 years, maybe even more than 100,000 years.[3] Humans have occupied the region on the north shore of Lake Ontario going back at least 11,000 years, if not even longer. During the Lake Iroquois stage – a prehistoric proglacial lake in the basin we now call Lake Ontario – water covered a much larger expanse and drained to the south via earlier versions of the Mohawk and Hudson Rivers. Downtown Toronto would have been submerged. During the subsequent Lake Admiralty phase, the water filled only about one-third of Lake Ontario's current size, placing the northern shore some 10 kilometres south of the modern shoreline in spots.[4] Accordingly, many Paleo-Indian archaeological sites are now far inland while others are submerged in the lakebed.

We know no details of Lake Ontario's first human beholders. But we know that some of their descendants eventually became a permanent ecological presence in the region. Their distant ancestors seem to have caused massive changes to the animal and plant life of the entire set of the Americas, hunting out much of the megafauna. The smaller iconic herbivores that have long been associated with northern North America – bison, elk, caribou, muskox, bighorn sheep, moose – were also earlier invaders from Asia. Many of the descendants of those first generations of hunters became dependent on the above-listed co-invasives. Over several millennia, no doubt subgroups of First Peoples came and went. Some of these groups eventually established themselves in the Lake Ontario basin, developing living modes and cultures uniquely attuned to the local ecological context.

In the Lake Ontario basin, archaeologists know a good deal about the late Woodland period, running from about 600 AD through European contact. Before the arrival of Europeans, the southern side and western end of Lake Ontario were predominantly Iroquoian speaking. The Haudenosaunee, which means "people of the longhouse," was a confederacy of five Iroquoian nations: Mohawk (Kanien'kehà:ka), Onondaga (Ononta'kehà:ka), Seneca (Shotinontowane'à:ka), Oneida (Oneniote'à:ka), and Cayuga (Kaion'ke-hà:ka). Later they were joined by the Tuscarora (Skarù:rę?). Primarily occupying what is now the northern tier of Upstate New York, they developed villages that featured palisaded longhouses, domesticated agriculture, and engaged in varied hunting and fishing practices.[5]

The Michi Saagiig (Mississauga) Anishinaabeg, an Algonquian-speaking nation, frequented the northern margins of Lake Ontario and its watershed both before and after the arrival of Europeans. *Mississauga* translates as "people of the river's mouth," and their appellation for Lake Ontario was "Chi'Niibish," meaning "big water," while other Anishinaabeg groups called it "Niigaani-gichigami" (leading sea) or "Gichi-zaaga'igan" (big lake). Wendat, Wenro, and Neutral nations also occupied the western end of Lake Ontario for many generations. The Wendat, a fairly sedentary Iroquoian-speaking group, shaped the surrounding landscape: they lived in longhouses, maintained agricultural fields, and cut down parts of the heavily forested region. Their maize fields were extensive. The Niagara River was a trading crossroads and Niagara Falls was an important spiritual and physical resource. The predominant Indigenous group around the Niagara River at the time of contact was the Neutral Confederacy. Composed of Iroquoian speakers, the French called them "Neutral" because of their relations with the Wendat and Five Nations, though the former called them Attiwandaron. They may have been the largest Indigenous society of the eastern woodlands in the early seventeenth century. Yet by the latter half of the same century the Neutrals had ceased to exist as a distinct cultural group because of disease, conflict, migration, and forced adoption, with a cooling climate also a potential factor. Consequently, relatively little of their history has been recorded, especially compared to the Anishinaabeg or Haudenosaunee Confederacy.

The cosmology, and population density, of these original inhabitants resulted in a light ecological footprint compared to contemporary society. Their impact was not entirely benign, however. The area around Lake Ontario was, to be sure, a type of managed landscape affected by Indigenous agriculture, their use of fire, hunting and gathering, and weirs and fishing technologies. Many Indigenous peoples in the Lake Ontario region, happy to live within a shifting cultivation mode prior to the fur trade, routinely used fire to help make clearings for their crops. Such practices influenced the extent and character of forest cover, which in turn affected water flows. Exactly how much Lake Ontario was affected by these fire regimes is very hard to say, however.

Given the paucity of written sources left by Indigenous groups, not to mention colonial frameworks that mirror the physical displacement of these groups with their symbolic displacement, the Indigenous perspective has often been omitted, minimized, or oversimplified. In the field of environmental history, this elision sometimes stems from declensionist narratives – which, to be fair, this book is to some extent – that emphasize those forces that most damage an ecosystem while ignoring centuries of sustainable use. But we do have other types of sources with which to at least partially reconstruct the ecological state of Lake Ontario, and the practices of Indigenous peoples, prior to the influx of Europeans on a large scale: oral traditions, archaeological evidence, and scientific proxies such as sediment samples.

The North American landmass is called Turtle Island in both the Haude-nosaunee and Anishinaabeg creation stories. Oral traditions and new waves of Indigenous scholarship attest to their more-than-human worldviews, which attribute spirits to natural features like Lake Ontario together with the creatures that inhabited it.[6] For instance, according to the oral history of the Seneca, a great beast named Gaasyendietha dwelt in the deep sectors of Lake Ontario. This flying hydra-like snake could spew flames and when airborne was followed by a trail of fire; it was also known as the "meteor dragon" since it was borne to earth by an asteroid or shooting star.

Similar creatures are linked to other waterbodies, so it is unclear whether Gaasyendietha was unique to Lake Ontario. This nevertheless speaks to a particular view of the natural world held by the Indigenous peoples who lived around Lake Ontario. They shared a reverence for the sacredness of water and stressed the reciprocal and kinship responsibilities they had in re-lation to water and nature. Lake Ontario was a vast waterbody that, on the one hand, provided transportation and sustenance. On the other hand, the lake was also a powerful and potentially temperamental entity that could quickly take the lives of those who did not respect it or offended the spirit world. Underwater serpents were to be feared and could be appeased through the practice of offering sacrifices. According to a nineteenth-century account, before crossing Lake Ontario by canoe the Mississauga offered a prayer for safe passage, the propitiation complete when they threw a dog with a stone tied around its neck into the water.[7] As a further example, the Mississauga later alleged that Euro-American settlers taking too much salmon from the Credit River caused a flood in which the indwelling water creature fled for Lake Ontario.[8]

Nevertheless, Lake Ontario does not seem to have held a particularly no-table place in the pantheon of those groups who lived around or near it. The lake does make an appearance in the Haudenosaunee origin story. In their oral tradition, Deganawidah (the Peacemaker) was born in the Bay of Quinte. Travelling south across the lake in a white stone canoe, he bore the Great Law of Peace to the Haudenosaunee lands. This was an intricate legal and political system binding the different groups together into an organized confederacy, providing guidance about how to live interdependently with, and relate to, the land, which as the basis for life was something to be revered and protected.

Each of the five original Haudenosaunee nations was linked to a specific homeland in the southern portion of the Lake Ontario watershed, though

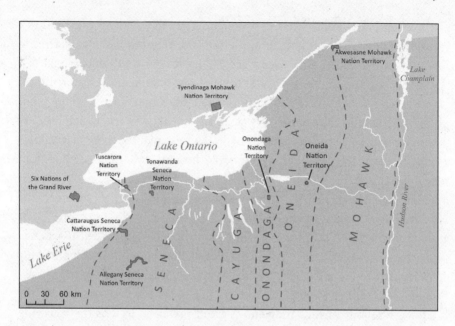

Figure 1.1
Map of Haudenosaunee territories. The dashed lines indicate the borders of historical homelands, while the labels indicate contemporary reserves and reservations.

the extent of these lands could be fluid (see figure 1.1). The Haudenosaunee generally placed their communities away from Lake Ontario on hillsides centred in the Finger Lakes region. Their social structure and lifeways formed in response to the nature of the Lake Ontario watershed and the local climate. Well south of Lake Ontario, summers are warm enough to allow excellent maize yields. Firewood, soil depletion, and other factors drove village relocation probably every twenty years or so. The available evidence indicates that the Haudenosaunee regularly came to Lake Ontario to hunt, harvest, and trade. They maintained fisheries at the mouths of streams and rivers. In 1655, for instance, Jesuits witnessed Onondaga and Oneida harvesting salmon, herring, brill, whitefish, pike, carp, sturgeon, bass, perch, bullhead, and catfish at the mouth of a river debouching into Lake Ontario.[9] Eel fisheries were also common. The Haudenosaunee clearly used Lake Ontario as a transportation route, canoeing along the shoreline – though it appears they rarely canoed directly across the lake.[10]

The Anishinaabeg were comfortable on the open lake because of their high-quality vessels and canoeing skills. The Mississauga could cross from their territory around the Credit River to the Niagara River in the span of a day when Lake Ontario's water was calm. They seasonally moved across a wide territory. Fall brought salmon, trout, and whitefish harvesting. During winter, ice fishing certainly took place, but more commonly during that season the Mississauga hunted game throughout the northern Lake Ontario watershed and beyond. In the spring they tapped maple trees. Many spent the summer near the mouths of waterways on Lake Ontario to acquire sustenance such as salmon and walleye, and they also planted crops at river flats and gathered other food: berries, roots, mushrooms, and wild rice (manomin or minomiin).[11]

The Mississauga names for the rivers flowing into Lake Ontario generally derived from associated physical features. Settlers later adopted or appropriated some of these: the name Credit River was derived from the Mississauga for "trusting creek," since it was there that they received credit from fur traders; the Etobicoke River's anglicized appellation comes from the Mississauga word for this waterway. The name "Toronto" was derived from an Iroquoian title, but various Indigenous groups referred to it as the "carrying place" and it fell squarely within Mississauga territory. This was an important crossroads, heavily trafficked with many village sites throughout what is modern-day Toronto.[12] The peninsula now known as the Toronto Island (or Toronto Islands in the plural) was used by, and had sacred significance for, the Indigenous inhabitants. The Mississauga brought their sick there to recuperate, for example. Other rivers in this region – the Don and the Humber – connected to portages out of the basin to waterways running north to Lake Simcoe and Georgian Bay, where the Mississauga had winter hunting grounds. The Huron also occupied parts of that region.

The Little Ice Age lasted from roughly the fourteenth until the nineteenth century in North America and Europe, and was at its coldest in the former during the latter part of this time period. Across this age, average temperatures were lower by 1°C to 2°C. Lake Ontario might have ameliorated some of the effects in its immediate vicinity – though the lake might have amplified other effects or feedback loops. At any rate, the Little Ice Age was not uniformly colder in this region. There was considerable variability from year to year, and decade to decade, with plenty of hotter- or wetter-than-average years mixed in. The frequent weather swings that undermined the stability of resource acquisition strategies probably proved more challenging than the climate trending slightly colder.[13] Some ecological changes provoked by this long-term cooling shift, such as fewer beech trees but more maples, could be adapted to by humans without great difficulty. But a higher frequency of summer droughts in which crops failed, or extremely heavy snows making it harder to hunt animals, posed more consequential challenges for Indigenous and settler societies alike.[14]

ALLIANCES AND CLASHES

Unpacking the contact era of the Lake Ontario region involves a complex stew of geopolitical contingencies, pre-seasoned with a climate swing, and thickened by the ecological realities of the Great Lakes–St Lawrence region. Newcomers from Europe began arriving in the Great Lakes region in the sixteenth century. These explorers were of course not really "discovering" anything, just setting eyes on what had been unknown to their cultures. Accompanying these newcomers were worldviews fundamentally different from those of the local peoples; settler attitudes and practices would eventually have severe repercussions for the Lake Ontario region.

Europeans also brought something else that would have more immediate impacts: diseases that were totally unfamiliar to Indigenous immune systems and thus frequently fatal and devastating to their communities. In the Great Lakes region, these diseases often arrived well in advance of their original hosts. By the latter half of the seventeenth century, Indigenous numbers had severely declined, mainly because of disease but also due to factors such as conflict and possibly the climatic cooling that inhibited resource acquisition. More than half, maybe much more, of the Haudenosaunee succumbed to pathogens. Some estimates put the continental Indigenous death from infection as high as a shocking 90 per cent.

In fact, a recent study contends that this mass Indigenous dying, and the resulting land use changes that resulted from decimated population numbers, are at least partly responsible for the aforementioned climatic downturn.[15] After Indigenous populations plummeted, there was a great rewilding; in the Great Lakes region "the land drifted into different kinds of habitat, mostly closed-canopy forest."[16] The increased tree canopy offered a much greater carbon storage capacity, meaning there was less carbon dioxide released into the atmosphere. This theoretically could have contributed to the cooler clime, though this line of argument remains speculative. At any rate, the combination of Indigenous death, their seasonal movements, and colonial thinking made Lake Ontario's shorefront seem relatively uninhabited and, from a European perspective, open for the taking.

Samuel de Champlain's time in the New World coincided with one of the coldest troughs of the Little Ice Age in the Great Lakes region. Based in Quebec, Champlain encountered Indigenous peoples who told him about a great lake to the west. Rather than Lake Ontario, the closest Great Lake, they were referring to a waterbody that we now separate into Lakes Huron and Michigan. Looking at the map of the whole region that Champlain made in 1612 based on what he was told, he seems to have blended the Ottawa River with the St Lawrence, and Lake Ontario is unidentifiable. This misinformation was not the result of Indigenous errors; rather, the opposite, as they hoped to keep him away from their rivals, the Haudenosaunee. Champlain did make a trip a few years later across the east end of Lake Ontario, escorted by the Huron and encountering the Haudenosaunee.

The French became the primary Europeans to the north of Lake Ontario, which they claimed as part of New France, with the Dutch and British to the south. Even so, throughout the contact period, Europeans were outnumbered by, and less powerful in the Great Lakes country than, the various Indigenous empires. Iroquoia continued to dominate the southern margin of Lake Ontario as well as territory far beyond that. As the fur trade expanded, Haudenosaunee groups asserted control over much of the lake, dealing with the Dutch and English while blocking or controlling passage to Montreal for other Indigenous traders, such as the Odawa and Wendat.

The fur trade, whose rivalries and economics led to the reorganization of societies and empires in the Great Lakes region as well as the over-hunting of fur-bearing animals, is at least partly attributable to the Little Ice Age. Not only did a cooler climate help drive the desire for pelts across the ocean, but back in North America it also affected pelt thickness. All this motivated other Indigenous groups to look at migrating into Haudenosaunee territory. The resilience and flexibility of Iroquoian food acquisition strategies, exemplified by three sisters agriculture (maize, beans, squash), may well have been one of the reasons they were able to hold their ground.

Indeed, the Longhouse Confederacy did more than just hold their ground: during the Beaver Wars they drove most other groups away from the region, transforming themselves into one of the most dominant empires the continent had ever seen. Consequently, the French tended to avoid Lake Ontario – until it acquired its permanent title, the French called the lake other appellations such as "St Louis" and "Frontenac" – for a good stretch of the seventeenth century. Instead, they journeyed to the upper Great Lakes region by way of the Ottawa River–French River–Georgian Bay route. Coureurs de bois operating independently of the French crown continued to frequent Lake Ontario, however.

By the later seventeenth century, some Haudenosaunee had moved to at least half a dozen sites spread along the north shore of Lake Ontario – the French called them "Iroquois du Nord" – which had been abandoned by the Mississauga who shifted north to escape disease and conflict. There is debate about whether the Haudenosaunee's motivation for expansion was declining beaver populations south of the lake. Possibly, but the move to the north shore also involved considerations such as replacing their own depleted numbers by adopting captives from "mourning wars" with groups such as the Wendat, establishing staging bases for hunting expeditions further north, or diverting furs headed to Montreal. The latter frustrated the French, who invaded Mohawk lands after coming to peace terms with the rest of the Five Nations in the wake of New Netherland's absorption by the English. Employing a different tack, Sulpicians established a short-lived mission at Kenté (Quinte) to minister to the Cayuga there. These missionaries reported wide-ranging winter fur hunting expeditions by the Haudenosaunee north from their Lake Ontario settlements. Ongoing conflict eventually influenced the decision of the Iroquois du Nord to move back south.[17] The Mississauga then reasserted their position on the northern side of Lake Ontario.

The French tried to gain some control of lake navigation with the 1673 construction of Fort Frontenac, the site of present-day Kingston at the confluence of Lake Ontario, the St Lawrence River, and the Cataraqui River (see figure 1.3). About this time they attempted two short-lived forts, Conti and Denonville, at the mouth of the Seneca-controlled Niagara River; later, in 1726, they would build Fort Niagara here.[18] Other French forts or trading posts were installed at locales such as Irondequoit Bay.

At Fort Frontenac, the missionary Hennepin reported in the late 1670s that just a hundred acres were under cultivation, and those much plagued by grasshoppers. He also complained about the humidity. The explorer La Salle, who had overseen the fort's construction, directed a shipbuilding program to further a project of westward expansion not entirely approved by the French authorities. Using Fort Frontenac as a base, La Salle set out to explore Lake Ontario and the upper lakes. He and Hennepin were among the first Europeans to reconnoiter the Niagara River.

It is important to remember that, in the seventeenth century, such European posts were only possible if Indigenous nations tolerated them. The French often had Anishinaabe support because of the former's utility to the latter's trade and political ambitions. For the Anishinaabeg, allying with the French offered a counterweight to the Haudenosaunee, themselves more tightly linked to the British and their colonies through a covenant chain. These alliances would shift after the Great Peace of 1701, which ended the Beaver Wars. As part of this accord, the Haudenosaunee and Anishinaabeg nations agreed to a peace treaty based on the "dish with one spoon" principle. Though the precise nature and extent of this concept is debated, it generally holds that the land (the dish) should be peacefully shared to the mutual benefit of the people using its resources (the spoon), who also retain their independence and sovereignty.[19]

After the Great Peace, Haudenosaunee diplomacy focused on staying neutral in European conflicts and fostering a three-way balance of power between themselves, the French and their Indigenous allies, and the English. The result was a half-century of relative stability and increasing trade opportunities.[20] The Five Nations became the Six Nations by adding the Tuscarora in 1722. This confederacy collectively retained control of most of the terrain south and east of Lake Ontario, with the Seneca, Cayuga, and Onondaga territories directly abutting the lake. Some Haudenosaunee returned to, or remained on, the north side of Lake Ontario.[21]

The British raised Fort Oswego in 1727 on the west side of the eponymous river's mouth, then added Fort Ontario and Fort George on the surrounding bluffs in the 1750s (see figure 1.2). They sited smaller forts and trading posts at the mouths of rivers such as the Humber and Credit, and other suitable locales such as Carleton Island at the head of the St Lawrence. The Mississauga regularly traded at the French and then British forts at the site of present-day Toronto. In return for furs, Indigenous traders received metal goods, wool garments, alcohol, and guns. Fur-bearing animals were soon hunted out in the vicinity of Lake Ontario. But furs came from further afield: Odawas, Menomimees, Potawatomis, and Chippewas from the upper Great Lakes traded at Oswego and Frontenac, or at Montreal. These transactions often involved travel via Lake Ontario, where the local Indigenous powers exacted a toll.

The ecological impact of the fur harvest was considerable, and Indigenous tribes played supplier, middleman, or provisioning roles in exchange for European goods or alliances. Pulled into this type of market-based trade, Indigenous acquisition patterns could also become unsustainable. As early as the 1630s, the Haudenosaunee had hunted out many animal species in their lands to trade furs for European goods, such as Dutch firearms. The depletion of beavers in particular would have had manifold ecological knock-on effects.

Figure 1.2
"A South View of Oswego, on Lake Ontario, in North America," ca. 1760. Despite the painting's title, this view is looking north to Lake Ontario. Note the fort on the left, the land formation jutting out into the mouth of the river, and the high bluffs on the right (east) side.

Figure 1.3
"A View of Cataraqui on the Entrance of Lake Ontario in Canada." This painting depicts Cataraqui, later to become Kingston, in 1784. Note the Indigenous encampment in the foreground, and the different vessels on the water.

The impoundments created by beavers serve as critical habitats for many species, block the upstream migration of other species, raise the water table, and recharge aquifers. It is possible that the extirpation of many of these animals led to faster tributary flows to Lake Ontario or other localized impacts.

What the Europeans call the Seven Years' War (1756–1763), and Americans call the French and Indian War, has been described as "an arms race on Lake Ontario."[22] While that may have been true as far as the naval aspects of the Seven Years' War go, recent scholarship argues that Indigenous nations were the pivotal players with their own agendas, while French and British interests were often peripheral.[23] Though this war is traditionally framed as a European battle for global supremacy, including control of North America, in the Great Lakes region it can be understood, at least in part, as a pan-Indigenous effort to stem the tide of English advances, with the French as allies. Initial Six Nations neutrality meant that the Lake Ontario front was fairly quiet for extended periods of the conflict. Nevertheless, in 1756 the French and their Indigenous allies took Fort Oswego and the other two forts the British had built there. Very soon afterward, however, a British counterattack regained them Oswego and then Forts Frontenac and Niagara, and eventually Quebec and Montreal, too.

The cessation of Indigenous support for the French spelled the end of their North American escapades. With their victory, the British took over the territory of New France. Of course, such a statement falsely implies that the bulk of the territory that fell under the aegis of New France had ever been remotely close to being controlled by the French.[24] Or, for that matter, by the British in the decades immediately after 1763. Though the process of Indigenous dispossession was set to accelerate, Euro-American settlements were still veritable islands in a sea of primarily Indigenous-controlled territory. Unable to envisage maintaining far-reaching military control over this vast and distant area, the British government's 1763 Royal Proclamation declared all land west of the Appalachian watershed, including the Great Lakes, as a sort of protectorate for Indigenous peoples. But it also established a process for land surrenders that had to go through the Crown. This left many White colonists suspicious of Britain's motives and long-term goals. Many of the Great Lakes Indigenous nations that had allied with the French remained mistrustful of the British, a sentiment that found expression in Pontiac's War.

After the British conquest of New France, they put up Fort York to guard the western entrance to the bay where the French had placed the short-lived

Fort Rouillé (see figure 1.4). Then a settlement grew a touch to the east along the shoreline. It was named Toronto, then York, then later Toronto again. The British took over the French fort at the Niagara River. But the British quit this fort for the west side of the river after the American Revolution, where they would be joined by United Empire Loyalists fleeing the new republic. The settlement around this fort at the mouth of the Niagara River was named Newark for the brief period when it was the inaugural capital of Upper Canada; it then became known as Niagara and then Niagara-on-the-Lake.

Europeans had certainly not rushed to settle by Lake Ontario during the New France era. For its part, the British government was rethinking its relationship with its Atlantic colonies. Those colonists harboured designs on land to the west, so recently reserved for people they saw as heathens unable to use the land to its maximum potential. Many of them also hotly resented the British toleration of the well-established Roman Catholic grip on the newly acquired territory that had been New France; indeed, a central purpose of the Royal Proclamation was to assimilate the French population, though the 1774 Quebec Act soon superseded it. The eventual result of clashing views amongst English-speaking peoples here was the Revolutionary War, which came by the winning side to be called the American War of Independence.

Figure 1.4
"York Barracks on Lake Ontario, May 13, 1804." A recreated Fort York exists in present-day Toronto, though now further inland because of shoreline extension.

Lake Ontario was the Great Lake most involved in the Revolutionary War, with Oswego seeing more action than any other forts or settlements.[25] Little of that action took place directly on the lake, however, compared to its southern watershed and the territory to the east. Fort Ontario was burned after the British abandoned it (though they would reoccupy the fort until the 1794 Jay Treaty). Today, a historical plaque and gravesite on Spy Island in Mexico Point State Park, at the southeastern end of Lake Ontario, tells the contemporary visitor that it was at this spot that one Silas Towne overheard British plans, allowing the rebels to defend Fort Stanwix and win the Battle of Oriskany. That this subterfuge warrants commemoration speaks to the lack of direct fighting at or on Lake Ontario.

After initially declaring neutrality, four of the Six Nations ended up fighting with the British, while the Tuscarora and Oneida sided with the revolutionaries. Raids by Loyalists and their Haudenosaunee allies in the frontier area hampered the Continental Army. To neutralize the Longhouse Confederacy, George Washington ordered the murderous Sullivan Expedition of 1779. American forces marched through western New York, destroying Haudenosaunee villages and food supplies. Though the expedition did not achieve its main strategic objectives, namely knocking the Haudenosaunee out of the war, many of the Six Nations subsequently migrated out of their traditional homelands. This would make settler expansion easier after the war. So too would claims about the ongoing threat presented by the Six Nations, which served as a convenient pretext for appropriating their land. Considering the brutality with which the Sullivan Expedition was waged against the Haudenosaunee, there was considerable irony in framing them as violent and vengeful savages.

The victory by the upstart Americans set in motion a reorganizing of the political map of North America. As I have endeavoured to show in this chapter, the land and water upon which those divisions were drawn had previously been gouged and shaped by glaciers, and then occupied by a unique mix of flora and fauna. That mix was still evolving and shifting when the first human inhabitants arrived there. Those original occupants developed societies, beliefs, and lifeways attuned to the ecological opportunities and constraints of the Lake Ontario basin. After many generations had populated this region, disease, warfare, and a shifting climate thinned the numbers of those Indigenous societies, partially opening the door to the intrusion of White settlers.

Though the settler societies drawing the new maps were still far from being able to dominate the Great Lakes region, and the wider continent, they had started down a colonizing path that would result in the marginalization, assimilation, or removal of the First Nations population. The settler goal of fully eliminating the Indigenous inhabitants, however, would never be achieved. Nevertheless, market economies based on exploiting the lake, the creatures in it, and the land around it would gradually overwhelm Indigenous worldviews of kinship, reciprocity, and obligations towards the more-than-human world. Slowly in the beginning, but then faster and faster, newly arriving colonials would set about remaking the shorefront – clearing forests, planting fields, constructing towns – and taking advantage of Lake Ontario's abundance. Within a few generations, the accelerating pace of these extractivist activities would make apparent some of the lake's environmental limits.

CHAPTER 2

Settlers and Ecologies

In his 1871 pioneer history of New York's Orleans County, which fronts Lake Ontario, Arad Thomas noted the local environmental degradation that had occurred over the previous century: "Quails, raccoons and hedgehogs are nearly exterminated in Orleans County. A rattlesnake is very seldom seen. The beavers were all destroyed by the first hunters." He added salmon, quail, raccoon, bear, and fox to the list of animals that had been mostly extirpated. Before the pioneers, Thomas asserted, streams were twice as large and had a more consistent year-round flow, and large tracts of land cultivated to grow grass and grains had once been extensive marshes too wet for trees. Moreover, before humans obliterated those wetlands and cut down the trees, winters were milder, with less snowfall.[1]

Such recollections suggest the extent to which the Lake Ontario environment was reordered in the century after the American Revolutionary War. Other nearby counties also produced written histories to commemorate the US centennial that conveyed similar observations. So too did naturalists and historians in the newly minted Dominion of Canada.[2] However, it is worth pointing out that, unlike Arad Thomas, these human-induced environmental and climatic changes were usually spoken of approvingly, conveying a confidence in the superiority of Euro-Americans and their taming of nature. Many settlers believed that human actions could cumulatively affect long-term climate and weather patterns. Like Thomas, they worried that certain land-use practices had made for colder winters, which they attempted to counteract with other techniques intended to hasten a warmer climate. Leaving aside the question of whether their conjectures about climatic causes and effects were accurate, they were certainly attuned to local ecological changes.

Such observations imply a larger truth: that, over the long term, Lake Ontario's climate has never been static. Human adaptation to changing conditions was an ongoing, albeit uneven, process. Colder conditions could threaten growing seasons and extreme winter weather might endanger human life; winter was, to be sure, a major limiting factor of the Lake Ontario environment. But, particularly before certain types of settler agriculture became widespread, slightly colder weather could also have some benefits: more fur-bearing animals, for example. Heavier ice cover on Lake Ontario, along with consistently cool winter weather, could make transportation easier, whereas a thaw might leave mired roads passable by neither sleigh nor wheeled cart. Climatic pressures induced new shipbuilding and transportation innovations while encouraging the diversification of agriculture and food production such as new wheat strains hardy enough to survive in the cold. In turn, such adaptations and changes to modes of production altered the types of liberal capitalist democracies that emerged over time around Lake Ontario.

TREATIES AND TERRITORY

After the end of the Revolutionary War, Lake Ontario was the Great Lake most fully incorporated within the new American nation, with the lion's share of its south shore becoming part of New York State. But that integration was still minimal until later in the nineteenth century, for the Great Lakes remained peripheral to the heavier concentration of settlement on the Atlantic seaboard. Conversely, as one of the designated destinations for United Empire Loyalists leaving the new republic, Lake Ontario became the Great Lake most central to what remained of British North America. Though the Euro-American population density remained quite sparse, over the coming century both the lake and the surrounding First Nations would come to pay the price of expanding settler colonialism.[3] A mix of treaties, land purchases, perfidy, commercial penetration, wars, and ethnic cleansing would eventually bring most of the Indigenous territory surrounding Lake Ontario under colonial control. The British and American governments would ground all this in legalized measures, which they defined and interpreted to suit their purposes – after the fact if, necessary. Even then, these colonial governments

rarely lived up to either the letter or the spirit of the laws created to disen-
franchise Indigenous nations and take their land.[4]

The 1784 Treaty of Fort Stanwix, signed between the United States and the
Haudenosaunee Confederacy, followed the War of Independence. Though
it recognized the Six Nations as sovereign states and created the first Indian
reservations in the United States, the treaty required them to surrender land
in western New York, Pennsylvania, and Ohio. But Massachusetts and New
York still had to resolve competing claims to the southern Lake Ontario
watershed. Their original colonial charters very grandly suggested that their
domains extended all the way to the Pacific, without making clear upon what
lines the territory in question would be divided.

The Treaty of Hartford in 1786 established that New York got political
jurisdiction over the disputed territory but that Massachusetts got the right
to sell off those Haudenosaunee lands to colonists. Massachusetts sold a huge
tract through the Phelps and Gorham Purchase of 1788, which included the
pre-emptive rights to six million acres south of Lake Ontario. However, this
land syndicate was only able to acquire title from the Haudenosaunee to
about a third of the territory and other developers subsequently became involved. Within a few years, the Holland Purchase obtained for a group of
Dutch investors the western two-thirds of the initial Phelps and Gorham
Purchase. The Holland Land Company then began dividing up and selling
lots to settlers.

The Six Nations never actually ratified the Treaty of Fort Stanwix, which
they had been pressured into signing. To address Indigenous title and
smooth the way for White settlers, New York State and the federal government negotiated other treaties with the Six Nations. The 1794 Canandaigua
Treaty recognized Haudenosaunee sovereignty and restored lands ceded
by the Treaty of Fort Stanwix. However, the 1797 Treaty of Big Tree saw the
Seneca surrender almost 3.5 million acres, which made up most of their
homeland.[5] By the time all was said and done, the Haudenosaunee were
restricted to six tiny reservations in Upstate New York, a mere fraction of
their former territories (and the government later tried to force them out
of New York State entirely). Several of these reservations are in the Lake
Ontario watershed, though none are directly on, or even close to, the lake.
Spatially confining the Haudenosaunee to these reservations had many
detrimental impacts and severely constricted the creative role that mobility
had played in their society.[6]

Most of central and western New York was now theoretically open to settler occupation. However, that occupation was slow at first because of frontier problems: a lack of roads, the land was heavily wooded, the Lake Ontario shoreline and its many wetlands were considered dangerous on account of disease, the continuing Indigenous presence, and the fact that the British lingered at forts in American territory.[7]

During the decades before and after the American Revolution, the British Crown also used treaties and purchases, force, and genocide to move the Indigenous inhabitants of the Lake Ontario region out of the way to free up land for settlers. In the 1760s, the Seneca ceded some land to the British Crown for certain uses around Fort Niagara; the terms of this acquisition, and the fact that the British sought permission to use Lake Ontario harbours and rivers, indicates that water touching Indigenous territory still remained under their control.[8] That Niagara concession was followed in 1781 by the Niagara Purchase, which acquired for the British the Mississauga's land along the west side of the Niagara River. Other land surrenders over the next quarter century pertaining to Lake Ontario included Crawford's Purchases (the Quinte–Kingston region), the Between the Lakes Purchase (including the area that became St Catharines), the Johnson-Butler Purchase (also known as the Gunshot Treaty, it covered a strip of land about twenty kilometres deep extending along Lake Ontario between the Humber and Trent Rivers), the Brant Tract and Head of the Lake Purchase (encompassing the west end of the lake), and the Toronto Purchase. The latter was first drafted in 1787 but redone in 1805 – covering about 250,000 acres – since the original was declared invalid. Putting all these together, the British Crown had acquired almost all the land along Lake Ontario that was not part of the United States.

Many of these land deals were controversial because of legal irregularities, imprecise geographical limits, and shady dealings. Moreover, Indigenous peoples and settler governments had different understandings about land tenure and the exact nature of these transactions. The British believed they were acquiring ownership of land and extinguishing Indigenous rights. First Nations generally believed they were simply sharing the land while retaining sovereignty and traditional activities. What's more, Indigenous peoples did not believe that territorial surrenders applied to water and aquatic resources. Indeed, there were clauses in many of the land purchases explicitly outlining that they kept fishing rights in particular waterbodies. The Mississauga contended that they retained access to the fisheries of the Credit River, Etobicoke

River, Twelve Mile Creek, and Sixteen Mile Creek. Mississaugas at the eastern end of Lake Ontario claimed the same for rivers there, such as the Trent and Moira. Moreover, they never thought that they were ceding the lakebed of Lake Ontario, the islands in the lake, or the Bay of Quinte.[9]

However, colonists kept encroaching on Indigenous territory and impeding their ability to exercise hunting, fishing, and resource harvesting rights. The Mississauga population near Lake Ontario declined, as did the numbers of other First Nations in the region. The Province of Canada passed some legislation to protect the fisheries of the Credit River Mississaugas. But Whites drove Anishinaabe fishers away, while sawmills fouled the waters, and no government was interested in enforcing Indigenous rights in the face of growing agricultural settlement. When the Mississauga lodged legal petitions and complaints, settlers and their governments generally obfuscated, delayed, or simply disregarded these claims. Treaty rights to continue traditional subsistence strategies were ignored and Indigenous fishing techniques were later criminalized, namely jacklighting, certain types of nets, and fishing at the mouths of Lake Ontario tributaries.

The Mississauga in the Toronto area left or were driven out of most of their remaining territory. Though some persisted with a community along the Credit River, upstream from Lake Ontario, seeing the writing on the wall in terms of resource depletion and settler expansion, by 1840 they had moved south of Brantford. Here they joined Mohawks, who had earlier been granted the Six Nations reserve on the Grand River, forming the community of the New Credit.[10] Though these Indigenous territories along the Grand are not too far from the western end of Lake Ontario, they are in the Lake Erie watershed. Mississauga from the eastern half of Lake Ontario were able to retain access to traditional resource territories for longer. Some briefly settled on Grape Island in the Bay of Quinte, but then moved to the Alderville reserve near Rice Lake, whose waters ultimately drain to Lake Ontario.[11] Other Anishinaabeg who frequented the mouths of eastern Lake Ontario tributaries eventually gathered on other reserves north of the lake but still within its watershed: the Hiawatha First Nation by Rice Lake as well as the Scugog Island First Nation and the Curve Lake First Nation elsewhere in the Kawartha Lakes chain.[12] However, they never agreed to relinquish many of their traditional hunting and fishing territories along and in Lake Ontario.

These Mississauga reserves fell within the territory later covered by the Williams Treaties of 1923 and Treaty 20.[13] The Williams Treaties were intended to finally deal with Anishinaabeg lands that had remained formally unceded, which included parts of the northeastern shore of Lake Ontario. However, the Mississauga believed that these 1923 agreements protected their hunting, trapping, and fishing rights in those unceded areas, while the Crown interpreted them as extinguishing any previous treaty rights. A court case later affirmed the government's stance that Mississauga First Nations had no traditional hunting or fishing rights off reserve. Litigation about land and harvesting rights arising from the Williams Treaties was only settled in 2018, along with an apology. Other legal settlements for past purchases and treaties have recently taken place between First Nations and Canada, a partial acknowledgement of the improprieties in the initial agreements. For example, the Mississauga of the Credit accepted $145 million to settle claims concerning the Toronto Purchase and the Brant Tract between Burlington and Hamilton.

The territory of the Mohawks of the Bay of Quinte (Tyendinaga), dating to a Crown grant of 1784, was the only Indigenous reserve or reservation placed directly on Lake Ontario in either Canada or the United States. The Mohawks had been promised land by the British Crown for their loyalty during the American Revolution. About 130 of them under the leadership of John Deserontyon selected the Bay of Quinte and arrived to take up a large area – perhaps 37,000 hectares, though the precise size is unclear. However, some of the first Loyalist communities were established nearby, and settlers progressively and illegally whittled down Tyendinaga's land base to a fraction of its former extent. The government sold off parts of their territory in the first half of the nineteenth century, including their hunting grounds to the north, and leased lands to settlers. They did retain reserve land fronting on the Bay of Quinte, but many of their resource lifeways and treaty rights were eroded or ignored. In 1845, for example, it became illegal to fish for salmon on any tributaries of Lake Ontario, while the government allowed White fishermen to encroach on Tyendinaga fishing grounds.

Settler pressures only increased as the Canadian state took shape. In 1841 Upper Canada and Lower Canada became the Province of Canada, with the former renamed Canada West and the latter Canada East; a quarter-century later, they would become the provinces of Ontario and Quebec. As of 1860, Indigenous peoples constituted less than 1 per cent of the two million inhabitants of Canada West and Canada East (though it should be pointed out that these political jurisdictions did not include the vast majority of what is now northern Ontario and northern Quebec).

ACCELERATING SETTLEMENT

In the decade after the Declaration of Independence, several thousand people who had stayed loyal to the British Crown started to take up His Majesty's offer of free land. In 1784 the middle of the St Lawrence River became part of the new boundary between British and American territory. Settlers were dispatched to the northern shores of the St Lawrence and Lake Ontario and further west to the Niagara Peninsula. When the displaced migrants, or United Empire Loyalists as they became known, arrived they called the land around Lake Ontario "wilderness." The British government generally located them in parties according to whichever military officer they had served under, an administratively practical albeit agriculturally arbitrary procedure. The lands on the northeastern shore of Lake Ontario were avidly taken up by a movement proceeding west from Kingston, including early communities such as Bath and Adolphustown. There was also eventually incentive enough for settling along the St Lawrence River's first fifty miles, flowing northeast from Kingston. In fact, settlement in that segment initially went counter-current, from east to west. The explanation is environmental.

Geological forces had in the deep past forced ancient hard rock upwards through the St Lawrence Lowlands bedrock formation, the so-called Front-enac Arch. Even though barely twenty miles wide at its narrowest, the arch connects the Canadian Shield and the Adirondack Mountains. The St Law-rence had cut through this relatively promptly in geological terms, leaving in its wake the Thousand Islands archipelago extending from Kingston down the river to Brockville. The Loyalists allocated to the St Lawrence were first settled well east of the Thousands Islands section because its banks were so rocky and there was almost no good soil to speak of nearby. At any rate, there was lots of land suitable for agriculture outside of this granite area. The trade that developed up and down the river is as much a part of the story of Lake Ontario as the cut so exquisitely made by the river through that upthrust portion of the Canadian Shield. But, unlike the river, the commercial story flowed both ways.

The British had taken over the site of Fort Frontenac, where they estab-lished Kingston as a military centre (briefly "King's Town"). The presence of Kingston must have given the shore-hugging Loyalists confidence, as well as customers. It is astonishing how quickly these new colonists – mostly relo-cating from New York but also from New England – were able to transform the look and character of the areas where they settled. Before their first winter they usually had made rudimentary dwellings and planted wheat fields. They created a kind of replica of the colonial settlements many of their forebears had made and then abandoned.

In the more fluid early days of settlement, attempts were made to extend limited social mobility even to the enslaved people brought by some Loyalists. In 1792, forty-one years before the formal abolition of slavery throughout the British Empire, Lieutenant Governor Simcoe proposed it to the Upper Canada Legislative Assembly. In this he failed, as racial prejudices remained widespread, but he did manage a ban on bringing in more slaves and a law mandating freedom at age twenty-five for all children of slaves. Later the "underground railroad" took slaves across Lake Ontario from New York harbours like Pultneyville, Rochester, and Oswego, while busier terrestrial lanes of this hidden highway went around the lake, especially through the Niagara region.[14]

At first, those who took up Crown grants along Lake Ontario chose to build very near the water because there were no roads to move people, farm animals, and goods from one place to another. There were Indigenous trails, but these needed to be widened and smoothed out for the purposes of people living almost entirely by agriculture and accustomed to using carts. Some early settlers at the neck of what is now the Prince Edward Peninsula, knowing there had been a portage route connecting the Bay of Quinte to Presqu'ile Bay, used log rollers to move their heavy, flat-bottomed, Quebec-designed "bateaux" across it.

Asa Danforth, an American surveyor, was commissioned in 1799 to make a road from Kingston to York, which he finished in three years. He had to settle for a ferry crossing to get travellers onto the Prince Edward Peninsula from the east, but other parts of his road survive today (from Port Hope west to Newcastle). He completed his work faster than the settlers and their offspring created their new communities, and so nature reclaimed much of its approximately 175-mile length for a time. Water transportation remained the easiest way to move people and goods.

The growth of any given cluster of settlers depended on the erection of mills, with flour mills and saw mills being the most important. Of the earliest settlements, some eventually became leading cities, while others all but disappeared off the map. Bath never grew beyond a small town. An 1802 plan to place the capital of Upper Canada at Newcastle on Presqu'ile only got as far as the building of a courthouse and jail. In 1804 a schooner from York, carrying amongst others the solicitor general, sank there with all hands, dashing Newcastle's aspirations to be a notable centre. The French name Presqu'ile, literally meaning "nearly an island," gives an idea of the coast's shape thereabouts. Nothing of the sunken schooner was ever found, and the whole region is dotted with scores of wrecks of sundry vintages. Many newcomers underestimated Lake Ontario's winds and waves; to be fair, they would not have experienced a freshwater system with this much sheer power elsewhere in western Europe or eastern North America.

Apart from a few sites, the shoreline west of Port Hope is rarely convenient for loading boats, consisting of a narrow backshore fronted by high sandy bluffs. So it is no surprise to find that, until discouraged by an 1823 law, it was speculators not settlers who first took up those lands. Testifying to continued crossborder migrations, a 1795 notice tried to attract readers in Upstate New York to hang their shingle here:

Upwards of 30,000 Acres of most excellent land on the north side of Lake Ontario, in the Township of Whitby, about 18 miles East of the new Town of York, now building for the seat of Government, 20 miles west of the Bay of Canty [Quinte], and 30 north of Niagara – divided into 200 acre lots – will be disposed of on moderate terms by Wm. Willcocks Esq., who will give good Encouragement to the first 10 industrious settlers that close with him before the first day of November next; apply to him at Niagara or York or to the printers of the Mohawk Mercury at Schenectady.

N.B. This township is nine miles front on Lake Ontario and twelve deep, it has three Good Harbours and several capital Mill Sites.

Like many absentee owners, Judge Willcocks got few if any takers. Those who know the coast here or look closely at marine charts can begin to guess why. Only one of the harbours could hold many vessels, none drawing more than a few feet. Willcocks knew the size of his township well enough, but the distances he gives to the Bay of Quinte and Niagara are seriously misleading understatements. Likely accurate measurements had not yet been made. Decades later a posh town, the county seat, arose in this advertised area. Regardless of its failure of purpose and internal defects, Willcocks's document truthfully points us to a time in Lake Ontario's history when geological, meteorological, and ecological factors conspicuously dictated the structure of human activities.

The York/Toronto district was geographically attractive because a series of shifting sand bars and shoals formed a protected harbour, plus the rivers flowing into it could be used to travel northward to portages out of the basin. Elizabeth Simcoe, the wife of the inaugural Lieutenant General of Upper Canada, described the area thusly in the 1790s: "A low spit of land, covered with woods, forms the bay and breaks the horizon of the lake, which greatly improves the view, which indeed is very pleasing. The water in the bay is beautifully clear and transparent."[15] She noted a Mississauga village, Taiaiagon, near the mouth of the Humber River, which had retained the name bestowed by its former Haudenosaunee occupants.

In the surrounding territory, wherever the steep shoreline was broken by a creek or spit, or where it was less abrupt, small towns sprang up at the water's edge, engaged in building ships, milling grains, collecting wool, and harvesting timber. An illustrative example comes from the journal of Timothy Rogers, a Connecticut Quaker who fetched up at Pickering near York: "In 1807 I bot a mil place in Picorin ... This town Picorin lays on about the senter of Lake Ontarao where emtys a fine streme cold Dofins Crik. This is a fine streme and I bilt my mil, so a bote cold com 3 mils from the Lake Shore and land at my mil dor, a fine fishery it is." Some of the best mill local sites were located a bit upstream from the lake, on the Napanee and Cataraqui Rivers for example. At Glenora, the location of a car ferry today, various milling and industrial stone buildings (textiles, plaster, foundry) were erected. Some were powered by water flowing downhill from the mysterious Lake on the Mountain on the ridge above. The speed at which these early clusters of buildings grew is testimony to how much these newcomers and late Loyalists already knew about homesteading. These were hardly pioneers; borrowing a phrase from molecular biology, we might call them replicators.

Along the southeastern end of Lake Ontario, in New York State, many settlers came from the same parts of the United States as the Loyalists. In cultural terms it would be not entirely wide of the mark to call the immediate settler hinterland of Lake Ontario a second New England. This helped facilitate the strikingly amicable commercial relations that emerged between the descendants of the newcomers to the lake despite their different political loyalties. That this area remained, intermittently, a war zone into the next century does present a paradox, albeit one that is more easily resolved if we think of those conflicts as civil wars of a type.[16]

In many places east of Sodus Bay, almost all the way round to Stony Point, the American backshore included extensive marshes and lagoons. These were allegedly rife with malaria. Moreover, settlers were still wary of the Haudenosaunee. Consequently, settlement near the lake was initially delayed compared to the process on the British side. A settler from Connecticut started in 1797 to make good near where Oswego now stands, in the middle of the least marshy strip of the southeast coast. But it would take some time before many others joined him, besides those required to be there for military purposes. The latter category briefly included the not-yet-famous novelist James Fenimore Cooper, who found about thirty buildings and fort ruins at Oswego.

Starting about 1800, settlers from New Hampshire worked hard to establish what became Watertown. This community is named after the multitudinous falls in the Black River. That waterway flows briskly west into Lake Ontario one bay south of the huge and sheltered Chaumont Bay, the heart of a domain locals now call the "golden crescent." During the War of 1812, right on the lake near a point on the south side of Black River Bay, the United States built a major naval base in Sackets Harbor, named after a New York City speculator who had started the town in 1801. By the war's end it was one of the biggest military and naval bases in the United States and one of the largest centres in New York State. It remained important through the nineteenth century. Today, it is mostly a sleepy village that bustles with tourists and naval enthusiasts during the summer.

At its east end, Lake Ontario offered a multiplicity of safe havens to ships – and often enough to smugglers. But it was less generous along the rest of its American shore, where trade frequently had to make do with the mouths of rivers and creeks. The completion of canals and railways in the nineteenth century would help make up for that early deficiency. Rochester and Oswego emerged as main ports on the south shore. The first mill at the future site of Rochester was established in 1789 by the upper falls of the lower Genesee River, followed by other grist and saw mills and businesses of various types. Other similar settlements peppered the map between the Finger Lakes and Lake Ontario. The route of the Erie Canal would eventually determine which of these settlements, competing with each other for ascendance, became significant population centres.

Figure 2.1
"Attack on Fort Oswego, Lake Ontario, N. America, May 6th, 1814, Noon."
The view is looking south from Lake Ontario toward the mouth of the Oswego River.
Note the fort on the bluffs.

The lower Great Lake basin was a central theater in the War of 1812. Pivotal land clashes took place along the Niagara and St Lawrence Rivers, with other confrontations on and around Lake Ontario: the Americans sacking Newark and York; naval battles near the Genesee River and Burlington Bay; attempted British invasions of Sackets Harbor; successful captures of Forts George, Niagara, and Ontario; and minor skirmishes at the likes of Pultneyville and Troupville.[17] The lack of decisive naval engagements on Lake Ontario was not because of the lake's unimportance. Quite the opposite: as a critical transportation route and the site of important naval bases, retaining at least a partial hold on the lake was of the highest strategic value. Both sides therefore put considerable resources into building up their naval capabilities there, especially at Sackets Harbor and Kingston. Losing a full fleet battle on Lake Ontario would have been disastrous, with the victor in such a confrontation perhaps winning the entire war or at least controlling the Great Lakes. The result was more or less an arms race standoff on Lake Ontario as the fleets only flirted with a major naval encounter.

The lake itself was a military actor, alternatingly an ally or an enemy, that restricted what was possible. Ice and inclement weather typically made naval manoeuvres more or less unthinkable for nearly half the year; the winter of 1813–14 was a partial exception since it was milder than usual. Storms, winds, or precipitation could determine the feasibility and success of campaigns: two American warships, the *Hamilton* and the *Scourge*, sank in a sudden summer squall north of Port Dalhousie in 1813. A lack of appreciation for the lake's capriciousness could mean disaster, while those commanders who respected the local environment had the upper hand.[18]

The Treaty of Ghent ended the War of 1812. It also put paid to the protracted era of conflict that has been called the Long War period, which stretched back through the Seven Years' War, the American Revolution, and the wars of Indigenous extermination. Aside from some annexation bluster from time to time, this meant the end of direct hostilities between the United States and Britain and its North American holdings. That meant settler stability for the Lake Ontario region. The 1794 Jay Treaty had put the border through the approximate middle of the lake, while the Rush–Bagot Treaty of 1817 underlined how permeable that border was. This 1817 accord reduced naval armaments on the Great Lakes, and the demilitarization of the Lake Ontario border encouraged transnational migration and cultural and economic contacts.[19] Historians have long argued about whether the colonies tried to retain their economic and cultural links to England in the face of an expansive United States; in truth, British Canada strengthened its links to both countries. Each of the two larger nations might have periodically exerted a stronger push or pull, but there was a sort of equilibrium. Which country neo-Canadians leaned towards at different times was often determined by economic self-interest: whichever would give the top price for wheat or corn, or whichever could offer the best deal on a new stove or plow.

York slowly grew, despite the setback of American occupation and razing during the War of 1812. Eventually York, retitled Toronto as of 1834, emerged as the capital of Upper Canada, then Canada West, and then the Province of Ontario; along with Kingston, it also served as one of the capitals of the United Canadas. For a time, Dundas looked like it might become the principal port at the head of Lake Ontario, connected as it was by a military road running to the forks of the Thames River. But another nearby United Empire Loyalist settlement, Hamilton, eventually took on that role.

Running east from Hamilton to the Niagara River, Loyalists started other communities and farms between the lakeshore and the Niagara Escarpment, including Beamsville, Grimsby, and Stoney Creek. The fall of the escarpment, or "the Mountain" in local parlance, offered good milling sites. It also created, in combination with latent heat from the lake, a unique localized climate that, along with sandy soils, was advantageous for tender fruit cultivation. The Neutrals and Senecas had grown corn, beans, peas, watermelons, and pumpkins here. As early as 1779, peaches were harvested near the mouth of the Niagara River, possibly planted by the French. Early settlers grew apples, pears, and cherries. Nevertheless, wheat became the settlers' predominant agricultural crop, with apples the most valuable fruit product; by 1875, three-quarters of the apples harvested here were shipped to Britain.[20]

CONSEQUENCES OF COLONIZATION

Clearing the forest – mostly hardwood but also the coveted white pine that grew abundantly in the sandy soils – was one of the first tasks of the Lake Ontario newcomers. Elizabeth Simcoe relayed to her diary that:

> The way of clearing land in this country is cutting down all the small wood, pile it and set it on fire. The heavier timber is cut through the bark five feet above the ground. This kills the tree, which in time the wind blows down. The stumps decay in the ground in the course of years, but appear very ugly for a long time, though the very large, leafless white trees have a singular and sometimes a picturesque effect among the living trees. The settler first builds a log hut covered with bark, and after two or three years raises a neat house by the side of it. This progress of industry is pleasant to observe.[21]

Of course, Simcoe's perspective reflected the settler's gaze, which held a low view of both Indigenous Peoples and unimproved wilderness. The same was true of Susanna Moodie's recollections. Writing a few decades after Simcoe's diary entry, Moodie remembers that the northeastern shore of Lake Ontario was initially rather "uninviting," for it "appeared to be covered everywhere with the dense unbroken forest." However, upon landing, she found that narrow strips of "primeval forest" had concealed most of the land already cleared for houses and farming concessions.[22] That the forest clearing kept advancing is made manifest by the remarks of James Elliot Cabot near the mid-nineteenth century. He accompanied renowned naturalist Louis Agassiz on his 1848 journey to Lake Superior, publishing his own travelogue in conjunction with Agassiz's magisterial 1850 study of the largest Great Lake's natural history. In those pages, Cabot lamented that Lake Ontario was "as tame as the edge of a duck pond," ascribing this "character" to the fact that the lower lakes were surrounded by "prairie country."[23]

Clearing the forest freed up land for agriculture, wheat especially. Early farm lots were elongated so as to maximize shore access. During the early days of photography, trees we would now classify as gigantic (near ten feet in diameter) were still nearby. Large enough building stones, fairly easily quarried, tended to be used only for foundations by the 1830s because limestone blocks were being transported (usefully doubling outbound as ship ballast) even a hundred miles from Kingston. People keen to use bricks instead of limestone for construction were generally able to have them made locally. However, some items had to be imported. Millstones from France continued to be favoured because those made from Canadian Shield rock were slightly too soft, giving off a kind of sand that ruined the flour. Clay and salt came across the lake from New York.

But British Canada had exports, too. Ports at larger communities such as Toronto and Kingston, as well as smaller ports like Oakville, Whitby, Port Credit, and Belleville, exported timber and wheat, primarily to Britain and the United States. These ports also served as distribution points inland for imports and trade as agricultural settlements crept away from the lake. In addition to lumber, felled trees could become potash for fertilizer, glass, and soap. Port Britain, in Ontario, was at the peak of its prosperity from annually sending two hundred first-class timber masts overseas to the Royal Navy. Just a few miles to the east of Port Britain, wharves facilitated the loading of ships with "Port Hope Whiskey," consumed throughout Europe.

An Upper Canada sheriff recalled in his memoirs seeing passenger pigeons – once the most populous bird in North America but destined to be extinct by the early twentieth century – "flying in such numbers that they almost darkened the sky, and so low often as to be knocked down with poles." There had been so many ducks, he reminisced, that they "made a noise like the roar of heavy thunder" when rising from a marsh.[24] However, such spectacles were a thing of the past. Elk and bison had persisted in parts of the Lake Ontario watershed for some time, the latter until near the start of the nineteenth century. But by the later 1800s most of the larger fauna were hunted out. Arad Thomas's historical recollections, which opened this chapter, confirm that the same clearing and decimation of wildlife was taking place in New York State.

The extensive land clearing transformed much of the lake basin from woodland to farmland. On the cleared land, settlers replaced native species with non-native flora and fauna. In a process characterized as the Columbian Exchange, Europeans brought over many life forms in their ships, both domesticated animals (cattle, chickens, pigs) and plant seeds (grain and nonnative flowers). The number they chose to bring was not particularly large, a dozen or so, but a host of other mostly small life forms accidentally came along as well: rats, earthworms, dandelions, crabgrass, and so on.

Historically, the First Peoples near Lake Ontario had deliberately selected seed stock every growing season, cultivating the best varieties of a range of plants (maize, potato, beans, squash, tomato, etc.). Partly for that reason, the crops original to the Americas lent themselves especially well to a shifting mode of cultivation and rapid transposition – within limits, of course. Nobody has found a strain of maize that can mature in the Arctic. However, the earliest inhabitants of the Great Lakes region had so deliberately selected maize varieties over many generations that not one of the hundreds of subtly different varieties now resembles wild types.[25]

The Indigenous groups also hunted, fished, and gathered edible portions of wild plants, achieving a well-balanced diet while maintaining their wooded landscapes, which were neither extensively cut over nor plowed. The Euro-colonizers of the Americas chopped down copious swaths of forests, drained wetlands as much as possible, and installed drainage tiles to dry out fields. After a few generations of initial hardship, the Euro-Americans found that the agricultural system they had imported worked well, from their perspective, in no small part because they incorporated elements of Indigenous agriculture and food-getting strategies. Of course, this success was facilitated by taking the lands upon which Indigenous peoples had employed those strategies.

Additionally, good timing from a climatic perspective may also have been integral to settler success. After all, the Little Ice Age was releasing its grip as Euro-Americans began settling the Lake Ontario basin in greater numbers.[26] Without this climatic shift, colonists might have avoided the area or their early agricultural efforts might not have been as productive. If that had been the case, the history of not only the Lake Ontario basin, but that of the two countries sharing it, might have played out very differently.

As I previously noted, Lake Ontario was the only Great Lake in which Atlantic salmon were native since Niagara Falls blocked their ability to move upstream. Though no firm numbers exist for salmon populations in the late eighteenth century, plenty of anecdotal accounts affirm their abundance. Haudenosaunee and Anishinaabe communities harvested salmon using torch-and-spear methods, nets, and weirs.[27] Settlers fished for themselves or purchased salmon from local peoples, preserving them in barrels. At first, settlers caught salmon chiefly for local consumption, mostly near the shore and in bays and tributaries. But with growing populations that needed protein, and later canals and railroads that could move the catch, commercial fishing expanded. What may have been the first primarily commercial fishery in the Great Lakes, which focused on salmon, was established in the American share of Lake Ontario – Chaumont Bay specifically – close to the War of 1812.[28]

Both Upper Canada and New York State passed laws protecting salmon spawning as early as 1801. Upper Canadian legislation to conserve not only certain fish species but settler fishing, at the expense of Indigenous harvesting, suggests that larger fishing operations were developing.[29] Fishing for

Figure 2.2
Sackets Harbor Battlefield State Historic Site in 2021. The water visible on the right is Black River Bay.

profit took place in Burlington Bay, and certainly by the 1830s a commercial fishery operated in the vicinity of the Toronto Islands. With their other lifeways increasingly circumscribed, Indigenous peoples also turned to participating in the commercial fishery.[30] Salmon caught in Upper Canadian waters were regularly exported to the United States. Many people also fished occasionally or seasonally to supplement their diets. At this time, Lake Ontario boasted the largest commercial fish harvests out of any of the Great Lakes. Of course, this was mainly because it was the first of these lakes to be heavily populated by settlers. By the twentieth century, Lake Ontario would be the least productive of all the Great Lakes when it came to commercial fishing.

After 1830, the introduction of pound and gill nets, and then trap nets, allowed for higher fishing yields. Spearfishing was conducted in streams, weirs were placed near river mouths, and hoop nets were used at river mouths and wetlands; eventually fishing technology included seines on beaches, pound nets for inshore shoals, and trap nets in shallow-water locales with soft bottoms further from shore. Then angling and gillnetting from boats allowed the exploitation of deeper offshore waters. By the midpoint of the nineteenth century, New York State alone had passed twenty-four laws that included prohibitions for specific waterways on dams, weirs, and certain types of nets; requirements for fishways around dams; and closed seasons. Upper Canada instituted fewer fishing regulations in the same period. But those it did implement tended to be more rigid, such as a closed season on salmon in the eastern end of Lake Ontario. Moreover, regulations seem to have been better enforced in Upper Canada than in New York State – at least, according to the reports and letters of J.W. Kerr, Canada's inaugural fisheries overseer, and the annual reports of the federal fisheries agency.[31]

The industrialization of watercourses was prioritized over their vitality as spawning sites. As salmon continued to decline, cisco became the dominant commercial species, along with walleye. By the end of the nineteenth century, lake sturgeon and blackfin cisco were on the verge of extirpation. Consequently, other species were targeted.[32] The proliferation of species foreign to the lake, such as alewives, also hurt some fish populations. Scientific investigation has concluded that alewife consumption led to an overconcentration of the vitamin thiamine in salmon and lake trout, causing mortality and reproductive problems.[33] At the same time, the alewife's abundance resulted in it becoming a keystone prey species for salmonids and walleye.

Human activities that changed water speeds and temperatures, or increased the nutrient loading of phosphates and nitrates, had repercussions throughout the aquatic food web.[34] One of the chief culprits in the nineteenth century was mills and mill dams. By the middle of the nineteenth century there were eighty-seven mills on the Credit River alone and over 7,400 saw mills in the State of New York.[35] According to *The Jesuit Relations and Allied Documents*, in 1749 Lake Ontario's water was "very transparent; at 16 and 18 feet, the bottom can be seen as if one saw it through polished glass."[36] But over the following century, tributary and nearshore waters became noticeably cloudier and turbid. Twenty-first-century scientific studies have found that around 1840 the composition of lacustrine sediments in places such as Frenchman's Bay, near Pickering, shifted to wood debris, soil, and other organic matter.[37] All those dams slowed water speeds in creeks and rivers, raising the temperature as well as sediment loads, as did erosion and deforestation. Mill waste, sawdust in particular, smothered spawning grounds in tributaries, the life cycle of the salmon making them particularly vulnerable.[38]

Removing shade-giving trees also raised water temperatures, while the terrestrial erosion from tree removal resulted in streams becoming wider, shallower, and murkier. None of this was conducive to the reproduction of salmonids. By the middle of the nineteenth century, fully one-third of the forest cover of southern Ontario was gone; by the First World War, it was 90 per cent gone.[39] According to a recent archaeological study of fish fossils, forest removal on this scale disrupted Lake Ontario's nutrient dynamics.[40] By the 1830s, if not earlier, Lake Ontario's nitrogen and trophic cycles were already changing, causing ripple effects for energy, nutrient, and food webs alike. Nutrient loading and pollution affect plankton at the base of the food chain. Phytoplankton, single-cell plant-like organisms such as algae and diatoms, are key producers of biological energy in the lake. Zooplankton, which are very tiny animals, consume these and then become food energy for amphipods, mollusks, and fish such as herring, alewives, and smelt, which become prey for higher-order fish species, such as trout and salmon, as well as birds and vertebrates. Impacts on plankton therefore have noticeable reverberations up the food chain.

Nutrient influxes can benefit phytoplankton and some aquatic plant species. But, overall, the cascading effects from anthropogenic pollution tend to be disruptive, particularly for species highly valued by humans. When nutrient levels in the water rise, so do levels of algae. When algae dies, it is consumed by bacteria and fungi, liberating those nutrients for other organisms. But too much decaying algae uses up the dissolved oxygen in the water, killing off other life, a process known as eutrophication.

Figure 2.3
"Wellington on Lake Ontario (Fishing Nets)," 1842. Wellington is located in
Prince Edward County, Ontario, where a sand bar, pictured here, separates Lake Ontario
(left side of the painting) from West Lake (right side of the painting).

In the latter half of the nineteenth century, industrial activities poured
out an array of pollutants, many of them new to the lake. Alkali runoff from
making potash afflicted waterways coursing into Lake Ontario. On tributaries
north of the rich fishing grounds of the Bay of Quinte, iron ore and gold
mining leached lead, arsenic, and sulfuric acid.[41] Deseronto emerged as an
iron-smelting centre near the end the nineteenth century, with the ores initially sourced from the Madoc-Marmora area to the north, persisting as such
until the end of the First World War. (After the Second World War, iron ore
from a new mine at Marmora owned by Bethlehem Steel was sent to Picton,
from where it was shipped across Lake Ontario to steel mills at Buffalo.) In
the late nineteenth century, new sewer systems would begin shunting the
untreated effluent of growing urban centres to the lake. This included not
just human and animal waste but other pollutants such as the byproducts
from the manufacture of coal gas for street lighting.

Heavy industry, sewers, street lighting – these all speak to how much the
human footprint at Lake Ontario had changed over the course of a century.

Lake Ontario and humans had both imposed themselves on the other. At the beginning of the nineteenth century, Lake Ontario still did more of the imposing. But by the later part of the century, the roles were reversing. The Euro-American settlement of the area led to a litany of environmental insults being poured into the lake. The draining of wetlands, deforestation, mills and industrial processes, overfishing, urbanization, pollution, and warmer temperatures from the fading of the Little Ice Age all had repercussions for the ecology of Lake Ontario. Well before the twentieth century, these were already combining to impair the lake's energy flows and biological processes.

The consequences of colonization were disruptive for Lake Ontario, but were even more severe for the Indigenous peoples who lived around the lake. Robbed of their territories, they were forced onto small reserves and reservations, where they tried to adapt to new realities while maintaining their traditional modes of living as best as possible, their ability to do so often restricted by the proximity of White settlers. The settler societies rapidly expanded, fuelled by their voracious appropriation of the lake's resources. Those resources, and Lake Ontario itself, would soon become integral to the emergence of the new Canadian nation-state and the Province of Ontario.

CHAPTER 3

Canals and Ships

James Fenimore Cooper, the famed American writer who penned the Leatherstocking novels, arrived at Oswego in 1808. Here he spent the better part of two years as a midshipman in the US Navy and helped launch the brig *Oneida*, the first American warship on Lake Ontario. In the meantime, Cooper became enamoured with the lake. Several decades later, the author set his fourth installment in the Leatherstocking saga, *The Pathfinder*, at the eastern end of Lake Ontario during the Seven Year's War.

A recurring subtext in that novel is a seaman, Charles Cap, who cannot bring himself to admit that this sweetwater sea is comparable to the ocean. "Just as I expected!" he proclaims when first laying eyes upon Lake Ontario, "A pond in dimensions and a scuttlebutt in taste."[1] But Cooper is satirizing Cap's hubris and condescension, as well as the disbelief of those who could not comprehend the power, size, and majesty of this Great Lake. The author's own sentiments are more likely captured in the words of another character, Mabel, who asserts that "[Lake] Ontario and the ocean appear very much the same."[2] In one of Cooper's scene-setting descriptions, the lowest Great Lake is a veritable sea surrounded by green wilderness, "the eye turning from the broad carpet of leaves, to the still broader field of fluid, from the endless but gentle heavings of the lake, to the holy calm, and poetical solitude of the forest, with wonder and delight."[3]

The Pathfinder is set during an era when Lake Ontario was at its most strategically important and water transportation was the most viable form of mobility. Prior to the War of 1812, more Euro-American shipping and commerce took place on Lake Ontario than on all the other Great Lakes combined. During that conflict, the navies of the combatants built up their fleets to considerable size. Soon after the war, the first steamship to operate in the Great Lakes, the *Frontenac*, was launched at the Port of Bath. From Sackets Harbor another steamship, the *Ontario*, came into service. The earliest screw-propelled vessel on the lake launched from Oswego in 1841. Meanwhile, canals and railways were being built all around Lake Ontario. Aside of ports such as Rochester and Oswego, rail lines in New York State were routed further away from Lake Ontario than those on the Ontario side.

This chapter partly overlaps with the previous chapter, albeit with an emphasis on transportation and mobility. Canals, ships, and railways enabled the migration of people, the exploitation of resources, the movement of goods and trade, and the formation and consolidation of political territories. Lake Ontario shaped economies, peoples, and nations; in a mutually constitutive relationship, humans shaped the lake, along with the attendant environmental consequences.

AMERICAN CANALS

Let's return to the beginning of the nineteenth century when various transportation routes were established to connect the nascent settler communities popping up all over Lake Ontario. From York, primitive roads were hacked out in multiple directions, while turnpikes and plank roads were laid down on the US side of the lake. The waterfront was the means by which most people arrived and departed, the conduit by which resources and supplies were sent in and out. Lake Ontario was also a source of protein, and a receptacle of waste. People often disposed of their trash in the lake or nearby waterbodies; in the winter they deposited their waste on the ice so that it would sink after the spring thaw. Communities on the lake, and on both sides of the border, became linked by frequent packets: an 1830s service, for example, connected Oswego to Lewiston, Toronto, Kingston, and Rochester, as well as Ogdensburg, Cleveland, Detroit, and Buffalo. The lake was a lifeline and the equivalent of the modern freeway, the settlements like islands separated by a terrestrial sea. Consequently, coastal communities on opposite banks of the lake were often better connected to each other than to communities within the same territory but only linked by land routes.

Liquid networks instilled a pan-lake identity, which canals and transborder shipping would enhance. The lake's destiny was shifting to resemble the Sea of Japan or the Mediterranean Sea; these waterbodies fostered long-standing and complex maritime trade patterns that were highly significant locally, even though many of the commodities involved were on their way out of the basin. Because of such cross-border linkages, and the comparative ease of moving by water, Lake Ontario was more of a bridge than a barrier in this era. Its porous border and the lack of good ground transportation, at least until later in the nineteenth century, facilitated transnational interconnections. A spirit of easy ambivalence pervades the area to this day, as the border between Canada and the United States bisecting it remains one of the world's loosest.[4]

A number of small pioneer canals were dug in the United States during the eighteenth century, modelled on European technology. The British also carved out shallow locks around several sets of rapids in the St Lawrence River. The Western Inland Lock Navigation Company installed locks on parts of the Mohawk River in New York State, foreshadowing the Erie Canal, and eyed up navigation improvements in the Oswego River. In fact, one of the leading plans for the Erie Canal foresaw it connecting to Lake Ontario at Oswego, working in tandem with another canal avoiding Niagara Falls (as late as the 1950s, some interests were still agitating for a Niagara ship canal on the American side).[5] The conclusion of the War of 1812 signalled the start of several decades of canal mania, led by the Erie plan.

When federal funding for the Erie Canal was not forthcoming, the State of New York decided to proceed alone with the artificial waterway, which it did between 1817 and 1825. It opted to build the route without utilizing Lake Ontario. Construction began first on the easier middle sections, and navigation commenced before the entire length of 363 miles from the Hudson River to Buffalo was complete (see figure 3.1). When finished, the canal featured eighty-three locks plus eighteen aqueducts to carry it over other waterways. Towpaths on each side of the waterway allowed draft animals to pull vessels along. Near its western terminus, the canal required flight locks and a deep cut through rock in order to climb the Niagara Escarpment.

Historians have attributed the Erie's inland route to fears about exposure to British North America, with whom the US had recently been at war, and the desire to draw off shipping and trade that would otherwise go via Lake Ontario and the St Lawrence. That latter motivation may have been exaggerated in retrospective efforts to stress the nation-building thrust of the canal. The path of the Erie served the interests of certain political and economic elites, but many Upstate New Yorkers would have been just as happy if the canal had used Lake Ontario. Indeed, Lake Ontario had made it easier

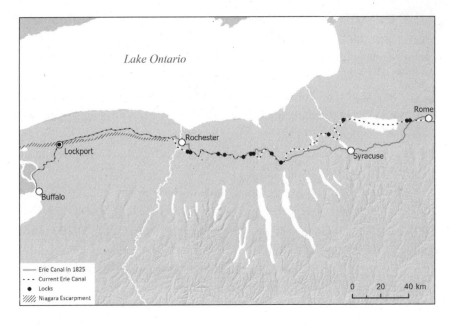

Figure 3.1
The Erie Canal. The dashed line indicates the current route of the canal, and the dark line shows the canal route in 1825.

for them to trade across the border than with other parts of their own state or country. For that reason, many Upper Canadians welcomed the prospect of the Erie Canal. Its final alignment avoiding the lake ultimately proved beneficial to both sides of the border, especially once other canals were built that linked with the Erie.

The Erie Canal was the megaproject of its day, and one that was considered an unalloyed success. The canal made New York City the primary Atlantic port. As many promoters had hoped, the canal served nationalist goals by suturing together the still-fledgling republic. In doing so, it provided the conduit opening up western New York State and the Midwest to settlement; people and manufactured goods moved west on the canal, while wheat, grain, and wood from new homesteads flowed east. About 24,500 people lived in western New York in 1810; a decade later, the population had more than quadrupled.

Religious fervour swept through the parts of New York within Lake Ontario's watershed, facilitated by the canal. Most of the area from Syracuse westward was considered the "burned-over district," part of a Protestant religious revival named the Second Great Awakening. Near Palmyra, east of Rochester, Joseph Smith received his visions that led to the establishment of the Mormon Church. Shakers and Quakers were active, as were utopian or progressive movements such as the Fourierists. Rochester became a hub of inspired activism in subsequent decades, led by the likes of abolitionist Frederick Douglass and women's rights advocate Susan B. Anthony; the 1848 Seneca Falls Convention, which launched the suffrage movement, took place in the eponymous Finger Lakes community that was connected by another canal, the Cayuga–Seneca, to the Erie Canal.

Significant economic interchanges across Lake Ontario – salt, timber, and potash – had preceded the Erie Canal and soared after its completion. The artificial waterway proved so successful that work on its enlargement began in the 1830s, though this was not complete for several decades. By the 1850s, the canal carried two million tons of freight a year. Whether measured by population, agricultural production, or industrial output, the canal helped

Figure 3.2
Canal aqueduct over the Genesee River at Rochester in 2021. A vehicle bridge was built on top of the aqueduct, which is the lower level of the structure with arches crossing over the water.

make New York preeminent within the union, giving truth to the Empire State nickname.

A number of smaller canals were built to link up with the Erie Canal. In northern New York, a canal connected the Black River to the Erie by climbing the western Adirondack foothills via more than 100 locks. Though this Black River Canal was an impressive engineering achievement, it was not a financial success.[6] The Oswego Canal essentially followed the line proposed by earlier advocates of an Erie Canal route that utilized Lake Ontario.[7] A private hydraulic canal to power mills and grain elevators had been built at Oswego in the 1820s, and the state then took it over and expanded this system. A much longer navigation canal was installed between 1825 and 1829. It ran from Oswego on Lake Ontario to where it joined the Erie Canal west of Oneida Lake and north of Syracuse. About half of this canal's thirty-eight-mile length used the Oswego River at a depth of four feet; fourteen locks overcame an elevation change of 123 feet. Supporting infrastructure needed to be built, changed, or replaced: dams, aqueducts, weirs, culverts, bridges, etc. Like most of the other canals, the Oswego was accompanied by a towpath so that boats and barges could be dragged by draft animals. Local interests undertook some small improvements at the mouth of the Oswego River to try and make the harbour more amenable to shipping and commerce. Sand bars, which had limited the draft of ships that could transit the mouth, needed remedy. But the government purse proved necessary: the Army Corps of Engineers put in long piers stretching out into the lake in the 1830s.[8]

Several other canals – Genesee Valley, Cayuga–Seneca, and Chenango – ran south from the Erie Canal.[9] The Oswego was the only one of the lateral canals that proved financially successful in the long run, partly because it brought the product of the salt works near Syracuse to markets and took tourists to Niagara Falls and beyond as part of the fashionable Northern Tour. To be sure, after the canal's completion, Oswego was a boomtown for several decades. In 1848, its port cleared over two million bushels of salt, and the amount of grain and lumber it handled during its peak years was far larger.[10] (Salt was produced by evaporating the brine collected from springs near Onondaga Lake, making Syracuse the salt capital of the United States.) Oswego then enjoyed a period as one of the nation's largest flour milling centres, along with timber and later corn starch. But after the Civil War it began a decline that took it from a leading lake port to a small regional centre – in 1870 the eleven grain elevators there handled 11 million bushels of grain;

Figure 3.3
Mouth of the Oswego River in 2021. This view is looking north to the mouth of the river emptying into Lake Ontario. The Oswego Canal and a lock are on the right; the old hydraulic canal is on the left.

by 1890 it was only half a million bushels – though some grain and coal would continue to be shipped through Oswego in the twentieth century.

The canals themselves were also tourist attractions. However, Lake Ontario did not become a draw for visitors to near the same extent as other nearby destinations such as Niagara Falls, the Adirondacks, and the Thousand Islands. The Erie kept increasing its annual cargo even after the initial spread of railways, which began replacing canals elsewhere. In fact, Erie Canal tonnage peaked in 1872, but declined fairly swiftly afterward.[11] Many of the feeder canals connecting to the Erie fell by the wayside, and those that remained operational, such as the Oswego, limped along. More and more farmers abandoned marginal and stony farmlands in Upstate New York and decamped to the fertile lands further west; the upside was that their deserted farms began to rewild, and many of these later became state forests or wildlife areas.[12]

CANADIAN CANALS

Canal mania was not restricted to the United States of America. The Welland Canal connected Lakes Erie and Ontario, bypassing Niagara Falls. Though the British colonial elite may have viewed the Welland as a rival to the Erie and an attempt to defend against American economic and military might, locals in the Niagara frontier were just as likely to view Canadian and American canals in the Lake Ontario basin as complementary and interlocking. In practice, the Welland proved to be as much an extension of the Oswego Canal as a competitor.[13] Goods could move through the Welland to the Oswego and then join the Erie, as well as move between Montreal and New York City via Oswego. In 1834, for example, the Welland Canal conveyed 40,634 bushels of wheat to Montreal while sending 224,285 bushels to the American market through Oswego. Appreciable amounts of wheat were also shipped from the United States to British Canada via Lake Ontario; when this grain was milled in Toronto or Montreal, it could be classified as "Canadian" and escape duties or prohibitions if shipped elsewhere in the British Empire, such as Caribbean plantations that sent products like sugar in return.[14]

The Welland Canal also allowed ships to sail straight between Oswego and Great Lakes ports such as Detroit, Cleveland, and Chicago without having to break cargo, transship into smaller vessels, or offload passengers, especially after Britain dropped colonial tariff preferences and the 1854 Reciprocity Treaty came into effect. At times, about 80 per cent of the foreign goods entering Upper Canada came through the Port of Oswego.[15] While the Erie was primarily a barge canal, the Welland and Oswego canals could accommodate deeper-draft vessels powered by wind and steam. Indeed, at the time, this trifecta composed what was arguably the most important canal network, in terms of cargo carried, on the continent.

The first Welland Canal left Lake Ontario at Port Dalhousie. A privately financed undertaking, it went through what became St Catharines, whose downtown developed on the canal several miles inland from the lake, and then scaled the ridge of the Niagara Escarpment. It continued south, joining with the Welland River (also known as Chippawa Creek), which acted as a feeder canal bringing water from the Grand River. Turning to the east, at first it emptied into the Niagara River at Chippawa just upstream from Niagara Falls. This detour to the Niagara was soon obviated by an extension that took the canal south to Port Colborne on Lake Erie. That augmentation gave the canal a total distance of forty-four kilometres (twenty-seven miles), with forty wooden locks.

But there were soon complaints, as there were about the Erie and Oswego canal system, that the Welland needed to be bigger. By 1841, the Upper Canadian government had bought out the Welland Canal and began improvements to deepen it to nine feet and build larger locks from stone. The second version of the Welland would be followed by a third version, opened in 1881, that boasted a depth of fourteen feet and followed a different path up the Niagara Escarpment; this route was shorter than its predecessors and made use of twenty-six stone locks. This would not be the largest nor the last version of the Welland Canal.

At the head of Lake Ontario, the short Burlington Bay Canal cut through the sandbar separating the eponymous bay from the bigger waterbody. Burlington Beach (or the Beach Strip) was a sand bar four miles long and thirty-five to ninety metres wide, never more than ten feet above the level of Lake Ontario, with a small gap in the middle. This outlet was filled in, and the new canal cut, in the 1820s. The Desjardins Canal was completed in 1837 to connect the town of Dundas to the west end of Burlington Bay through the Cootes Paradise marsh. Despite repeated efforts to improve it, the Desjardins Canal soon fell into relative disuse as Hamilton beat out Dundas as the main port at the head of Lake Ontario.[16]

Geopolitical considerations generated two of the British Empire's more ambitious continental engineering projects at the eastern end of Lake Ontario: Fort Henry and the Rideau Canal. Opened in 1832, this canal connected the lake to the Ottawa River at Bytown.[17] The southern section of the Rideau Canal utilized the Cataraqui River, which debouches into Lake Ontario at Kingston and the Royal Naval Dockyard, protected by Fort Henry.[18] About 90 per cent of this canal's roughly 200-kilometre length took advantage of natural waterways, using forty-five masonry locks. A series of fifty stone or wood dams – including Jones Falls, the highest dam in North America at the time – submerged wetlands, marshes, falls, and rapids, creating a slackwater navigation route. Dams flooded out almost the entire Cataraqui and its rapids, turning the river into a chain of lakes; the raised water level expanded the canal's watershed to encompass waterbodies that otherwise would have drained through the Gananoque River and then into the St Lawrence River.

The motivation for the Rideau Canal was primarily military: it provided a route from Lake Ontario to the Ottawa River, and then to Montreal via several other canals installed in the Ottawa River, which avoided exposure to the Americans on the upper St Lawrence. The rebellions of 1837 in Upper and Lower Canada suggested what continued exposure could bring, and attested to the continued crossborder permeability of Lake Ontario. In Upper Canada's rebellion, William Lyon Mackenzie advocated far-reaching democratic reform, generating admirers across the lake. Consequently, an American group from Oswego crossed to join in the failed invasion that was the Battle of the Windmill near Prescott; Americans then smuggled some of Mackenzie's supporters across Lake Ontario to safety. Soon, colonial authorities made Kingston the first capital of the United Canadas. After two years, fearing the proximity to the large American naval base just down the lake at Sackets Harbor, they moved the seat of power to Montreal. Later it would be sent northwest to Bytown, the emerging urban area at the terminus of the Rideau Canal that was renamed Ottawa. Though the Rideau never became a significant transportation route, it did move lumber and other resources while helping develop the inland sections of eastern Ontario (later in the century, my paternal ancestors would settle in Smiths Falls, one of the main communities along the canal).

The Lachine Canal, one of the artificial waterways that aided transportation in the St Lawrence upstream from Montreal, opened in 1825. Further west in the St Lawrence, British engineers had built several canals: Cascades, Rocher Fendu, and Coteau-du-Lac. These were later replaced by the Soulanges Canal, which in turn was superseded by the Beauharnois Canal. By the 1850s, canals and locks in the St Lawrence River provided a minimum channel depth of nine feet from the Atlantic Ocean to Lake Ontario; this would be fourteen feet by the early twentieth century. After Confederation, a royal commission called for improving the existing canals. The Cornwall Canal and the Williamsburg canals (Farran's Point, Rapide Plat, Iroquois–Galops), installed in the mid-nineteenth century, were expanded to aid navigation through the upper St Lawrence in Ontario.

The first locks in the Trent River, which connects the Bay of Quinte to Rice Lake, had been built in the late 1830s. These were some of the earliest infrastructural elements that would emerge piecemeal over the next century as the Trent–Severn Waterway, linking Georgian Bay to Lake Ontario via Lake Simcoe, the Kawartha Lakes, and Rice Lake (see figure 3.4). The Murray Canal, replacing the portage between Presqu'ile Bay and the Bay of Quinte, had been completed in the late 1880s. Decades earlier, Belleville had become the preeminent urban centre in the Quinte region – about 4,000 resided there by mid-century – facilitated by the lumber trade and then the arrival of the Grand Trunk railroad.

The Trent–Severn canals cut across Anishinaabe lands extending from Lake Ontario to Lake Huron. According to Doug Williams, an Anishinaabe elder from Curve Lake, this canal struck "a devastating and destructive blow to Michi Saagiig Nishnaabeg life, leading to the extermination of salmon and eels from our territory, flooded burial grounds and camp sites, the decline of fish and animal relatives, the near destruction of minomiin – the cornerstone of our food system – and an overwhelming increase in settlers."[19]

The middle sections of the Trent–Severn waterway near Bobcaygeon and Peterborough, where the well-known lift lock was finished in 1904, offered commercial links to the hinterland. Around the turn of the twentieth century, consideration had been given to a canal from Rice Lake to Port Hope. Ultimately new dams and locks were installed in the Trent River Valley, in large part because of hydroelectric considerations.[20] Further work on the Trent lasted about a decade, continuing until 1918. This included five hydro power plants on sites leased from the federal government; though these were initially built by a private concern, they soon came under the control of the Province of Ontario. By the time the western end of this canal system finally reached Georgian Bay in 1920, the Trent–Severn system was mostly used for pleasure boating and recreation (which was also the case for the Rideau Canal).

The 1871 Treaty of Washington, intended to settle outstanding US–UK problems, gave Canada and the US reciprocal access to a number of waterways in the Great Lakes–St Lawrence system. In the next few years, the US Army Corps of Engineers Lake Survey examined and made charts for Lake Ontario and the international section of the St Lawrence, establishing the mean level of the lake at 246.21 feet.[21] Amidst the flurry of canal proposals and developments in the last decades of the nineteenth century, the first serious conceptions of a deep St Lawrence waterway allowing access to the continent's interior were articulated. In the 1890s, the two countries formed the International Deep Waterways Commission to study the feasibility of constructing waterways that would allow ocean-going vessels to pass between the Great Lakes and the Atlantic Ocean. Each national group released a report in 1897. The American contingent suggested linking the Great Lakes to the sea through American territory, such as down the Hudson River; the Canadian report favoured the St Lawrence. The idea of expanding the Great Lakes

Figure 3.4
Lake Ontario and the waterway system to the north, 12 April 1838. This map shows the
waterway system running northwest from Lake Ontario, which provides the route for
the Trent–Severn Waterway.

navigation connection to New York City would persist, however. For example, in the 1920s an "All American Canal" linking Lake Ontario to the
Hudson was pushed as an alternative to improving the St Lawrence.[22]

The federal government, led by Wilfrid Laurier's Liberals, established a
royal commission to investigate a comprehensive Canadian waterway system.
But it was abandoned in favour of expanding the Grand Trunk Railway,
which hugged Lake Ontario's north shore. Improvements to Canadian inland
navigation were nevertheless made, such as upgrades to the Trent Canal and
Lachine Canal. One of Laurier's planks in his unsuccessful 1911 re-election
campaign was a Georgian Bay Ship Canal that could connect the Ottawa
River to Georgian Bay via Lake Nipissing. This would have allowed ships
from the upper lakes to skip over Lakes Ontario and Erie, though there were
associated plans for a canal from Georgian Bay to Toronto.[23]

Although many of these canal schemes were abandoned or postponed,
the canals that were built in the Lake Ontario basin had a range of ecological
impacts. Some of the most obvious are introduced species and changes to
water quantity and quality.[24] Because of technological limitations, canals

built in the first half of the nineteenth century were not very deep, but those that followed required more extensive excavation. Canals large and small generally needed to either utilize existing rivers or tap nearby waterbodies so that there would be enough water to carry barges and boats. Many wetlands, swamps, creeks, ponds, rivers, and lakes were fully or partially sacrificed to create the artificial rivers, with predictably detrimental impacts for aquatic species. This also lowered water tables in surrounding areas. The Erie Canal separated the Montezuma Wetlands and the Galen Marsh, for example, from their water sources. Describing a stretch west of Utica where that canal had drained nearby wetlands, novelist Nathaniel Hawthorne wrote that the trees were "decayed and death-struck."[25]

Canals often became heavily polluted. Lake Ontario is at a lower elevation than the canals that flow into it; consequently, significant volumes of pollution from industry and manufacturing have been sent into the lake, particularly by the Welland, where abandoned stretches of the old canal routes became full-fledged waste outlets. Moreover, industry and manufacturing grouped along canals and waterways because of the transportation, power, and labour advantages. Mills were commonly found near locks because of the change in water elevation and shipping opportunities. Locks and control works changed water speeds and temperatures, and the byproducts and waste of sawmills, sawdust especially, smothered benthic communities at the bottom of waterbodies by robbing them of oxygen and burying spawning grounds. As Nancy Langston writes, such land use changes began to "unravel nature's assimilative capacity," and ecological alterations reduced aquatic resiliency.[26]

Pollution was just one way that canals altered species composition. Digging a canal destroyed habitat, while the resulting locks and dams blocked many species that needed to move seasonally through waterways. Canals built in the decades after Canadian Confederation, such as in the Trent River or newer iterations of the other canals, could take advantage of technologies that permitted even deeper blasting or dredging. As we will see, mid-twentieth-century canals could be several orders of magnitude bigger, with commensurate ecological repercussions.

By offering new connections between watersheds, these artificial waterways also opened the door for the introduction of new species. It seems certain that the Erie and Oswego canals let some non-native species into Lake Ontario. The Welland Canal removed the species separation between Lake Ontario and the rest of the Great Lakes afforded by the natural barrier of

Niagara Falls. That is, the Lower Niagara–Lake Ontario–Upper St Lawrence system had been biologically distinct from the other Great Lakes in some ways because of the fact that aquatic organisms could not move further upstream due to the waterfall. The earliest iterations of the Welland Canal, which tapped the Grand River and other waterways in the Niagara Peninsula, were not very conducive to invasive species transmittal. But subsequent changes to the water supply for the third version of the Welland created a more straightforward aquatic highway for species like sea lamprey by taking water out of Lake Erie and sending it to Lake Ontario. In doing so, the enlarged Welland Canal continued its predecessor's penchant for remaking many of the local waterbodies to supply the fluid required to move ships through. Of course, canals also facilitated the spread of the planet's most invasive species: humanity. Canals led to larger populations and more industrial activities, which cumulatively had myriad ecological reverberations.

The Erie Canal is an interbasin transfer, meaning that it moves water between separate basins, though it takes minimal amounts of water out of the Lake Ontario watershed.[27] Intrabasin diversions, in contrast, are those that move water but keep it within the same basin. The Trent, Rideau, and Welland are all intrabasin diversions at the scale of the Great Lakes–St Lawrence watershed, but at the scale of the Lake Ontario watershed they are interbasin diversions. However, the first two of these canals do not divert appreciable volumes of water in or out of the Lake Ontario watershed. The Welland Canal, for its part, currently sends about 20,500 million liters per day from the Lake Erie watershed into Lake Ontario.[28]

SEASONALITY AND SHIPPING

The fluid nature of canals reveals one of the more important limitations of water travel at northern latitudes: seasonality. Winter was the most conspicuous seasonal obstacle, as canals here had to close for a good chunk of the year, usually from December to April. Floods and spring freshets, or large precipitation events, could be problematic, destroying parts of a canal as well as adjoining infrastructure and property. A tremendous amount of maintenance was necessary, and there were many chokepoints, locks especially, where a small problem could block all canal traffic.

Lake Ontario rarely freezes over completely in winter. But once ice had frozen thick on its nearshore waters, as was more likely during the Little Ice

Age, the ice offered a cheaper and more flexible transportation platform than travel by boat. Paintings such as "Toronto Harbour in Winter" and "Winter Scene on Toronto Bay" (see figures 3.5 and 3.6) serve as a type of climate proxy, revealing how people adapted to colder winters. New designs and technologies emerged to take advantage of local materials and conditions: ice-boats, sleighs, and skates offered commercial, transport, and recreational possibilities. Even if someone hoping to travel or move goods could find an operating ship in wintertime, they would have to pay to get themselves or their cargo on a lake vessel or canal packet whose timing and destination were controlled by others; conversely, those with access to a horse and sleigh or wagon had better mobility options on ice. There was always the danger of falling through, of course, especially in the shoulder seasons when ice was congealing or melting, or during a mid-winter warm spell.

These paintings reveal another vital but easily overlooked winter resource supplied by Lake Ontario's bays and tributaries: ice for storing food and perishables. Until electrical refrigeration in the twentieth century, communities would cut ice for use throughout the year, and an extensive ice trade was carried out regionally. Ashbridges Bay served this purpose for Toronto, at least until that bay became a veritable garbage dump and cesspool, prompting ice-cutting for the city to move to Lake Simcoe. Other urban communities also looked farther afield for ice because of similar pollution problems.[29]

In the 1830s and 1840s, the iron horse of the railways galloped through the area, reducing the need to time mobility quite so closely to nature's clock. Many of Ontario's earliest railways radiated out from Lake Ontario ports, and the lake remained the prime hub in the spiderweb of lines that resulted from the rail craze of subsequent decades. But until the further proliferation of railroads in the basin during the second half of the nineteenth century, water remained the dominant form of long-distance transportation. Consequently, communities on Lake Ontario stayed dependent on the lake and frequently interacted with it in multiple ways – whereas today the lake is directly used only infrequently and by a small percentage of the total population.[30]

Another unique use of Lake Ontario's resources was stonehooking. Between Scarborough and Oakville, stonehooking became a common activity starting in the 1830s. Dundas Shale had eons ago formed in long terraces not far offshore. When pulled or pried loose from the lake bottom, flat slabs of this shale were ideal for use in various construction activities: house foundations and walls, for example. Much of the rock went to building Toronto.

Figure 3.5
"Painting of the Steamship Chief Justice Robinson Landing Passengers on the Ice off Toronto in 1852," by William Armstrong. In addition to the steamship, note the ice boats and horse-drawn sleighs on the ice.

Oakville, Port Credit, Frenchman's Bay, and Bronte became focal points of this industry, building more than 100 of the unique schooners that brought stone up from the lakebed (the "hook" in stonehooking referred to the special type of schooners).

Stonehooking destroyed spawning grounds for valued fish species, however, such as lake trout. Removing all that rock from the lake's bottom also allowed water to erode the foreshore more rapidly. This became enough of a problem for waterfront property owners that as far back as the late 1850s a Three Rod Law was passed prohibiting stone removal within about fifty feet of the shoreline. This injunction had little effect, however. Neither did signs at the Scarborough Bluffs, which had been posted because stone removal was so extensive there. Stonehooking became even more intensive over time: counting gravel and other rock, between 1890 and 1910 approximately 25,000 to 50,000 tons was taken every year from the lake bottom.[31] This practice died out around the First World War, when concrete became more widely available as a building material. Nevertheless, in addition to the other ecological impacts, taking so much lakebed rock for close to a century may have even lowered lake levels by a bit.

Figure 3.6
"Winter Scene on Toronto Bay, Looking from Taylor's Wharf East towards Gooderham & Worts Windmill," 1835, by J.G. Howard. Note the windmills in the background as well as horse-drawn sleighs, people skating, and ice cutting on the lower right side.

During the early colonization period, the sailing ships that plied Lake Ontario were ones specially designed to carry the type of resources harvested from the Great Lakes and also deal with wildly varying meteorological and surface conditions that obtained there. Fitting inside canals was another design consideration. After all, if vessels hoped to move beyond Lake Ontario, they needed to squeeze into locks, a consideration requiring ship dimensions that were long, narrow, and shallow. Roughly from 1825 to 1875, Lake Ontario (along with the other Great Lakes) saw the emergence and thriving of a distinctive maritime culture dedicated to the shipment under sail of a large variety of commodified products extracted from the landscape by one means or another. As Kingston-based historian and sailing enthusiast Colin Duncan explained to me, this was the golden age of sail on Lake Ontario. Grain, timber, coal, metal ores, and stone originating in the Great Lakes were sent throughout the basin as well as to purchasers located in more distant places such as Europe, the eastern seaboard of the United States, and the Caribbean isles.[32]

For the purposes of building sailing craft, the region possessed an advantage but also presented a problem. Because of the abundance of excellent ship-building timber trees, it was possible to build ships inexpensively. Little capital was needed, and the skills were initially imported but then locally refined. The big problem confronted by shipbuilders was the size of the Great Lakes, though not in the sense one might assume. Whereas for canoes the open lake could be impossibly wavy and large, for big sailing ships laden with cargo the lake was dangerously small, as one could rarely be sure of much room between the vessel and islands or the mainland. Sailing ships cannot easily go much upwind, square-sailed ones least of all.[33]

Lest ships go sideways too much, designers had for centuries attached various vertical board contraptions. The need to fit within canals ruled out putting these on the sides of the vessels, a traditional arrangement that was easy to construct and very simple to repair. Contrariwise, coastal ships in Europe had not been able to use what is called a centreboard because the lined hole in the bottom of the ship, out of which that kind of board protrudes when deployed, would fill with gravel and mud whenever the tide dropped the ship down on the generally shallow shores. But for Lake Ontario the locals perfected the centreboard design and introduced some distinctive modifications to the rig.[34]

While the Great Lakes see plenty of days with ferocious winds able to drive a ship to destruction on a leeshore, they also see days with very light winds blowing quite high above the surface of the water. The ships developed in this local golden age of sail, Duncan avers, carried extremely high rigs festooned with hemp rope lines to allow the rapid addition and reductions of a broad number of sails cut in varying shapes so as both to maximize manoeuvrability and keep the operational wind speed range as wide as possible. The cumulative breadth of canvas when fully rigged was stupendous. But no single sail was so large as to be very difficult to control or to strike down if the breeze suddenly picked up. The evidence suggests these ships were highly effective on the Great Lakes, safe enough and affordable enough for serious commerce in a number of different commodities. They were only relegated to barge duty once steam engines became practical.

This might also be considered the golden age of Lake Ontario lighthouses, as many of the best known of these infrastructural elements went up in this period. The first light beacon was installed on Galloo Island near Sackets Harbor, followed by towers at Oswego, Sodus Bay, and the mouth of the

Genesee.[35] Of these, only Sackets and other parts of the scalloped north-eastern coastline, such as Henderson Bay, offered protected natural harbours. A late 1820s Army Corps of Engineers survey identified the potential of the others, provided improvements were made. And improved they soon were. The Corps subsequently built navigational aids – harbours, piers, jetties – and dredged channels, removed sandbars, installed water gauges, and charted shoals and reefs. On both sides of the border, such efforts were mostly paid for out of the public purse. These public expenditures then facilitated private profits.[36] Several lighthouses were erected on the Canadian shore of Lake Ontario in the first decade of the nineteenth century, along with some harbour improvements at locations such as York and Kingston, and soon after the cessation of the War of 1812 a survey was made of British North America's shore.[37]

Few of Lake Ontario's harbours are easy to enter under sail. Until concrete was more widely available, there were not many piers (structures built out perpendicular to the shore) because nearshore ice destroyed them quite quickly. To work successfully in a harbour, a sailing ship had to be manoeuvrable. The sailors had to be highly skilled as well, but it is in the design detail of the ships that we see the distinctive refinement of solutions. The success of these ship designs led to a brisk trade in commodities going from one part of the lake to another. So frequent was the trade crossing the lake in both directions that by 1848 even diminutive Port Darlington had its own collector of customs. It also had a growing export trade as well. The region was an especially good source for pine timbers for masts, necessary in the time of European naval wars, as well as for other more generic goods. In 1851, two barrels of flour milled at Bowmanville won first prize at the London Exhibition in England.

The environmental realities of shipping on this lake and the seemingly ever-changing geopolitical context of diplomacy and trade meant that the Lake Ontario environment and the global political economy affected each other reciprocally. Relations between Britain and the expanding United States of America continued the up-down pattern established over the previous century, though in retrospect this was the start of the long period of comity that continues to this day. Sometimes the problems were generated at the formal diplomatic level, but not always. In the 1860s, American supporters of the cause of Irish independence from the United Kingdom conducted raids onto Canadian soil near Niagara and in southern Quebec, hoping to spark more rebellions. The Fenians, as these radical republicans were called, certainly complicated the official British view of America. So did American aggression against lingering Spanish interests on its southern edges and against Indigenous cultures in the western plains. Some of these, but not all, were sanctioned militarily. America's exceptionally violent and sprawling Civil War then threatened to spill north over the border, helping motivate the creation of the Dominion of Canada.

Compounding the problem of predicting future trade opportunities (and restrictions) amidst all these political complexities, rail networks expanded in North America. These tracks, mostly financed by British capital, crucially helped to make it seem to many Americans that their "manifest destiny" was to dominate the entire continent. Various groups and interests based in Montreal and Toronto conspired together to limit this. Canadian Confederation, achieved in 1867, was undertaken to solidify British North America's political distinctiveness from the United States under the overall rubric of continuing membership in the British Empire, itself still expanding throughout the nineteenth century.

Lake Ontario was key to Confederation. After all, the new dominion represented a consolidation of political and economic power along the Lake Ontario–St Lawrence axis, facilitated by the promise of far-reaching transportation infrastructure to suture together the dispersed parts of the new country. A transcontinental railway was deeply associated with the Confederation project, of course, but without the east–west water axis, Canada as an independent country would not likely have even been conceptually, much less physically or economically, possible. In Lake Ontario the new country built harbours and piers, removed shoals, dredged deeper channels, and installed lighthouses, while constructing new locks and canals in the St Lawrence. All this improved the transportation, communication, and trade links between central Canada and the other constituent parts of the new nation – as well as improved the links with the mother country, which still held the final say over many aspects of the young polity. At the same time, Lake Ontario continued to provide a vital connection to, but also a buffer from, the United States.

By the end of the nineteenth century, official relations between Canada and the US had attained the level of mutual toleration, even respect.[38] On personal levels, Americans continued crossing to the Canadian side of Lake Ontario for various purposes. Cobourg, built on a cedar swamp a few miles east of Port Hope, became a popular summer resort for industrialists and the well-heeled from the Pittsburgh area – "the Newport of the North" – claiming the best atmospheric ozone in North America.[39] In 1890, future American president William McKinley persuaded Congress to apply a killing tariff on barley, a crop that Prince Edward County farmers and merchants had made into fortunes by shipping to New York brewers across the lake. This financial disaster drove a mass switch in the county to fruit growing and canning, as well as hops and cheese. The northeastern basin of Lake Ontario, including parts of Upstate New York, became a dairy zone.

In the Great Lakes region, wood for steam power was plentiful before the railway network made coal transport feasible, but those types of engines only began to dominate the lake trade nearer 1900. Coal-powered steamers could run the fierce rapids in the upper St Lawrence, a feat sailing ships did not attempt, especially when moving upstream. Steamers deposited untold quantities of coal clinkers and ash into Lake Ontario, which tended to settle to the bottom (interestingly, those clinker reefs eventually became spawning habitats for certain fish species). The shape of vessels dictated by the Welland Canal were adopted by the designers of early steel ships operating on the Great Lakes. Too confident about the new material and too mindful of the canal-favoured shape, it was a winter storm in November 1913, nicknamed the White Hurricane, that found them out. Because of the unusual sheer duration and violently oscillating directional shifts of very strong winds over several days, immense waves developed, taking down many vessels. Long and thin as "lakers" were, the key variable determining their survival in the most extreme case turned out to be longitudinal strength.[40]

The size and scale of water transportation had undergone a massive change between the early nineteenth century and the twentieth century, moving from paddles to sails to fossil fuels. My sketch here of the history of Lake Ontario vessels is admittedly brief and impressionistic; for the curious reader, many books are available on ships and navigation that go into much more detail. As I have shown, a range of canals and other infrastructural changes to facilitate navigation were constructed and maintained, usually by the state. Important lake harbours were deepened over the course of the nineteenth century, and they required frequent dredging to maintain sufficient depth. Ship technologies were enhanced and improved. Most of the important canals, built in the first half of the nineteenth century, were subsequently expanded several times. True, railways began siphoning cargo and passengers away from the water. But it would not be until the twentieth century, and the advent of automobiles, that Lake Ontario would cease to be a primary transportation mechanism for people.

The various forms of water transportation kept people in contact with the lake. They also had the potential to affect Lake Ontario's ability to bridge the two countries. Nineteenth-century canals like the Erie kept trade and migration within a particular territory. But, when used in conjunction with other canals such as the Welland and the Oswego, they could also commercially and culturally tie together the two countries sharing the lake. Improved ship designs and harbour facilities could cut both ways: they facilitated Canadian integration with the United States while also making it easier for the colony to retain direct links with Britain. Often it was regulations, immigration laws, and tariffs that determined whether the artificial border through the lake was reinforced or obscured. The aquatic links offered by Lake Ontario allowed more settlers and supplies to arrive and enabled the political jurisdictions they occupied to become economically and politically powerful. As the United States expanded westward, Lake Ontario's place in the national imaginary, never that large, decreased. Conversely, Lake Ontario's role in the evolution of the Canadian nation-state, which included Confederation in 1867, kept increasing.

CHAPTER 4

Cities and Growth

I have stayed at vacation rentals in apartment towers on the Toronto waterfront several times in recent years. These towers provide commanding vistas of Lake Ontario and different parts of the downtown. At one, it felt like I could reach out and touch the CN Tower right from my bed. The thing is, a century or more ago, I would have been lying on the lakebed. That is how much the foreshore area has been extended – this now densely inhabited part of the contemporary city used to be out in the water.

Lake Ontario's environmental health in the last century has been markedly affected by the growth of urban zones, the most conspicuous of which by far is the Greater Toronto Area (GTA) and the wider Golden Horseshoe: the urban conglomeration that encompasses the western end of Lake Ontario, including the GTA. Given that half the Canadian population lives within the Great Lakes–St Lawrence watershed, the paucity of large cities directly on the Great Lakes is somewhat surprising. In fact, Lake Ontario is the only Great Lake with a big Canadian city – it hosts four of Canada's ten largest cities, including the largest (and the five largest cities in Ontario, besides Ottawa). Indeed, most of Ontario's population lives near Lake Ontario. The story is the inverse in New York State, however, where only a few small cities sit astride Lake Ontario tributaries.

The urbanization of the western end of Lake Ontario, and the requirements of such a large population, meant that industrial and utilitarian uses of the lake came to predominate. In the early nineteenth century, that heavily urbanized future was still a long way off; this did not mean, however, that small settlements could not have deleterious impacts on local environments, as we will soon see. This chapter begins by addressing the earliest cities that developed near Lake Ontario during the nineteenth century. Then I look at the more recent history of the Golden Horseshoe and Lake Ontario's other urban areas.

EARLY CITIES

When Toronto was designated a city in 1834, it was home to about nine thousand inhabitants. This population had been, and would continue to be, buoyed by immigration from the British Isles. Toronto was well on its way to becoming a primary port on the lake. The Welland, Erie, Oswego, and St Lawrence canals increased traffic, and beginning in the 1850s the railroads arrived in force. But the same landforms that protected Toronto's harbour also threatened shipping (see figure 4.1). Sand encroached; silt filled the bay. Dredging continued incessantly to keep Toronto's harbour at sufficient depth and to match the deepness of the various iterations of the Welland Canal. The resulting dredge spoil was often deposited elsewhere in Lake Ontario. Wharves and docks went up piecemeal, and the shoreline was reinforced with retaining walls.[1] In what would become a perpetual Toronto pastime, plans and reports to remake the waterfront were formulated and then shelved.

Beginning in the 1830s, hotels and resorts opened on the sand spit that curved around most of Toronto Bay. People lived there too, many occupied with hunting and fishing. The ever-shifting contours of this peninsula and its shoals continued to evolve. Over time, it became an island archipelago accessible only by boat or ferry, making the "Toronto Islands" (rather than the singular "Toronto Island") henceforth a more appropriate appellation. An 1858 storm severed the hook-shaped peninsula from the mainland for good, creating a new eastern entrance to the harbour in the process. The Toronto Islands supported commercial fishing and sport hunting, as well as myriad recreational and outdoor escapes. For many, the islands became a refuge from the side effects of an industrializing city. More elaborate resorts opened, one owned by rowing sensation Ned Hanlan, catering to the upper classes ferried across the bay.[2] Responding to the growing demand for more middle-class parkland and leisure attractions, the city created new islands and ponds, along with other amenities and venues. Granted, such efforts were also meant to exert greater control over the social, moral, and racial geography of water-related recreational activities.[3]

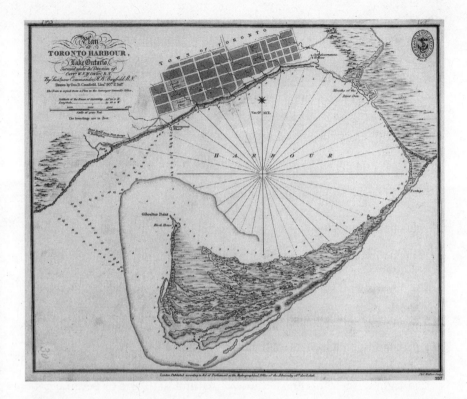

Figure 4.1
Plan of Toronto Harbour, 1828. The shape of the sand spit protecting Toronto Harbour,
which occupies the lower middle of this plan, is now very different.

Canals helped dictate the geography of settlement throughout Lake
Ontario. Communities on the US side mostly followed the Erie Canal axis,
creating an east–west line of inland communities, frequently ending in the
"port" suffix, ten miles or so from Lake Ontario. The Welland was a key factor
in establishing the spatial settlement of the Niagara Peninsula, accounting
for the urban centres strung along the canal corridor. It drew population and
business away from communities on the Niagara River and hastened the
decline of Niagara-on-the-Lake as a regional hub.[4]

Hamilton incorporated as a city in 1846 and became a manufacturing
centre and transportation crossroads, aided by its location on Burlington
Bay (officially Hamilton Harbour as of 1919) as well as the Great Western
Railway's decision to headquarter there. By 1851, Hamilton was already bigger
than Kingston and was surpassed in population only by Toronto. Hamilton
had been founded on the south side of the bay, though inland from the water

since the shoreline was marshy and saturated with inlets. For the railway, the existing shorefront was excavated, levelled, and extended out into the bay by some 222 metres.[5] The reclaimed portlands attracted industry and manufacturing, turning public bottomlands into private land, but also offering more social and recreational opportunities. The city later invested in new waterworks and sewage facilities, some of the earliest substantial works of their kind on the continent – the former brought water from Lake Ontario, the latter emptied into the bay.

The American shoreline of Lake Ontario never grew any large city comparable to those in Canada, such as Toronto, Hamilton, or Kingston, or comparable to American cities directly on other Great Lakes, such as Chicago or Cleveland. Instead, many small settlements at regular intervals along the lakefront focused on fishing, fruit, or agriculture. The north perimeter of Lake Ontario, conversely, was part of the Canadian heartland, and its population eventually dwarfed that of the American side of the lake. Most New York settlements that later became cities were a distance from Lake Ontario because of the Erie Canal as well as the topography: many of the rapids and falls on the lake's tributaries that made for good mill sites were upstream and inland. On the British North American side, settlements were more often placed right at the shoreline because of natural harbours or because good milling sites were situated closer to the lake.

The only American settlement of appreciable size directly on the lake was Oswego, which had a river with rapids conducive to mills near its mouth. Watertown, situated a bit off the lake at mill sites on the Black River, developed as a regional centre, with many industries that took advantage of the falling water. Watertown passed Oswego in population during the first decade of the twentieth century, aided by the proximity of Fort Drum. The eastern end of New York's Lake Ontario watershed developed more heavy industry than counties to the west, with the exception of the Rochester and Niagara areas. The largest US city in the basin, Rochester, was centred over a half-dozen miles from the lake; in the twentieth century, through annexation and growth, Rochester and its suburbs spread towards the lakeshore.[6] Other inchoate cities and towns, such as Syracuse, grew because of the Erie Canal's propinquity and then because of railroads which tended to follow the existing canal corridors and settlements.

Let's consider Rochester's development in a little more detail. Rochester was already exporting flour when the arrival of the Erie Canal turned it into a veritable boomtown. It was incorporated as a city a decade later. Water-

Figure 4.2
The High Falls at Rochester today. The tall buildings behind the waterfall are Rochester's downtown.

power from the Genesee River made Rochester, one of the fastest growing communities in the new west, a milling centre (see figure 4.2). But that river's destructive floods also made it a "treacherous benefactor."[7] Installing dams, diversions, and weirs helped mitigate some of that threat. All the waste cumulatively discharged into the river from mills, adjacent industries, and the public sewers must have impaired the water quality. However, whether it was enough to have a noticeable impact on Lake Ontario is open for debate.

The village of Charlotte and port facilities developed at the Genesee River's mouth, downstream from Rochester. Appreciable quantities of milled grain went out this river on its way to Canadian ports; the foremost chronicler of Rochester's history avers that its central trade asset following the War of 1812 "was not the river but the vast lake a few miles north."[8] By the year following the 1854 Reciprocity Treaty, $1.5 million in exports came from Canada through the Genesee port.[9] Crosslake trade was good during the Civil War years, too. But this area's time as a significant lake port had passed, and dreams that it would again become a shipping centre were never fulfilled.

Up to the late 1870s, Rochester's many mills together produced one million barrels of flour annually. But milling then moved further west. Scores of different industries came to characterize Rochester, shifting from the production of timber and wheat to shoes and clothing, then plant nurseries and seeds, and then two different industries that relied heavily on lenses: photography (Kodak) and optical (Bausch and Lomb). The nickname transition from the Flour City to the Flower City reflected Rochester's emergence as the centre of the mail seed and horticultural industry, as well as the hub for the surrounding fruit-growing district. Lake Ontario's moderating influence on the local climate offered a good growing season and ample precipitation in these parts – preventing late frosts in spring and early frosts in fall – while the Erie Canal and then railroads offered distribution for the produce and products. A slightly more temperate climate, the result of the Little Ice Age giving way, probably helped. By the mid-nineteenth century, Rochester boasted numerous plant nurseries, including the world's largest. The many local horticultural businesses distributed seeds, plants, and seedlings all over the growing United States by mail-order catalogue.[10] For a time, Rochester was also the centre of the country's major apple-producing region: almost half a million bushels were grown in 1855, while neighbouring Wayne County harvested even more, and Orleans and Niagara counties were also prominent producers. Other produce, including grapes, cherries, peaches, pears, and celery, were cultivated as well.[11]

Between the Niagara River and Rochester, no large towns developed right on Lake Ontario. Wilson and Olcott are the biggest communities, both with populations today of only a little over one thousand people. Olcott connects inland via Eighteen Mile Creek to Lockport, the site of the staircase locks on the Erie Canal. Olcott became a resort destination that used to feature a sizeable five-storey hotel and an amusement park with a roller coaster. The surrounding parts of Niagara County are fruit belt, as are the neighbouring counties running east to Oswego. Between the Genesee and Oswego Rivers, there is a smattering of lakeside villages and hamlets, such as Sodus Point and Fair Haven. Places like Putneyville spent some time as minor harbours, while today the whole of Orleans County does not even have a single village on the lake to speak of.[12]

By the later nineteenth century, a number of other amusement parks, camps, and resorts had joined Olcott on the south side of the lake. Most of these would continue to be popular into the early twentieth century. Ontario Beach, beside the Genesee River port, transitioned from a high-end resort into more of a working- and middle-class amusement park after the Civil War, earning the moniker the "Coney Island of the West" from boosters.[13] Just to the east, where Irondequoit Bay meets Lake Ontario, Sea Breeze amusement park opened in the 1870s. Indeed, most of the Lake Ontario shore on both sides of the Genesee River served as a recreational escape, with steamers, trains, and trollies bringing pleasure-seekers from Rochester and further afield. Sodus Bay, a bit further east, was also a popular spot for summer vacations. To the west of the Niagara River, Port Dalhousie was a resort destination known for its carousel, built on the filled-in part of a lakeside lagoon. Other camps and amusement parks could be found at Grimsby, Hamilton Beach, and Burlington.

The same climate that makes the south side of Lake Ontario a fertile orchard area also makes it a prime snow belt. Lake effect snow results from the unique combination of westerly winds, fetch across the lake, and the reluctance of the lake's open winter waters to freeze over. Cities on the leeward side of Lake Ontario, like Rochester, Oswego, and Syracuse, regularly get more of the white stuff than other cities in the country. The Tug Hill plateau, north of Syracuse, usually gets the most. The culture of northern New York is deeply influenced by these heavy snowfalls, adding another way in which Lake Ontario shapes the region.[14]

GOLDEN HORSESHOE

Over the course of the twentieth century, Toronto emerged as Canada's paramount city, the hub of a megalopolis – dubbed the Golden Horseshoe – that curved around the lake. At the start of the twentieth century, Toronto had a population of some 200,000 souls and was the second largest manufacturing centre in the country; the city proper would be over ten times larger by the end of the century, and that does not count the millions more in the surrounding parts of the Golden Horseshoe. Cities like Rochester and Syracuse continued to grow until the midpoint of the twentieth century, then began to plateau or drop despite absorbing nearby communities. The same was true of Upstate New York in general, which became the east end of what is pejoratively referred to as the rust belt. This is an unfortunate moniker that is also quite inaccurate in its implications; after all, not only is the Great Lakes

watershed an economic powerhouse but, because of the lakes, the predominant colour of this belt is actually blue.

By the late nineteenth century, Toronto was already starting to turn its
back on Lake Ontario. The federal government, which had held the Toronto
Islands since the dubious Toronto Purchase, sold these land formations to
the City of Toronto the year of Canadian Confederation. Shortly after,
Toronto moved its waterworks to the lake side of the Toronto Islands to bring
in potable water. But persistent typhoid problems prompted authorities to
extend the intake several times further and deeper out into the lake and
continue to improve the capacities and technologies of the waterworks.
Since the city sent its effluent into Toronto Bay – including the waste from
the stockyards that provided the basis for the porcine nickname "Hogtown"
– pollution remained a noxious problem. By the early 1880s, if not earlier,
fish were already impaired by sewage and livestock manure in the bay.[15] Realizing that dilution was not a sufficient solution to pollution, at least not for
a city with Toronto's population on a bay of that size, interceptor sewers were
constructed to take most of the city's outflows east of the harbour. There, a
new water treatment plant addressed the city's effluent. Still, in 1909 the city's
infant mortality rate was twice that of Rochester's, even if not all of those
deaths were attributable to polluted water.[16] A water purification plant was
built on the Toronto Islands in 1912, then quickly replaced by a larger plant
during the First World War. This plant filtered lake water through sand and
gravel, then piped it underneath the Toronto harbour to the city.

As part of an improvement scheme, the Don River was straightened and
enlarged, and its mouth was moved so that it debouched through the Keating
Channel.[17] A breakwater was erected between the harbour and Ashbridges
Bay, the marsh that the Don River had formerly run through before emptying
into the harbour. But this only created more stagnant water in Ashbridges
Bay, which was blamed for the city's cholera epidemics and other public
health problems. To address this, and create more industrial space, in the first
decades of the twentieth century the Toronto Harbour Commission oversaw
the almost total conversion of Ashbridges Bay to solid land. Like most of the
surrounding waterline, it was bordered by a constructed shorefront that hardened the ecotone, the transition zone between distinct biological areas such
as land and wetland.[18]

Indeed, much of Lake Ontario's shores had been marsh or wetland in the
past. More than half of the lake's shoreline wetlands have been lost since

European settlement, including almost all the wetlands in urban settings.[19] Estimates are that only 17,800 hectares of wetland remain along the Lake Ontario shoreline. That is very lamentable because wetlands are so biologically rich and serve many important ecological roles: providing habitat and spawning grounds for bird, fish, and invertebrate species, filtering out and holding contaminants and nutrients, absorbing high water levels, sequestering carbon, and recharging aquifers.

The Ashbridges Bay wastewater treatment facility was joined in 1929 by the North Toronto Treatment Plant in the Don Valley. In 1956, the Highland Creek wastewater plant was built at Lake Ontario in Scarborough, followed four years later by the Humber Treatment Plant. During the Second World War, the architecturally renowned R.C. Harris Water Treatment Plant at the east end of The Beaches neighbourhood joined the Island facility.[20] The First World War–era Island plant was replaced in 1977, preceded by Etobicoke's R.L. Clark facility in 1968, and followed closely by Scarborough's F.J. Horgan treatment plant in 1979. Four filtration stations now bring drinking water from Lake Ontario, the city's only source for public water supply.

In the later nineteenth century, the Toronto shoreline had been pushed south into the harbour by an additional 300 metres from Front Street, reclaiming 180 acres of the bay.[21] More infilling followed, often utilizing garbage and spoil from urban expansion projects or dredged material from the harbour. But less industry than expected actually relocated to these new port lands (see figure 0.1). Much of the reclaimed territory was used for bulk storage, and much of that was related to energy. The east-central portion of the waterfront in particular served as an energy conversion and distribution hub.[22] Every year, hundreds of thousands of cords of wood were stacked along the water before distribution to consumers. Coal from Pennsylvania and Wales was shipped and stored here in huge amounts: in 1891 the Ontario Coal Company alone imported 190,000 tons of coal, which accounted for 40 per cent of Toronto's consumption.[23] Facilities for gas, natural gas, town gas, and kerosene were prevalent, as well as electricity generation and transmission facilities (and later this was the site for the Richard L. Hearn thermal power station).

Consequently, the total amounts of contaminants leached into the surrounding water and ground are not precisely quantifiable, but surely legion. The Don River was already perhaps the most polluted river in the province, belching the outflow of city sewers, cattle yards, and industrial concerns into the harbour.[24] Furthermore, in addition to allowing the industrial expansion that produced so much of this pollution, all the terrestrial and aquatic modifications undercut the ability of the nearshore waterscapes, particularly marshes and wetlands, to deal with contaminants and nutrient loads.

The continued remaking of the shore cut off public access to the central waterfront, epitomized by the Esplanade. Begun in the 1850s, the Esplanade was originally intended to be both a public promenade and a railway corridor. But the latter became its primary purpose. Railways and other port developments further blocked Torontonians from the shorefront. At the same time, industrial developments also created or cloaked marginal spaces for non-prescribed uses, such as nude bathing by middle-class male youths.[25] Public bathing and recreational activities in Lake Ontario were relegated to a small number of officially designated spaces, such as Sunnyside Beach, Scarborough Beach, and the Toronto Islands, which eventually added amusement parks to their offerings. We might say that setting spaces like the Toronto Islands aside for specific recreational pursuits justified shutting the public out of other waterfront zones. But becoming seen more formally as a part of the city meant that the Islands were no longer as much a place on the periphery, and the area increasingly came under the gaze of authorities and their mores about class and gender.[26]

The gaze of the state also included race. I have already addressed efforts to erase the Indigenous presence from Lake Ontario. Given that some United Empire Loyalists were Black, and the Lake Ontario region was a well-travelled route on the Underground Railroad, there was a strong African American presence in places such as Niagara-on-the-Lake, St Catharines, and Toronto. Despite Canada's tendency to hold itself up as an exemplar of racial tolerance, compared to the United States, Black people in Ontario had always been subjected to informal and formal types of discrimination and segregation, which included access to Lake Ontario's amenities. Since they generally were not welcome at what were considered White beaches or recreational areas, those of African or Caribbean ethnicities created their own aquatic social spaces.[27] Across the lake at Rochester, a city with a large African American population, a history of legal and structural segregation also meant that beach and lake access followed racial lines.[28]

Physical control went hand in glove with social control: the footprint of the Toronto Islands complex was expanded and solidified. The Toronto Harbour Commission created Algonquin Island right before the First World War, for example. An airport opened at the northwestern end of the Islands on

Figure 4.3
Toronto, looking southwest toward Lake Ontario in 1918.

reclaimed land. During the Great Depression, the city allowed a small number of permanent dwellings on leased lots; by mid-century, the Islands had more or less become an integrated city neighbourhood, rather than a removed escape on the urban margins. But local government wanted to enhance public access to leisure facilities. Several decades of protracted battles about year-round residents on the Islands followed, with many losing their leases. Other controversies centred on bridges and tunnels to connect to the mainland, as well as the island airport. Permanent residences were gradually concentrated on just two eastern islands. The remaining islands were developed or reshaped for parks and attractions. Though the Toronto Islands had returned to their roots as a place of leisure for urban dwellers, the contours had changed over time: the bulk of the expanded footprint consisted of one large, crescent-shaped island – Centre Island – that almost totally enclosed the harbour and sheltered the smaller islands.

By the end of the Second World War, Toronto was on its way to taking over from Montreal as Canada's leading city. Though shipping and industry at the lake were in decline, the city's Bay Street was becoming the financial hub of the country, and light and heavy manufacturing proliferated all over

Figure 4.4
Sketching the Scarborough Bluffs, 1951. In the background is the Scarborough Bluffs.

the region. Hurricane Hazel struck in October 1954. Killing eighty-one people, it prompted Toronto to rethink some of its urban planning priorities, especially when it came to the waterways that coursed through the city on the way to Lake Ontario.[29] The subsequent history of schemes for redeveloping Toronto's lakefront has filled numerous books. Many of these plans did not come to fruition, but those that did included the Gardiner Expressway – running along the lake, it was completed in the mid-1950s – and the Don Valley Parkway, finished in the 1960s. Virtually everything was covered in concrete and non-permeable surfaces; this increased runoff and pollution during storm events, which went to the lake.

Other parts of Toronto's lakefront sphere were substantially reshaped as well. More than one thousand hectares of land have likely been reclaimed since the nineteenth century, and the shoreline in the harbour is now eight hundred metres from where it used to be at Front Street. And those figures do not even include the Leslie Street Spit. Starting in the 1950s, hundreds of acres of new land were created with construction debris and dredged materials, jutting out into the lake from the landform that had replaced Ashbridges Bay. This spine of land, which would eventually become known as the Leslie Street Spit, was initially intended as a breakwater and outer harbour for the increased shipping that the St Lawrence Seaway would bring. Those turned out to be misplaced expectations, since the Seaway never carried near the predicted cargo. The Toronto Port Lands had already started the slow process of deindustrialization and shipping traffic continued to decline.[30] More and more waterfront territory became vacant, leaving brownfields and contaminated sites.

While shipping may not have grown, the Leslie Street Spit did. Continual dumping and dredging added more landforms and lagoons to the original peninsula (see figure 0.1). There were other kinds of growth: flora and fauna colonized this locality on their own. At various points in subsequent decades, plans for this reclaimed land included industrial, tourist, and airport developments; these fell away, replaced by the idea of auto-free parkland. By the time the Berlin Wall fell and the SkyDome opened across the bay, the shoreward side of the spit was christened Tommy Thompson Park. Dumping continues to this day – approximately 60,000 tonnes are taken annually from the Keating Channel alone – making the spit bigger than New York's Central Park. Its ecological value as a nature escape, however accidental at first, has become its primary public benefit, along with accepting dredged material in the ongoing confined disposal units. The Leslie Street Spit is simultaneously a dump, park, artificial landform, and nature refuge, with all the contradictions such hybridity entails.[31]

Where the lake had previously served as a bridge, in the first half of the twentieth century it became more of a barrier. Waterfront communities in the past had looked to the lake for commerce, transportation, and food, as well as the focal point of recreation, community building, and identity. By the middle of the twentieth century, relatively few denizens actively interacted with Lake Ontario in direct or meaningful ways – for the majority, their most explicit connection to the lake was through drinking water and sewer systems. Indeed, Lake Ontario was viewed by many as a utilitarian sink.

To get across the lake now usually meant driving around it rather than travelling directly on it. To facilitate that, the Queen Elizabeth Way (QEW)

Figure 4.5
Toronto waterfront at dusk in 2021. This picture was taken from the western end of the Leslie Street Spit, looking north toward downtown Toronto, the skyline dominated by the CN Tower. Notice the rubble in the immediate foreground.

began during the Great Depression as a limited-access autoroute to carry traffic between Toronto and Hamilton. It soon expanded, running all the way to Fort Erie. It cut off easy access to the Lake Ontario shoreline between Hamilton and St Catharines, running right through the fruit belt. In the second half of the twentieth century, the QEW morphed from a parkway to a freeway: it was repeatedly widened, the speed limit raised, the number of intersections decreased, and most of the original ornamental aspects removed. The high-rise Burlington Bay (James N. Allan) Skyway, finished in 1958 and twinned in 1984, carried the QEW high over the Burlington Bay Canal. The Garden City Skyway did the same over the Welland Canal. Another transportation corridor developed west of the QEW at Burlington Heights; this isthmus, which separates Hamilton Harbour from Cootes Paradise, eventually carried six sets of railway tracks and ten vehicle lanes.[32] Toronto's network of 400-number freeways expanded in the 1950s. The 401 highway ran above Lake Ontario, replacing Highway 2, which was situated closer to the water, as the province's main east–west thoroughfare. Many new expressways, highways, railways, other types of public infrastructure, and hydro lines severed the lakefront from surrounding neighbourhoods. The new transportation routes, which needed to run *around* Lake Ontario, exemplified how the waterbody had become an impediment to mobility in the auto age.

The modern story of the Beach Strip (or Burlington Strip) at the western reach of Lake Ontario bears some similarities to the Toronto Islands. Both were peripheral areas caught in a tension between recreation for the masses versus playgrounds for the elite, but also as places for certain groups to live away from prying eyes. By the midpoint of the twentieth century, Hamiltonians of means had started to go further afield for their beach leisure, aided by the automobile and motivated by Hamilton Harbour's pollution. The Beach Strip became more of a working-class neighbourhood and, with the erection of the Skyway, even more of a transportation corridor. Like the Toronto Islands, this peninsula between Hamilton and Burlington was reconfigured and enlarged with infill during the twentieth century. The strip was noticeably widened, parts filled in (such as at the Burlington end), and others reshaped (the Windemere Basin at the Hamilton end). As the steel-making capital of Canada, Hamilton's port facilities continued their relentless encroachment on the bay, steadily moving north by infilling and reclamation. More recently, sections of Hamilton Harbour's industrial waterfront have been repurposed for public recreational amenities, which Nancy Bouchier and Ken Cruikshank have detailed in their history of this area.[33]

Hamilton's population more than doubled in the second half of the twentieth century. The stretch of territory between Hamilton and the Niagara River also grew during this period, if not quite as rapidly. St Catharines produced cars and served as a regional hub, adding a university in the 1960s that joined many other postsecondary institutions near the lake, a number of which opened to accommodate the postwar baby boom. Places like Grimsby, Stoney Creek, and Lincoln were attractive on their own or as bedroom communities for those working in Hamilton or elsewhere in the Golden Horseshoe.

The southwestern shore of Lake Ontario was already Canada's primary tender fruit district. Both wheat and apple acreage fell off considerably in the twentieth century, replaced by commercial fruit such as peaches. Unsurprisingly, canning was a chief employer in this area. Fruit acreage peaked about 1950 and has decreased since, in some cases replaced by wine grapes and greenhouse-grown flowers.[34] The coming of the QEW, and its later expansion, had a detrimental effect. In addition to directly converting large swaths of agricultural land to concrete, this limited-access freeway encouraged urban and suburban build up.[35] Over time, these communities further ate away at the agricultural land base. But the QEW did make tourist access to this region easier. Tourism remains a prime economic activity, especially along the Niagara River. Niagara-on-the-Lake had enjoyed a revival of sorts as a resort destination in the late nineteenth century. That too dissipated, only to be revived in the latter half of the twentieth century by the wine industry, the Shaw Festival, and the bed-and-breakfast scene.[36]

By the end of the millennium, the population of Toronto proper stood at 2.5 million and counting – with millions more in the surrounding GTA, which includes large lakeside cities such as Burlington, Oakville, Mississauga, Pickering, Whitby, and Oshawa. Within this megalopolis's borders are Canada's largest concentration of people, manufacturing, finance, and postsecondary education. There were signs that Toronto and other GTA cities had tentatively started to re-engage with Lake Ontario. Ontario Place opened in 1971 near the Toronto harbour's western entrance; it featured pods anchored beneath the water and protected by artificial reefs. As industrial buildings began to disappear from the waterfront, they were replaced by other types of buildings, like the new headquarters of the *Toronto Star* newspaper and a hotel.[37] Some lake filling permitted new parklands and recreational opportunities: in addition to marinas at Toronto Bay and the Leslie Street Spit, reclaimed land east and west of central Toronto enhanced public recreational opportunities and wildlife habitat at The Beaches, Bluffer's Park in Scarborough, Humber Bay Park, and Samuel Smith Park at Etobicoke. Other waterfront parks across the GTA were developed or improved, as were the public amenities on the Toronto Islands.

Nevertheless, the connections between the city and Lake Ontario remained tenuous. Water pollution, which will be addressed in chapter 7, was widespread. As one respondent to the Royal Commission on the Future of the Toronto Waterfront put it in 1989: "Torontonians' relationship to their waterfront is a sad one. We can no longer look to our waters as a physical and spiritual source of renewal. … Our water has become one-dimensional to us, a view or backdrop. It's too disturbing to think about what's underneath the surface."[38]

The 1990s ushered in new and more ecologically sensitive visions for revitalizing Toronto's waterfront; granted, more often than not, they never got past the planning stage. In the twenty-first century, the city has taken strides toward embracing the lake. The waterfront has become more publicly accessible, and some contaminated areas have been cleaned up. Several billion dollars are currently being spent on addressing stormwater overflows with a massive underground retention system and a new eye-catching and ultra-modern stormwater processing plant. The lower reaches of the Don River and Port Lands have been partly rehabilitated, with plans for more. Work has already begun on shifting the river mouth to prevent flooding, and the resulting island will have recreational, commercial, and residential space.[39]

But the Don also remains one of the more polluted rivers in the country, home to only the most resilient of aquatic species. Sewer overflows into the lake occur whenever there are large precipitation events, which are more common because of climate change, clogging the waterfront with whatever people flush down their toilets. After summer storms, many of Toronto's beaches need to be closed because of high E. coli levels. Remediation and restoration projects still get bogged down by politics, lack of funds, and inertia.

Whereas other Great Lakes cities such as Chicago reclaimed their lakefront in the post-industrial age with expansive public spaces and parks, Toronto has only done so in a partial way. Driven by Waterfront Toronto's spending, the Harbourfront shoreline south of Queen's Quay is now primarily parks, hotels, condos, restaurants, and marinas. The Port Lands is composed of brownfields, wharves, and extant industrial facilities interspersed with public spaces. The lakefront immediately west and east of the Toronto Harbour does now mostly consist of parks. An aerial reconnaissance of the wider GTA lakeshore from Burlington to Clarington reveals that it is chiefly occupied by a mix of residences and municipal parks.

Though many still complain about the state of Toronto's waterfront, contending that the condo towers and Gardiner Expressway cut off the city from the lake, others take a different view. Shawn Micallef, a renowned cultural commentator on Toronto's relationship to its water, points out that these towers mean the waterfront has become an actual neighbourhood where people live. A variety of businesses, restaurants, and grocery stores service this growing residential community within steps of the harbour, drawing in even more people. Micallef believes that more Torontonians are discovering Lake Ontario and creating a sense of community there.[40] He has noticed a growing lake culture in recent years, postulating that newer generations do not have the same hang-ups about Lake Ontario as an unclean or unsafe waterbody, or the waterfront as a place only for work and industry.

For every person willing to dip into the lake, however, there is another like the forty-something pizzeria owner in Port Credit who told me he would never go into the water. This restaurateur was of Middle Eastern descent, and despite his reservations about the lake, many ethnic communities, working-class folks, and marginalized groups have long sought out the water. Toronto is renowned as one of the world's most multicultural cities, and the White middle- and upper-class reluctance to swim and play in Lake Ontario – outside of certain activities such as sailing – provided openings for others with cultural connections to water and those without the means to escape the city in the summer or access its pools.[41] Many different ethnic communities in the Golden Horseshoe – for example, Caribbean, African, East and South Asian, Middle Eastern – have used empty waterfront recreational spaces, or created their own, to fish, swim, picnic, and play cricket.

Hanlan's Point Beach, on the west side of the Toronto Islands beside the airport, may have been the first nude beach in North America, making it, according to the *Toronto Star*, the "oldest continuously used queer space in Canada."[42] My recent visits to Toronto's waterfront confirmed the popularity of this beach, and elsewhere along the water the cultural diversity was unmissable. The COVID pandemic increased the number of people taking advantage of the beaches on Toronto Island and other areas. The problem now might be that central Toronto does not have enough official beaches to satisfy the demand. Consequently, there is a push to make existing beaches more accessible, perhaps build a new a pedestrian and public transit link to the Toronto Islands, and to permit public swimming in more places.

EASTERN SHORES

In contrast to the dense urbanization that characterized the western end of Lake Ontario, small cities and towns developed along the northeastern edge of the lake. Today, Trenton numbers 22,000, Belleville 50,000, and Kingston in the neighbourhood of 125,000.[43] Industry such as mills, tanneries, and lead smelters had historically grouped at Kingston's harbour. Many of these used docks and bulk storage facilities for commodities and fuels. A dry dock and new grain elevator went up near the turn of the twentieth century. At least fourteen large coal docks and wharves, which collectively might have been able to store as much as 100,000 tons of coal, appear on 1892 fire insurance maps, along with other coal merchants spread throughout the city.[44]

The per capita amount of coal and coal-handling facilities would have been similar for other places around the lake. Like other Canadian communities in the basin, much of Kingston's coal came across the lake via New York State ports such as Oswego and Rochester. Sodus Bay had a trestle to send coal out, beside which stood a malt house that imported barley from Ontario. In addition to furnace use, coal was processed at gasification plants from the mid-nineteenth to the mid-twentieth century. It was burned to power Kingston's new municipal water pumping system, which was opened in 1890. This private–public system used a steam pump to supply water from the lake for civic purposes and individual homes.[45] Reliance on coal meant that smog days were common in the Limestone City, as Kingston is known, as they also were in Toronto. Water travel largely died out in the first half of the twentieth century, replaced by ground transport; ferry travel to Wolfe Island and Amherst Island, Prince Edward County, and other nearby places has remained to the present day, with some ferries recently converted to electric.[46]

Like many other Lake Ontario cities, Kingston turned away from the lake, using the waterfront primarily for shipping or industrial purposes. Some shoreline infilling had occurred, though not on the scale of cities like Toronto or Hamilton. The LaSalle causeway across the bay was built during the First World War and reconfigured in the 1960s.[47] Presumably, this causeway circumscribed the hydraulic circulation from the inner to the outer harbour, much like a dam, with ecological consequences for fish and other species, as well as pollutant distribution. Ambitious plans were afoot during the interwar years to make Kingston the trans-shipment centre at the foot of the Great Lakes, including a massively redesigned inner harbour that involved joining Belle Island to the mainland. None of this materialized, however, with the city getting only a new Canada Steamship Lines grain elevator as a consolation prize. During the Second World War, the likes of DuPont and Alcan set up shop in Kingston.

Grain, coal, and heating oil still moved by ship in and out of Kingston until the 1950s. Nevertheless, Kingston had long been declining as a port. The opening of the St Lawrence Seaway did the city few favours, since it just meant that even bigger ships could now bypass it. During the decades following 1945, the few commercial activities that still occupied the waterfront disappeared. The upside was that much of the waterfront was freed for other uses. Railroads and buildings were removed and some brownfields were eventually remediated – though many potentially toxic sites remain, with landfills or sediments containing hazards such as mercury or coal tar.[48] Parks, recreational areas, wharves, hotels, and parking lots now characterize much of the downtown lakefront. Belle Island was eventually connected to the mainland:

Figure 4.6
Kingston in 2021. This picture looks westward from beside Fort Henry. The closest buildings
are the Royal Military College of Canada. The tall buildings in the background are at
Kingston's waterfront, with Wolfe Island on the left.

in the decades after the Second World War it was used as a municipal landfill,
then converted to parkland.

A similar pattern obtains for Belleville and Trenton. Heavy industries, such
as steel rolling mills and Portland cement, had long been operating in this
region. Nonetheless, the post–Second World War creation of provincial parks
benefitted the tourist economies of these cities, along with others such as
Picton, Cobourg, and Port Hope. Presqu'ile, a peninsula just west of Prince
Edward County, was the first provincial park on the lake, created in the 1920s.
In the two decades after the Second World War, Ontario provincial parks
skyrocketed from eight to almost 100, including several more on Lake
Ontario.[49] These included one at Darlington and several in the Prince Edward
County area, with Sandbanks the best known (see figures 4.7 and 4.8). Ad-
ditionally, there are a multitude of waterfront municipal and county parks
on each side of the lake. Tourists could pick up some locally made Hawkins
Cheezies to snack on while lounging on a Lake Ontario beach; first developed
in Tweed, production of this quintessential Canadian snack food moved to
Belleville in the 1950s. Both Cobourg and Port Hope have charming main

streets, though the former used its lakefront for recreation while the latter gave a good chunk of its waterfront over to a uranium refining plant.

The United States has far more acreage along Lake Ontario dedicated to recreation and parkland, reflecting its more rural character. But Canada is the only country with national parks directly on Lake Ontario, albeit with little acreage. Two small islands in eastern Lake Ontario, Main Duck and Yorkshire, are administered as part of Canada's Thousand Islands National Park. The Rouge National Urban Park encompasses the lower Rouge River watershed in Scarborough and narrows to less than a kilometre of frontage

Figure 4.7
Bathers at sand dunes in Prince Edward County overlooking Lake Ontario, 1951. The water pictured here is West Lake, which is separated from Lake Ontario by these sand dunes.

on Lake Ontario. There are also several national wildlife areas in Prince Edward County. While the United States has no national park on Lake Ontario, New York boasts more than twenty state parks or wildlife areas strung at regular intervals along the lake. The Lake Ontario State Parkway runs west from Rochester to carry vehicles to several parks and beaches. Furthermore, there are many other state parks on Lake Ontario tributaries and elsewhere in the watershed, including two of the nation's earliest and best-known state parks, Adirondacks and Niagara Falls.

Both the liquid and frozen waters of Lake Ontario offer opportunities for many sport and recreation activities. I have already touched on a good deal of the non-winter activities. In the cold seasons, sports like curling and hockey, or skating and sleighing, were possible on the gelid nearshore parts of the lake. Prior to the Second World War, these might bring out a whole community, offering mingling and courtship opportunities. Such scenes are common in artistic representations of winters at Toronto Bay, for example (see figures 3.5 and 3.6). Iceboating, too, has a long history at Toronto Bay, and at other places around Lake Ontario such as the Bay of Quinte, Kings-

Figure 4.8
Beachgoers in Prince Edward County in 2021. This picture looks west from the
Sandbanks park across Lake Ontario.

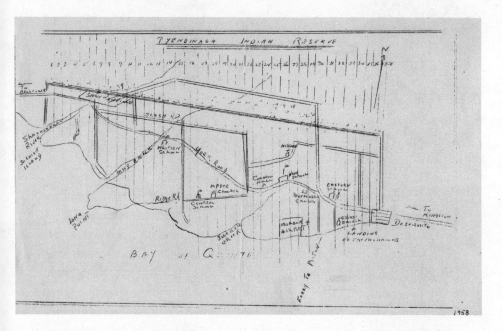

Figure 4.9
Map of Tyendinaga Mohawk Territory in 1958.

ton, and Sodus Bay, going back to the 1820s.[50] The unique craft that is the iceboat was used for ferrying purposes across Toronto's frozen harbour and for patrols by police and life-saving services. One account recalls twenty-four iceboats gathered at a Belleville event in the 1920s. Interest in iceboating declined in the middle of the twentieth century, but then seemed to pick up again. Climate shifts have reduced the viability of iceboating in recent years, however; Toronto's harbour rarely freezes over anymore, for instance. Nevertheless, places like Kingston still have a small but dedicated recreational iceboat community.[51]

The lack of harbour ice cover speaks to the ways that cities, which act as heat islands compared to the surrounding areas, can alter the local climate. Extensively built-up infrastructure, such as roads and buildings, absorb and re-emit the sun's heat to a greater extent than the greener parts ringing urban spheres. Accordingly, the dates of the first and last frost are different in cities than in the surrounding zones. In addition, the wastewater and effluent, along with road salt runoff, from cities alters the freezing and thawing of the waterfront, nearshore areas of the lake, and bays.

By the start of the twentieth century, the Tyendinaga Mohawks at the Bay of Quinte had already adapted to the surrounding market economy, facilitated by easy access to centres like Deseronto and Belleville. Many undertook wage labour in the nearby White communities. The government had pushed them to take up agriculture and drop hunting and fishing. However, they still retained traditional activities: mixed subsistence farming of garden crops like corn, berry picking, hunting, fishing, and muskrat trapping.[52]

As far as the federal Department of Marine and Fisheries officially saw it, according to an 1875 statement of their position, First Nations had no special fishing privileges outside of a reserve. Other branches of the federal government, and the provincial government, had conflicting stances on such questions of jurisdiction, which only further muddied the waters. Nevertheless, given the economic and cultural importance of traditional resource activities, the Mohawks of the Bay of Quinte had persistently asserted their rights by accessing traditional sites, purchasing licenses, or charging rent to White fishermen.[53] They continued techniques such as spearfishing, asserting their long-standing rights in the face of persistent settler persecution and the limitations of the federal *Indian Act*.

This pattern continued into the twentieth century. Government officials confiscated Tyendinaga seine nets, limited licenses and open seasons, changed bylaws, and in at least one instance directed that dredge spoils be dumped on fishing grounds in front of the reserve. Questions about reserve boundaries relative to the water line, as well as fishing seasons, continued to confuse things, as did the Mohawk right to take walleye in the spring. In response, White fishers sometimes tried to use physical intimidation.[54] Judicial rulings informed by imperialist notions and circular logic consistently went against First Nations, as did the 1923 Williams Treaties. To wit, in 1921 a fishery inspector confiscated the seine net of Eliza Sero of the Tyendinaga Mohawks for fishing without a licence. Sero took the case to court, claiming Mohawk sovereignty, since she deployed her net within Tyendinaga waters. But the judge could not countenance such jurisdictional claims and ruled against her.[55]

In the years after the Second World War, the Tyendinaga Mohawk became one of the first Indigenous communities in the country to gain control over band administration, meaning they no longer had to deal with a federal Indian Agent. Even after the 1973 *Calder* legal decision recognized that Indigenous peoples' inherent rights to the land predated the arrival of Europeans, subsequent Mohawk efforts to reclaim their land, at the Bay of Quinte (including most of Deseronto) and elsewhere, were stonewalled and then criminalized by the Canadian state.[56] Nevertheless, they were eventually able to reincorporate some of their former territory. Today, Tyendinaga is fairly rural, interspersed with woodlands and wetlands, and encompasses about 7,300 hectares with a membership of eight thousand.[57]

Children were sent to residential and day schools, where they were punished if they spoke the Mohawk language. Tyendinaga members nevertheless clandestinely maintained ancestral practices and traditions. In recent decades, they have been able to practice these lifeways more openly. There is a movement to regain facility in the Mohawk language and teach sacred practices. The Kenhté:ke Seed Sanctuary, for example, preserves rare heirloom crops like blue Cayuga flint corn and Jacob's cattle bean. According to one of the sanctuary keepers, who describes the process as one of "rematriation" because it involves returning women to their leadership and Earth-care roles, "Our connection to these seeds goes back to our creation story, which is the foundation of our origins, our language and our culture. That's how deeply significant the seeds are to us … it's seeds, foodways and reconnecting to our spirituality and sacred ecology."[58] Tyendinaga has recently become even more emboldened in its efforts to resist the settler state, evidenced by its 2020 blockade in opposition to a gas pipeline through Wet'suwet'en territory on the west coast. This First Nation has managed to hold on, resist, and thrive.

As I mentioned earlier, the Tyendinaga Mohawk Territory is the only Indigenous reserve directly on, or even very close to, the waters of Lake Ontario. There are several Haudenosaunee reservations within the Lake Ontario watershed on the New York side – Tuscarora, Tonawanda, Oneida, Onondaga – but these communities are a mere fraction of their former land base.[59] Nevertheless, these nations have defended their homelands and culture in the face of the persistent settler attempts to erase them. In the twenty-first century, the largest population of Indigenous peoples on Lake Ontario is in Toronto. Though drawn from many different First Nations, and not occupying a specifically designated territory, estimates put the number somewhere between 45,000 to 70,000.[60] This speaks not only to the resiliency of Indigenous peoples in the face of settler colonialism but to the fact that many still live near Lake Ontario. Indeed, the total number of Indigenous peoples living by the lake today might be higher than at any point in history, even if it is now only a very small percentage of the total population.

Since the population of the US shore of Lake Ontario is just a fraction of Ontario's, there is much less to say about urban development along the lake in New York State. At the start of the twentieth century, most of the American perimeter of Lake Ontario was still farmland or undeveloped. Rochester slowly expanded its borders, reaching Lake Ontario during the First World War.[61] While shipping via the Genesee River had severely fallen off, port facilities were improved and the river was dredged. Schemes to expand Irondequoit Bay as a significant harbour – in conjunction with a potential canal from Toronto to Georgian Bay – came to naught. But starting in 1907 the Ontario Car Ferry Company, cooperatively organized by the Grand Trunk Railway and the Buffalo, Rochester and Pittsburgh Railway, began a ferry service from here across Lake Ontario to Cobourg. The primary purpose of the ferry was to transport train cars loaded with Pennsylvania coal for steam trains on the Grand Trunk railroad, but it took other cargo and personal vehicles as well. It also carried passengers, mostly for summer excursions: in 1920, 63,811 of the 68,429 passengers rode between June and September. During the following five years, the ferry carried more than 350,000 persons. But between 1945 and 1949, coal traffic decreased by more than half, from 854,916 tons to 425,651; passenger traffic declined by roughly the same proportion. The last trip took place in 1949. Around then, another passenger steamer route that called at Rochester was shuttered.[62]

Even the prospect of the St Lawrence Seaway, addressed in the next chapter, did not excite enough Rochester leaders to spur port development; the larger Seaway ships bypassed most ports on Lake Ontario anyway. Coinciding with the Seaway's construction was the opening of the New York State Thruway, which ran east–west from Albany to Buffalo. This toll freeway's placement pulled most travellers, who now used automobiles, far away from the lake.

Coal traffic still went across the lake, though, and personal pleasure craft was clearly on the rise.[63] The majority of people who plied the waters of this sweetwater sea henceforth did so for recreation and fishing. Even though a much smaller percentage of the population now experiences the lake by watercraft, compared to previous centuries when that had been a primary form of mobility, the total number of people who move under the power of sail is today the highest it has ever been. While most sailboats also have a motor as a backup, and for getting in and out of port, a high percentage of boats rely exclusively on engines. Nowadays, these range from modest fishing watercraft to motorboats and runabouts, up to catamarans and luxury yachts, berthed at the many docking facilities, ports, and marinas that dot the lake.

Some mill sites on the Genesee River were converted to hydro power, while upriver from Rochester the Mt Morris flood control dam was finished by the early 1950s. At about the same time, after decades of considering it, Rochester began drawing its drinking water from Lake Ontario. Rochestarians continued to frequent resorts, beaches, and amusement parks at Charlotte and Irondequoit Bay, which had become suburbs of the city.[64] Nevertheless, the glory days of lakeside recreation had peaked before the First World War. The amusement park at Ontario Beach was torn down, except for a carousel, by 1920.

Greater Rochester remained the major urban centre between Syracuse and Buffalo. By the 1960s, Rochester had a population of more than 300,000; it then declined while some of its commuter suburbs grew larger. Rochester proper now has one-third fewer inhabitants, making it smaller than Buffalo but bigger than Syracuse. That said, the wider Rochester metropolitan area is home to one million people, about the same as Buffalo. Syracuse, about forty miles from Lake Ontario, is the urban hub in the southeast portion of the basin. Its population peaked in the 1950s at over 220,000, but it has since dropped to less than 143,000 – though its metro area population is over 400,000.

Rochester has never fully defined itself as a lake city; if anything, the lake decreased in importance for Rochester during the twentieth century. Oswego identified more closely with the lake. Granted, by the twentieth century, Oswego was already in relative decline. It was home to over 12,000 souls in 1850, two years after it became a city, and almost 21,000 two decades later; the population then plateaued, topping out around 24,000 in the 1920s. During the 1970s it dipped under 20,000, where it has remained.

In 1870, 900,000 tons of cargo had gone through the Oswego Harbor. Even though the salt, starch, and grain traffic started declining, timber imports from Canada took up the slack. But that too proved temporary, despite harbour improvements such as an outer breakwater and channel deepening. For the next decade or two, coal exports made up for some of the loss – 400,000 tons in 1900, 700,000 tons by 1913 – but that also tapered off.[65] In the 1930s, Oswego's inner harbour breakwater was removed along with some islands, the outer breakwater was given the arrowhead configuration that remains in place today, and the west harbour was deepened. Despite these improvements, the elevators and industrial buildings that once crowded the Oswego waterfront slowly declined. Cement still goes in and out of Oswego, though; in fact, the entire lake is studded with cement facilities.[66]

The types of land uses and the number of people around Lake Ontario changed dramatically between the nineteenth and the twentieth centuries. Undoubtedly the paramount shift was the growth and intensification of the Toronto area and the wider Golden Horseshoe. In fact, most urban centres near the lake but outside of the Golden Horseshoe decreased in population or significance over the past century; the Toronto region, in contrast, grew to become the most heavily populated part of Canada. With the population of the Ontario side of the lake dwarfing that of New York, it became more and more a Canadian lake. Benefitting from the resources and opportunities offered by Lake Ontario, Toronto passed Montreal as the financial, industrial, and political centre of Canada, further solidifying Lake Ontario's centrality to the nation.

The urban conglomeration called the Golden Horseshoe was both enabled and constrained by, and definitely embedded within, Lake Ontario's ecology. From food to drinking water, energy production to transportation, waste disposal to industry, the lake made possible the growth of the human societies around it. Lacustrine resources instilled expectations of abundance, sustaining the capitalist, liberal, and democratic political economies that hugged Lake Ontario's shores. But maximizing the exploitation of resources put enormous stress on Lake Ontario in myriad ways. Though its resilience was remarkable, considering all that humanity had thrown at it, the lake's vulnerability was becoming equally apparent. Particularly near the largest urban areas, Lake Ontario was showing the scars of its exploitation.

CHAPTER 5

𝕛𝕩

Energy and Megaprojects

"It has moved the ocean a thousand miles inland," proclaimed the *Globe and Mail* newspaper the day the St Lawrence Seaway and Power Project opened in 1959. "The effects of this cannot as yet be estimated, but we can be certain that they will be very great." The impacts of this megaproject were indeed great in magnitude, though the bad arguably outweighs the good when it comes to Lake Ontario. The navigation and hydroelectric benefits aided the industrial and economic expansion of the Lake Ontario basin. But by damming the upper St Lawrence, Lake Ontario was henceforth treated as a hydro power reservoir; by opening the gates of new locks to ships from across the globe, the Seaway allowed foreign species to infiltrate the lake.

The St Lawrence Seaway and Power Project represented the apogee of more than a half-century of efforts to re-engineer the hydraulic system of the lowest Great Lake and its outlet. At the same time that the river flowing out of Lake Ontario was being reconfigured in the 1950s, Canadian and American engineers were also cooperating to redesign the river flowing into Lake Ontario. The Niagara River had been at the forefront of advances in hydroelectric generation, and, after decades of prior attempts, in the 1950s its famed waterfall would be remade for both power and beauty.

This chapter will show that these water control projects, along with many others on Lake Ontario tributaries, had tremendous ramifications for the lake and for the political jurisdictions that surrounded it. In addition to physically remaking waterbodies, hydroelectricity fostered the belief that energy abundance could produce perpetual economic growth around Lake Ontario. That power abundance undergirded the political economy of not only the Province of Ontario but the larger Canadian nation. Though hydro-electricity from the Lake Ontario region was not as important, relatively speaking, in the United States as a whole, it was a key energy source for New York State. Hydroelectricity generated a broader belief in the efficacy of government intervention, and transnational cooperation, since it was the Canadian and American states that worked together to provide the expertise and financial resources to make these engineering megaprojects happen.[1]

HYDRO PIONEERS

By the later nineteenth century, Niagara Falls was the cradle of large-scale hydroelectric production and distribution. Allied industries such as aluminum and electrochemicals moved to the Niagara frontier to take advantage of the copious electricity. Canada and the US began discussing how to mutually refashion Niagara Falls for optimal energy and industrial production. Because of public fears about the growing ravages of industrializing the Niagara River, by the 1880s a transnational preservation movement had spurred the creation of protected parkland on both banks of Niagara Falls. The goal was to "free" Niagara so that the sublime experience was theoretically accessible to everyone.

Niagara's first hydroelectric generator was installed in 1881 by Jakob Schoellkopf, owner of the Niagara Falls Hydraulic Power and Manufacturing Company. Over the next decade or so, hydro power technology advanced rapidly. By 1895, the Edward D. Adams powerhouse had opened on the New York side of the Niagara River. It featured a revolutionary central station model: large generators produced all the power at one location and then transmitted it at high voltage over long distances. The Adams plant's ten turbines generated 50,000 horsepower (around 37,000 kilowatts) of two-phase electricity, more than any other hydro power plant globally. It was the first truly large-scale alternating current (AC) generating and polyphase transmission plant. The Niagara Falls Power Company sent three-phase AC (11,000 volts) some twenty-two miles from the Adams station to Buffalo, and then a few years later added a second powerhouse. Several different hydroelectric generating stations at Niagara Falls would subsequently lay claim to the mantle of the largest in the world.[2]

American hydro financiers looked across the Niagara River for more opportunities. The International Railway Plant produced the first hydro power on the Canadian side in 1893.[3] In 1898, the nearby DeCew Falls hydroelectric station became operational. Taking water from the Welland Canal, it emptied into Lake Ontario via Twelve Mile Creek, sending the electricity thirty-five miles to Hamilton. Three hydroelectric stations were subsequently completed on the Ontario side of Niagara Falls by the Electrical Development Company, Canadian Niagara Power, and the Ontario Power Company. The proliferation of hydroelectric companies was part and parcel of a larger continent-wide explosion in electricity. The Adams power plant alone was responsible for one-tenth of all the electrical power generated in the United States. This growth helped drive the shift from using electricity mainly for lighting to also powering machines. More widely available electricity in turn brought a transformation of both workplace and household labour, with the attendant range of social consequences.

The first big power station built on the Ontario shore of the Niagara River was the Canadian Niagara Power Generating Station, later known as the Rankine generating station. Featuring the largest generators in the world when it came online in 1905, this station was modelled on the Adams plant and was a subsidiary of the same parent concern, the Niagara Falls Power Company. As the company directors planned from the beginning, the bulk of the electricity was exported to the United States. Another new station, the Ontario Power Plant, was owned by the Ontario Power Company; however, the name is misleading, for this was an American company that signed export contracts to send the electricity across the river.[4] The Toronto Power Plant, owned by the Electrical Development Corporation, was the only Canadian concern among the new Ontario plants. However, a group of Toronto robber barons controlled it and sent most of its power to that city.

The United States was embroiled in protracted and intertwined debates concerning private versus public power, state versus federal control of power, and unbridled economic expansion versus the preservation of resources. Although the creation of the State Reservation at Niagara had pushed industry away from the waterfall, the New York legislature continued to grant charters for prospective hydroelectric developments that would take water from above the falls. To supply these generation stations, water was diverted from the upper Niagara River and around the waterfall through various conduits. The cumulative volume of the diversions had a noticeable impact on the amount of water flowing over the falls and thus on its aesthetic attraction for tourists.

Many called for the preservation of Niagara Falls, though precisely what constituted "preservation" had mixed meanings and motivations. Some argued that as much water as possible should be diverted for power production to protect the majestic Horseshoe Falls from constant erosion (three to seven feet per year on average). There were a variety of schemes to ostensibly enhance power generation and simultaneously protect the waterfall's scenic appeal. These included dams across the Niagara River at several different locations. One such proposal placed an enormous barrier across the Niagara River about a half-mile upstream from the waterfall that could divert all of the water for power production, except for the eight hours each day when Niagara Falls would be turned back on. Others suggested alternative iterations of this "intermittent waterfall," such as schemes allowing water to flow over Niagara Falls only on Sundays.[5] In the following years, the Deep Waterways Commission and the United States Board of Engineers also recommended a dam across the Niagara River at its mouth to counteract the lower levels throughout the Great Lakes basin caused by the Chicago Diversion.[6]

HYDRAULIC DIPLOMACY

The hydroelectric works in the Niagara region were on the cutting edge globally. They required advancing the scientific understanding of how interconnected the Great Lakes hydrological system really was – for example, would diversions in or out of the upper Great Lakes be discernible at the power stations in the lower Great Lakes basin? Attention focused on the Chicago Sanitary and Ship Canal, which was the first large-scale diversion out of the Great Lakes basin when it opened in 1900 to provide sewage disposal and public health benefits for the "Windy City." This engineered waterway reversed the flow of the Chicago River *away* from Lake Michigan, and thus out of the Great Lakes watershed, eventually to the Mississippi River and then the Gulf of Mexico. The "Chicago Diversion" refers to the volume of water allowed to be withdrawn by the Sanitary and Ship Canal. Canada and the other American Great Lakes states strenuously objected to the Chicago Diversion, arguing that it would lower levels throughout the Great Lakes, including Lake Ontario, hurting shipping and hydroelectric generation. It became a thorn in the side of US–Canada environmental diplomacy, periodically disrupting interstate politics and foreign relations for over a century.

These types of transborder water issues called for greater international coordination or cooperation. In the 1890s, the three North American countries had entered into talks about some sort of international agreement to govern shared waters. The International Waterways Commission (IWC) set the stage for the International Joint Commission (IJC). The IJC was created when the US and Great Britain (on behalf of Canada) signed the 1909 Boundary Waters Treaty (BWT). This treaty was a pioneering piece of water resource management. But it was equally a bilateral agreement intended to make it easier for both sides to exploit their shared waterscapes for economic development. Essentially, under the treaty any changes in the level of a boundary waterbody needed agreement through the IJC (or a special agreement between the federal governments outside of the IJC, which would happen with the 1954 St Lawrence Seaway agreement and the 1950 Niagara River Diversion Treaty). The BWT outlined an order of precedence for border waters uses: 1) domestic and sanitary purposes, 2) navigation, and 3) power and irrigation. However, no mention was made of industrial, recreational, or environmental uses, though these were recognized and incorporated over time, particularly after the Second World War.

The IJC is made up of six commissioners, three appointed by each side. Commissioners are intended to act not as representatives of their national government but in the common interest of the citizens of the basins the IJC works in. The BWT provided for public-input mechanisms, such as public hearing sessions that take place in the concerned watershed (rather than just in national and provincial/state capitals), so that locals affected by a particular matter could have their voice heard. The BWT can be seen as ushering in the modern age of environmental regulation for Lake Ontario, and the IJC would be central to future Lake Ontario ecopolitics concerning both water quantity and water quality.

In the first few decades of the twentieth century, gigantic new hydro power stations were built on both sides of the Niagara River. The Schoellkopf station in New York was the largest private hydroelectric station in the world, while the Queenston-Chippawa station opened in the early 1920s by Ontario Hydro (also known as the Hydro-Electric Power Corporation of Ontario, or HEPCO for short) was the largest hydro power station of any type globally. Bilateral engineering studies investigated how to maximize electricity production while modifying Niagara Falls to disguise the impact of diverting more water. In 1929, Canada and the United States signed a convention and protocol for the preservation of Niagara Falls. This brief treaty had two crucial concerns: construction of remedial works and additional water diversions. The agreement provided for remedial works to ensure un-interrupted crestlines at all times on both the Canadian and American falls and enhance their scenic beauty. However, this treaty could not get through the US Senate.

Even though this accord stalled, the two countries cooperatively under-took other navigational and hydro power improvements that had implications for Lake Ontario. They agreed to dredge deeper channels for navigation in the Thousand Islands. This coincided with the creation of the Beauharnois canal and hydro dam, which was constructed in the St Lawrence just west of Montreal between 1929 and 1932. The new Welland Canal, the fourth, also opened in 1932. Titled the Welland Ship Canal, it was built over almost twenty years: work had begun in 1913, but progress was halting because of the economic impact of the First World War and other factors. In the meantime, the Erie and Oswego canals, along with other linked canals, had been improved and renamed the New York State Barge Canal. By the second half of the century, however, this fluid artery that had played such an important role in Upstate New York's history was primarily the domain of recreational users.

The fourth iteration of the Welland Canal reduced the number of locks from twenty-six to seven, including a guard lock, with a controlling depth of twenty-five feet.[7] It also featured three consecutive twinned flight locks that marched straight up the Niagara Escarpment rather than approaching it at an oblique angle, as the previous Welland routes had done. The route remained much the same from Port Colborne to Thorold. However, from the Niagara Escarpment it ran north to a new Lake Ontario connection at Port Weller. Here two piers stretched 1.5 miles out into Lake Ontario. Building these piers was challenging and time-consuming work, requiring massive amounts of material dumped onto the lakebed, which Lake Ontario storms and ice habitually threw back or eroded. The early Welland canals had attracted industry, including shipbuilding and some of Canada's biggest textile, paper, and grain mills. After the Welland's twentieth-century expansion, other heavy industry and manufacturing began locating near it, including steel and vehicle manufacturing plants as well as a shipbuilding yard at Port Weller.

This much larger Welland Canal involved a new water supply system and a new hydroelectric station, all of which further reworked the area's hydrology. Some domestic wells dried up, and in some cases public water supplies were contaminated; even industries taking water from the canal found it too polluted or turbid. Chippawa Creek, also known as the Welland River, was diverted and taken under the canal by a syphon culvert. Several other culverts took watercourses under the new shipping channel. The valley of Ten Mile Creek was obliterated, and multiple wetlands were filled in. Beaverdams Pond linked with the Lake Gibson and Lake Moodie reservoirs to supply water to the DeCew generating station. Ontario Hydro acquired this station in 1930, upgraded it, and added a second station during the Second World War.[8]

Many smaller power stations were built throughout Lake Ontario's watershed in its many tributaries and canals. Just as mill dams had prevented fish passage, created pollution, and affected water flows, smaller hydro stations cumulatively had an appreciable effect on water quality and quantity. The Trent River now has close to ten hydroelectric stations, more than any other Lake Ontario tributary. The Cataraqui basin hosts small power generation plants at Jones Falls, Brewers Mills, Washburn, and Kingston Mills. A series of ice control dams were built into the Moira River in the vicinity of Belleville during the later decades of the twentieth century; in 2008 one of them was retrofitted to generate hydro power. In Upstate New York, small and micro hydro stations are scattered across the Lake Ontario basin. The biggest are in the Genesee, Oswego, Salmon, and Black River basins, often where mills used to operate, though all but a handful produce less than ten megawatts. Additionally, there are scores of dams in the counties touching Lake Ontario that do not produce hydro power, many creating slack water for flood control, water supply, and recreational purposes.[9]

In the wake of the failed 1929 Niagara treaty, there were other prospects for a transborder agreement. The Great Lakes–St Lawrence Deep Waterway Treaty, signed in 1932, outlined a twenty-seven-foot deep seaway as well as hydroelectric development in the St Lawrence River. The treaty also dealt with a range of other boundary water issues in the Great Lakes basin, including remedial works at Niagara Falls and other diversions, such as those from Chicago and the Albany River basin (the Long Lac and Ogoki diversions). Over the course of 1933, the treaty was debated and studied. It became ensnared in US domestic politics and in the conflicts between the regions and interest groups that had bedevilled the St Lawrence project in the United States for decades.[10] When the time came for a vote in March 1934, a majority of the US Senate approved the treaty, but not the two-thirds majority required for ratification.

Though the passage of the 1932 Great Lakes–St Lawrence Deep Waterway Treaty had failed, the door was not definitively closed. But the prospects were not bright. President Franklin Roosevelt told Prime Minister Mackenzie King that he wanted to subsume the Niagara issue within a wider agreement to replace the unratified 1929 and 1932 accords. But Ontario's new premier, Mitchell "Mitch" Hepburn, had campaigned on a "back to Niagara" platform. Hepburn hatched a plan to supply Ontario with power from Niagara, supplemented by diversions into Lake Superior from Ogoki–Long Lac. Roosevelt and King did not want Niagara addressed outside of a revised comprehensive Great Lakes–St Lawrence agreement, with the St Lawrence Seaway as a centrepiece.[11] Matters remained at an impasse until the outbreak of the Second World War. Canada needed more power, as did the US, even though it hesitated to join the conflict. In fact, the United States and Canada together would lead the globe in expanding hydroelectric capacity during the war.[12]

By early 1941, both countries were ready to sign a new comprehensive Great Lakes–St Lawrence agreement. President Roosevelt had decided this should take the form of an executive agreement rather than a treaty. The resulting Great Lakes–St Lawrence Basin Agreement again centred on the construction of a St Lawrence deep waterway and power development, and again included other basin issues such as remedial works at Niagara Falls. The agreement was attached to an omnibus bill, but before the House of Representatives could approve it, Japan attacked Pearl Harbor. With the United States joining the war, Congress deferred the bill until the end of the global conflict.

Nevertheless, the United States agreed to the Ogoki–Long Lac diversions during the war. This allowed Canada to increase the size of these diversions into Lake Superior and thus escalate water withdrawals for electricity production hundreds of miles downstream at the Niagara stations.[13] Upon completion, Ogoki and Long Lac together comprised the largest diversions *into* the Great Lakes basin, bringing in a little more water than the Chicago Diversion removes, essentially balancing things out.[14] These diversions elevate the mean level of each of the Great Lakes, raising Lake Ontario specifically by 6.7 cm (0.22 feet).[15] As is usually the case when water is manipulated on a large scale in the Great Lakes–St Lawrence basin, particularly for hydroelectric developments, Indigenous peoples, who historically used sites conducive to hydroelectric developments, bore the brunt of the direct impacts.

During the war, Ontario and New York authorities also moved to enact some of the Niagara provisions from the 1941 agreement. Infrastructural improvements were made to Niagara generating stations and their intakes while the two countries expanded their mutual power interchanges. Both increased their diversions and built a submerged, stone-filled weir to raise the level by about a foot above the falls.[16] They agreed to ignore the limits on Niagara River diversions so that all Niagara generating stations could be used to their total capacity for the duration of the war. Most, if not all, of the extra power produced in Ontario was exported to the United States. During the war, diversions rose well above the limits set by the Boundary Waters Treaty; undoubtedly, both nations would have approved more if necessary, but these water volume caps reflected the full capacity of the existing generating stations.

MEGAPROJECTS

As we have seen, over the first half of the twentieth century Niagara Falls negotiations were often intertwined with St Lawrence hydropolitics. But after all the failed diplomatic agreements, the Niagara issue was dealt with separately: Canada and the United States signed the Niagara River Diversion Treaty in 1950. This accord authorized the two countries to divert most of the Niagara River's water around Niagara Falls for hydroelectric generation, as well as to construct multifarious remedial works to compensate for and forestall erosion while hiding the aesthetic impact of stealing so much water from the waterfall. The 1950 treaty restricted the flow of water over Niagara Falls to no less than 100,000 cfs during daylight hours of what was deemed the tourist season (8 a.m. to 10 p.m. from April to mid-September, and from 8 a.m. to 8 p.m. during the fall), and no less than 50,000 cfs during the remainder of the year. Given that the average flow of the Niagara River was about 200,000 cfs, this meant that the United States and Canada together could take the majority of the total flow over the falls for electrical production. In other words, tourists at Niagara would be witnessing, at best, half of the water that would otherwise drop over the great cataract; if someone visited the falls outside of the prescribed tourist hours, they were treated to only one-quarter of the Niagara's flow making the plunge.

Since diverting such massive quantities of water around Niagara Falls would surely impact the waterfall's scenic appeal, the treaty authorized a series of remedial works to mask the effect.[17] As I detailed in my book *Fixing Niagara Falls*, the primary engineering objective was to ensure a satisfactory "impression of volume" and an unbroken "curtain" of water at the crestline while allowing for the diversion of water for electricity production.[18] A 1,550-foot control dam was built out from the Canadian shore, featuring sluices equipped with control gates. The purpose of this structure was to control

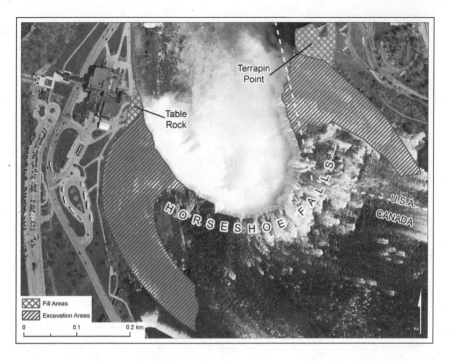

Figure 5.1
Modifications to the Horseshoe Falls in the 1950s. The bordered areas at the flanks of the
Horseshoe Falls with the horizontal lines indicates where the waterfall was excavated and
deepened, while the cross-hatched areas indicate where the lip of the Horseshoe Falls was
shrunk at Table Rock and Terrapin Point.

water levels as well as spread out the flow for appearance's sake and to prevent
erosion. Engineers relied heavily on scale models to plan the waterfall's face-
lift, making sure that the water had the correct shade of green and a "sceni-
cally satisfactory flow per foot."[19] Excavation took place along the flanks of
the Horseshoe Falls – about 90,000 cubic yards total – in order to create a
better distribution of flow.[20] To compensate for the smaller volume of water
going over the lip, the crestline of the Horseshoe Falls was shrunk and filled
in (fifty-five feet on the Canadian side and three hundred feet on the American), parts of which were fenced and landscaped to provide prime public
vantage points (see figure 5.1).[21] Unlike other high modernist dams of the era
that imposed themselves on rivers and turned them into artificial lakes, which
was about to happen on the St Lawrence, at Niagara technocrats sought to
retain the "natural" appearance of the waterscape as much as possible, mainly
because the tourism industry was so dependent on it.[22]

As a result, the waterscape of Niagara Falls was strikingly manipulated, a hybrid of the natural and the artificial. To take advantage of the rationalized water regime, the Power Authority of the State of New York (PASNY) and Ontario Hydro built massive new hydroelectric facilities during the early Cold War period. In 1954, Ontario Hydro opened Sir Adam Beck No. 2 (1,328,000 kilowatts) beside its existing Queenston-Chippawa plant, which was rechristened as Beck No. 1. After a protracted political fight, which gained additional urgency when the Schoellkopf generating station dramatically collapsed into the Niagara gorge in 1956, PASNY finished its new Niagara power plant in 1961. The biggest hydro power station in the western world at the time, it was named after Robert Moses, the chairman of PASNY. Moses, the legendary builder of roads, parks, and infrastructure in New York City, had been brought in to oversee New York's share of the St Lawrence and Niagara power projects because of his expertise in ruthlessly shunting people aside. This came in handy during PASNY's fight to locate the reservoir for the new Niagara station on Tuscarora land. Moses effectively mobilized the resources of the settler state to try to intimidate and bully the Tuscarora, who ultimately were not able to stop the reservoir, though their lengthy resistance and legal challenges did compel PASNY to reduce its size.[23]

The new PASNY and Ontario Hydro generating stations were both situated several miles downstream from the falls to utilize the full drop of the Niagara Escarpment; they were fed by huge tunnels abstracting water from the upper river. The water still moved from Lake Erie to Lake Ontario, but it did so in a decidedly unnatural way. Measured by volume, the biggest waterfalls at Niagara now took place inside the penstocks of the power stations. Furthermore, the new energy sources attracted even more industry to the Niagara corridor. The effluent of these factories, much of it toxic, was destined for Lake Ontario.

As the renovation of the Niagara River was underway, Lake Ontario's distributary, the St Lawrence River, was also about to be reconfigured. Canada and the United States had been talking about building a deep waterway since the 1890s, and a seaway was the focal point of the failed 1932 and 1941 diplomatic agreements. After the Second World War, policymakers and politicians touted the economic and continental defense advantages of a St Lawrence canal and hydroelectric development. During the first half of the 1950s, the St Lawrence topic became one of the most contentious issues in Canadian–American relations. Frustrated by American delay and realizing the nation-building and nationalist appeal of going it alone, Ottawa opted to pursue an all-Canadian Seaway. In June 1952, pursuant to the 1909 BWT, the two governments applied to the IJC for approval to construct the hydro power project on behalf of New York State and the Province of Ontario, who would jointly build and operate it. Approval came in October. But it would not get underway until 1954 since the US used the requisite domestic license for New York State's share of the hydro project, which legally had to be granted by the Federal Power Commission, as a bargaining chip to help force Canada to consent to a joint Seaway. Because of the likely negative ramifications for the bilateral relationship if Canada resisted American pressure, the two nations ultimately agreed on a joint navigation project through a bilateral 1954 St Lawrence agreement.[24]

My book *Negotiating a River* covers the political and environmental history of the massive Seaway and Power Project, which was jointly built between 1954 and 1959 by Canada and the United States. It is a both a navigation (Seaway) and hydroelectric (Power Project) undertaking. The 181.5-mile-long Seaway, which runs from Montreal to Lake Erie via the St Lawrence, Lake Ontario, and the Welland Canal, cost US$470.3 million ($336.5 million contributed by Canada, $133.8 million by the US). Including the cost of the hydro power phase, the bill for the entire project was over $1 billion.

This megaproject wrought huge changes in the St Lawrence basin, but it also had direct and indirect implications for Lake Ontario. The Seaway allowed in large vessels from across the world, and they would have a variety of impacts on Lake Ontario shipping and ports. Larger ships from abroad would also bring foreign biological invaders. The hydroelectric aspect, for its part, used Lake Ontario as an extension of the reservoir created in the upper St Lawrence, with the new dams intended to control and smooth out levels on the lake.

The Moses-Saunders powerhouse, a gravity power dam with thirty-two turbine/generator units that generated 1,800 megawatts, was bilaterally built near Cornwall, with the Canadian and American halves meeting in the middle. Two other control dams were installed in the river, turning part of the upper St Lawrence into a lake while deepening it for navigation. Lake St Lawrence inundated some 20,000 acres of land on the Canadian side, along with another 18,000 acres in the US, flooding out many communities and a wide range of infrastructure.[25] On the more populated Canadian side, this included 225 farms, the Lost Villages, eighteen cemeteries, and cottages, while highways and railways were relocated or replaced. Two different First Nations reserves were directly affected by the creation of the St Lawrence Seaway and

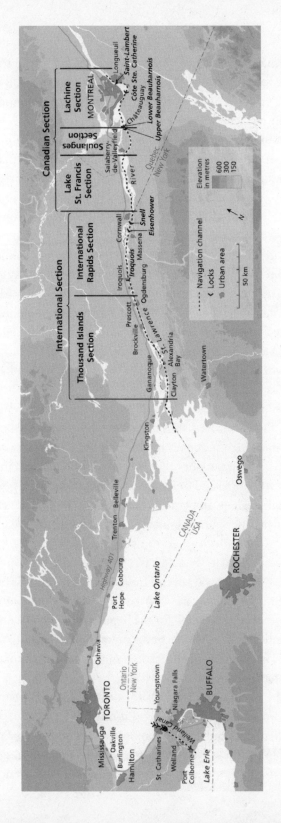

Figure 5.2

St. Lawrence Seaway. The Seaway runs from Montreal through the upper
St. Lawrence to Lake Ontario and then through the Welland Canal.

Power Project: Kahnawake Mohawk Territory near Montreal and the Mohawk Nation of Akwesasne (St Regis) that straddles the Canada–US border near Cornwall. The project was especially harmful for these communities – yet another example of hydro colonialism.

Flooding out thousands of people was justified in the name of progress and for the benefit of the wider populace.[26] Locals were promised that their sacrifice would allow the upper St Lawrence to become the industrial heartland of Canada – a promise that would prove to be empty. This primarily agricultural and small-scale manufacturing district was spatially reconceived, with the small villages, hamlets, and farms consolidated into several modern towns. The intention was that these communities would grow significantly, reoriented away from the river to serve as key nodes on a new freeway system. Government planners reconceptualized the St Lawrence as a water highway connecting Lake Ontario and the continental interior to the rest of the world. As it turned out, the Seaway would primarily move a few types of bulk cargo – such as iron ore from the Ungava region and wheat from the west – while the new freeways would transport many other types of cargo that had previously moved by water.

The enlarged Welland Canal was incorporated into the St Lawrence Seaway. The canal was then improved with the Welland Bypass, which opened in the early 1970s, marking the fourth iteration of this artificial waterway. There were plans for what we might call version 5.0 of the Welland that featured an entirely new channel and one large superlock to tackle the Niagara Escarpment. Though designs and land expropriations were finalized, this new canal was ultimately not pursued since the Seaway never carried enough cargo to justify it.

Indeed, compared to the cost–benefit cargo numbers used to warrant its construction, the Seaway has always been a tonnage failure. This was because claims about the traffic it would carry proved to be greatly inflated, partly because the locks were built too small for the bigger transoceanic container ships just coming into use. The Seaway never came close to paying for itself through tolls, as had been intended, on account of the relative lack of traffic. After a slow start, it had better years cargo-wise in the 1970s but then declined. Since the start of the twenty-first century, the Seaway has never conveyed more than 50,000 tonnes in a year. In 2009 it only carried about 30,000 tonnes, and since then it has only topped 40,000 tonnes once. Lake Ontario is nowadays plied almost exclusively by large vessels taking bulk cargoes to and from different points in North America. Remaking the St Lawrence with public money for the benefit of the shipping industry means that the Seaway could therefore be seen as a giant subsidy to the corporate concerns that own the ships or use them to move their products.

The environmental repercussions of constructing the St Lawrence Seaway and Power Project were enormous, and its legacy can only be fully measured if we include the ecological and social impacts. The reconfiguration of the local ecosystem inherent in the St Lawrence project disrupted the aquatic environment, which included circumscribing the success and mobility of numerous species. (Granted, some species did benefit from the rejigged water environment.) Certain fish communities were ruined for decades, some permanently.[27] Other ecological damage done by the St Lawrence project includes decreased water quality, loss of land by various types of erosion and island drowning, marshland flooding, weed growth, redistribution of pollutants, and concentrated pollutants in fish.[28] The copious amounts of cement used in dams emit greenhouse gases, as does the decomposing vegetation submerged by large reservoirs. Changed flow and ice regimes altered scouring, sedimentation, and erosion processes. During construction, many islands were removed or reshaped, with new islands added. Channels were enlarged, deepened, and widened to accommodate flows from the power dam and to facilitate navigation. The dams allowed the levels of the river, and Lake Ontario, to be artificially regulated. I will address this, and the influx of destructive invasive species made possible by the Seaway, in more detail in upcoming chapters.

The colossal hydraulic projects built into the St Lawrence and Niagara Rivers represented a new stage in the history of using Lake Ontario's natural bounty to create prosperity. They also represented a new stage in the hubristic belief in humanity's ability to impose itself on nature in general and Lake Ontario specifically. After all, the explicit goal was to improve and control this enormous lake and its connecting rivers. Though preceded by decades of diplomatic debate, these hydraulic projects ultimately fostered transnational cooperation and intensified crossborder integration. Remodelling this water system for hydroelectricity and navigation prioritized industrial, commercial, and state-sponsored uses and users of the lacustrine environment over other uses and stakeholders, as well as over the lake's ecological health. These megaprojects transformed Lake Ontario into a hybrid envirotechnical system, its ecosystem and natural functions – water regime, aquatic chemistry, habitat quality, species composition – shaped by human and nonhuman forces alike.

CHAPTER 6

Fisheries and Invasives

It was one of those overcast but still mornings when the lake and the sky meld into one steely blue horizon. We were on a family vacation, staying on Lake Ontario near the mouth of Oak Orchard Creek, approximately halfway between the Niagara and Genesee Rivers. A lone birch tree stood along the shoreline, its gold-spun leaves hanging on in the late fall. A mink scampered along the rocks; several gulls hovered nearby; in the distance, a fish breached the water's smooth veneer with a loud splash. I find fascinating the notion that, over the past millennia, other people from very different cultures and worldviews must have witnessed, and appreciated, a similar tableau. But though Lake Ontario's placid surface may have looked the same, what swims underneath it has changed significantly: the dominant fish species of a century or two ago are mostly gone, replaced by other species, many of which are not native to the lake.

I touched on Lake Ontario fish during the pre-modern period in previous chapters. The modern history of lake fisheries, the subject of this chapter, can be characterized as one of rapid change in habitat and species composition. Put more plainly, humans decimated natural fish stocks in Lake Ontario. Previous to the arrival of Europeans, fish communities in Lake Ontario likely had not changed much since the post-glacial period. But, as I showed earlier, previous to the most recent glaciation, the aquatic composition of the water-body that we now call Lake Ontario was appreciably altered over many millennia. However, those changes generally occurred on time scales far slower than what has been provoked by human activity since the colonial period. If we were to take a snapshot of the composition of Lake Ontario at the start of recent centuries, fish communities would look very different in 1800, 1900, and 2000. Over the past two hundred years, extensive shifts to fish populations were obvious even over shorter durations: comparing the changes every half, or even quarter, century reveals some dramatic transformations.

DECLINE AND DISAPPEARANCE

By the time of Canadian Confederation, most desirable fish species in Lake Ontario were disappearing, such as salmon, lake trout, and whitefish. By 1880 there was barely a salmon to be caught in Lake Ontario. The last reported sighting, at least until stocking efforts in the next century, was in 1898. Breeding and pisciculture (fish farming) became popular ways of trying to replace the fish. Despite the enthusiasm with which many took it up, artificial propagation was not really successful. But it was a way to justify overharvesting.

Fish hatcheries at Lake Ontario had a populist bent, with Samuel Wilmot the most famous Canadian proponent of fish stocking. He turned fish propagation from a hobby into a state-sponsored enterprise, spreading hatcheries across eastern Canada. Working in Newcastle, just east of Oshawa, Wilmot initially focused on salmon. These fish were stocked in most of the lake's tributaries in Ontario, with four million juvenile fish planted in 1879 alone. But Wilmot had given up within a few years: "I cannot disguise from myself that the time is gone by forever for the growth of salmon and speckled trout in the frontier streams of Ontario."[1] He shifted his focus to whitefish and other types of trout, hoping these would help Great Lake commercial fishing. That approach changed in the 1890s when Wilmot retired. Ontario won a share of fisheries jurisdiction from the federal government and established its first provincial fisheries administration, which was geared more toward promoting recreational fishing.[2] American shad, rainbow trout, brown trout, and striped bass were all intentionally introduced into the Lake Ontario basin, and potentially alewives as well.[3]

When it came to whitefish, the Canadian Department of Marine and Fisheries lamented in 1869 that "[t]hese rich and beautiful fish at one time so numerous in Lake Ontario, are now almost wholly gone."[4] John W. Kerr, who had become the fisheries overseer for Upper Canada a few years before Canadian Confederation, contended that whitefish were still abundant in the 1880s. He kept a voluminous diary and records of his correspondence, which constitute a rich resource on the nineteenth-century Lake Ontario fisheries.[5] By the 1890s, there was no disputing that whitefish were disappearing. Granted, in certain places like the Bay of Quinte, harvests stayed strong well into the next century, but this was also because of intensifying efforts, better technology, and fry planting.[6] The majority of the commercial catch in eastern Lake Ontario went to US markets. Nonetheless, it was becoming clear that the fisheries of all the Great Lakes were in decline after decades of overharvesting – single seines had been taking in over a million pounds of fish per year – with Lake Ontario the most impaired.

While this decline was related to dams, grain and wood mills, and overfishing, some fish ecologists have suggested that there was no big detrimental change to the lake's water chemistry until the influx of municipal and industrial waste in the early twentieth century.[7] Other scientists disagree, however, and their evidence is more convincing: the pollution, especially of nearshore Lake Ontario, by timber extraction, mills, agriculture, and wastes from settlements had already rendered those waters suboptimal, if not worse, during the nineteenth century. Sediment, for example, covered nearshore gravel beds used for spawning.

Both nations undertook their own studies, and cooperated in forming the Joint Commission Relative to the Preservation of the Fisheries in Water Contiguous to Canada and the United States. In 1894 this commission conducted a massive survey of fishing in Lake Ontario. During these interviews, those involved in New York's commercial fishing industry complained about the recent state regulations, which they said favoured anglers as well as Canadians. In fact, a number of interviewees had consequently stopped fishing because of state laws or had found work as guides for sportfishing, which was on the upswing. Views were mixed about the hatcheries and artificial propagation. Most lamented the state of the overall fishery in Lake Ontario. A Pulaski resident noted that salmon were already growing scarce by 1850 because of nets placed at river mouths.[8] Several pointedly identified pound nets as the main problem.[9] According to two Stony Island fishermen, "The fishing has not amounted to much for nearly 20 years. The whitefish are not here now and could not be taken by any means, except in small numbers."[10] Others said similar things about trout and sturgeon. Another postulated that dead alewives – a non-native species prone to mass die-offs from seasonal or nutritional stress, which can result from rapid water temperature changes – ruined whitefish spawning grounds. C.M. Clark spoke to the extent of the alewives: "One still day in August the dead fish were so thick that the lake had the appearance of a field of ice."[11] A few interviewees spoke about pollution. For example, a Nine Mile Point fisherman relayed that "[t]rash from the Genesee River is frequently found in the nets,"[12] while others said the same about many other rivers flowing into the lake.

The commission's final report identified pollution problems but concluded that overharvesting, especially with seine nets, was the prime culprit. It therefore recommended uniform commercial fishery regulations across the border. The report went largely unheeded, however. But both nations did step up their fisheries regulations in an attempt to cope with overharvesting, such as closed seasons and changed licensing requirements. But in New York State, enforcement was difficult because juries tended to find in favour of accused fishermen when charges went to court. Since most of the catch in Canadian waters was controlled or purchased by American interests, fisheries policy was effectively set by the demands of the US market. Canada and the United States did negotiate an Inland Fisheries Treaty in 1908 as part of the attempt to regulate these fisheries, but failed to ratify it.[13] Discussions between the US and Canada about establishing crossborder regulations continued on and off, leading to another rejected fisheries treaty in 1946. Finally, a diplomatic agreement was inked in 1954, creating the Great Lakes Fishery Commission, though it would primarily focus on dealing with sea lamprey.

From the 1880s to the end of the First World War, herring was the top catch in Lake Ontario, followed by whitefish and lake trout, as well as northern pike, catfish, and yellow perch. This was mostly in the northeast sector of the lake. Whitefish, among other species, were rebounding and in the 1920s passed herring; the latter then returned the favour, but subsequently disappeared. In urban centres such as Toronto, the working class – including immigrants who followed the Catholic "meatless Fridays" prohibition – purchased low-value fish refused by those of better means. These cheaper fish had become relatively more abundant through human abuse of Lake Ontario. The bigger taxa of the salmonid and percid (perch) families were replaced by types that did not grow as large and could better tolerate moderately degraded habitats.[14] Consequently, the Lake Ontario fishery generally moved away from smaller catches of high-value fish to larger catches of lower-value fish.

The lake's main coldwater species – cisco, deepwater chubs, whitefish, lake trout, and burbot – all had collapsed by the middle decades of the twentieth century.[15] Lake Ontario's offshore waters are also more habitable for walleye, compared to salmonids, because of nutrient enrichment from Lake Erie's outflow.[16] Eliminating some keystone species must have significantly altered the circulation of biotic material and energy throughout the lake, catalyzing knock-on effects for other fish types and organisms. Fish that fed in near-shore areas were the food source for many deep water varieties, and the disappearance of either, or both, of these energy vectors would have had repercussions for energy flows through different horizontal and vertical layers of the lake. The various geographic sections of the lake were also affected in different ways: the fish composition of certain basins, such as the Oswego and Trent, became different from the rest of Lake Ontario.

The conventional thinking from governments and the fishing industry was that environmental conditions alone, not overfishing, hurt stocks. Thus, an open-access fisheries policy continued, de facto if not de jure. There were scientific voices, however, arguing against this approach.[17] The crash of Lake Ontario whitefish and other species in the other Great Lakes further supported this notion. By the 1970s, fish biologists were reporting that alewives and rainbow smelt dominated the open waters of the lake; both are non-native species, and humans only intentionally catch the latter.[18] There also seemed to be a correlation between smelt abundance and whitefish decline. It became clear that fish depletion was the consequence of numerous interlinking and complex ecological factors – but most were driven by human actions. These factors included a changing climate, though that was not yet readily apparent to ecologists. Nevertheless, an ecosystem approach began to find expression in government regulations.

Chemical contamination was undoubtedly a problem. This was addressed to some extent by the Great Lakes Water Quality Agreements (signed in 1972 and 1978), which will be addressed in the next chapter. Concerns about mercury levels in fish were severe enough that they led to the closing of the eastern part of Lake Ontario to commercial fishing in the early 1970s. During that decade, catching several different fish species was temporarily outlawed because of contaminants. Since phosphorus inputs had declined by the 1980s, the deep part of the lake returned to an oligotrophic state, meaning that it had a low productivity rate on account of low nutrients, though with abundant dissolved oxygen. This had all sorts of complex ripple effects for aquatic species and biogeochemical flows. It led to a decline in prey fish production and biomass (such as alewife and rainbow smelt), which led to a decline in predator fish. On the other hand, these conditions favoured the rebound of ciscoes and sculpins, which became prey for top predator species.[19]

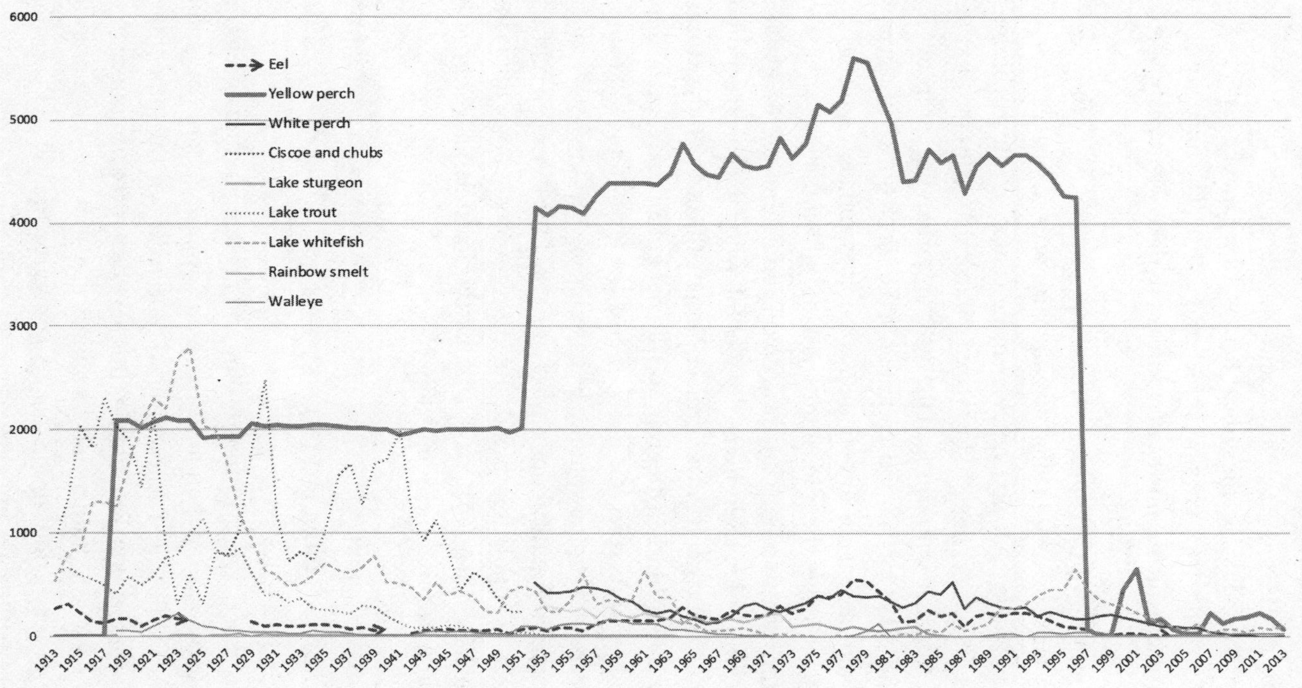

Figure 6.1
Selected fish catch in Lake Ontario, 1913–2013. Derived from Norman S. Baldwin et al., "Commercial Fish Production in the Great Lakes, 1867–2006" (Great Lakes Fishery Commission).

The two countries' enthusiasm for modern fish stocking waxed and waned. In the later twentieth century, stocking in Lake Ontario increased considerably, including for various types of salmon, trout, and other species.[20] For the last few decades of the Cold War, the annual haul in Lake Ontario was just two million pounds – chiefly perch, sunfish, eel, and catfish. The majority of the catch was still taken from the northeastern area of the lake, where many species maintained larger populations.

Eels have been called the "quintessential Lake Ontario fish" – they prefer to spend most of their time in shallow and warm waters, such as bays and tributaries – and once made up a noteworthy percentage of the fish biomass in the Lake Ontario watershed.[21] They were an integral food for the First Nations in the region. Eel may have been the most important fish for Iroquoian peoples around Lake Ontario, and a number of the Six Nations had eel clans, indicating this species' significance to their cosmology and lifeways. The high oil content of eel makes them ideal for smoking, allowing them to be preserved for winter consumption. Surprisingly, eel populations in Lake Ontario experienced record-high levels in the decades following the construction of the St Lawrence Seaway and Power Project. Despite the fact that the Moses-Saunders power dam blocked the river, and did not initially have fish ladders, the shallow edges of its reservoir likely offered the type of aquatic habitat preferred by eels. Substantial volumes were still being captured, with much of this catch exported, until about the last quarter of the twentieth century, when the lake's eel population then declined precipitously. Since the 1980s, their numbers have collapsed. Ontario ultimately closed its eel fishery early in the 2000s and declared them "endangered."[22]

CHANGING SPECIES

During an October day, the sky mostly blue and the temperature unseasonably warm, I drove around the southeastern end of Lake Ontario. Stopping at the Oswego, Salmon, and Black Rivers, I repeatedly saw the same thing: anglers casting for salmon. Fall salmon runs have been occurring since time immemorial, these fish dramatically leaping as they move up tributaries to breed and die. However, the salmon that do it now are primarily of the Pacific variety, rather than the Atlantic type originally native to the lake.

Anthropogenic actions have changed the species composition of Lake Ontario fisheries not only through the purposeful introduction of species,

Figure 6.2
Fishing in the Salmon River in fall 2021.

illustrated by the Pacific salmon, but by creating vectors and scenarios in which invasive species can arrive and thrive. Of course, "invasive" species is a loaded term that connotes species types we do not like because of their negative impacts. When we do not mind the effects of a non-native species, or even benefit from them, we call them by more benign terms such as "introduced." Or when it comes to the many species we purposefully brought to North America, we do not use any adjectives for them at all, since most people assume they are native to the area. Approximately 180 non-native aquatic species have arrived in the Great Lakes–St Lawrence basin since the early nineteenth century; it is estimated that about one-third have done so since the St Lawrence Seaway's opening.[23]

Let's dive into some of the more prominent of these foreign species. Sea lamprey were found in Lake Ontario as early as the 1830s. As a recent book on this creature attests, scientists are still divided about whether the Atlantic lamprey came into Lake Ontario through routes like the Erie Canal or the Finger Lakes, or had made their way there via the St Lawrence River hundreds or thousands of years earlier (maybe they were even native to the lake).[24] The same question goes for the alewife, a small fish abundant in Lake Ontario by the early 1870s. Both lamprey and alewife populations were likely limited by salmonids. But when the latter's population crashed and human actions altered the water temperatures and quality of spawning tributaries, the lake became a more suitable habitat for lamprey, and alewife numbers skyrocketed.[25] Changes to the water supply for the Welland Canal resulted in these two species using that conduit to get to Lake Erie and the other Great Lakes; the first lamprey was found above Lake Ontario in 1921 (though there is evidence they were in some of the upper lakes decades earlier). The lamprey became a pernicious threat to many larger fish favoured by humans, especially lake trout. Akin to a vampire eel, the lamprey latches onto fish and drains their bodily fluids. They sometimes also grasp onto humans: lamprey harassed sixteen-year-old Marilyn Bell when in 1954 she became the first person, or at least the first we know about, to swim across Lake Ontario.

The Great Lakes Fishery Commission, formed the same year as Bell's famous swim, tested over six thousand chemicals to eradicate lamprey. The commission eventually landed on TFM, a chlorinated compound, as a lampricide to kill juveniles in their spawning streams without harming other organisms. It did not completely eliminate the sea lamprey but kept their numbers in check. That control was achieved in Lake Ontario by 1971. Whether this approach should be considered a sustainable long-term solution, however, is debatable: not only does the chemical need to be continually applied, but it can bioaccumulate and harm other organisms. The upside is that it is *more* toxic to lamprey.

Lamprey had helped eliminate the predators for alewives, namely lake trout. Alewives may have already been the most abundant fish species in Lake Ontario before the close of the nineteenth century, and by the early Cold War they had come to dominate the biomass in all the Great Lakes except Superior, which was too deep and cold for their liking. The prevalence of alewives hurt other native fish species (perch, whitefish, herring) that relied on the same plankton, which along with lamprey led to the decimation of the lake trout. The alewife population exploded, sometimes experiencing massive die-offs. Their stinking carcasses covered Lake Ontario beaches throughout the 1960s.[26]

The introduction of Pacific salmon, which feasted on the alewives, helped bring their numbers down. Indeed, there were eventually worries that the alewife population, which had become valued because of their importance to sustaining the Pacific salmon stock, was too low. Various salmonids had been introduced to Lake Ontario as far back as the nineteenth century, but they did not stick. But Pacific salmon introduced to Lake Michigan tributaries in 1966 took hold, with human support and copious alewives to feed on. This approach was subsequently applied to Lake Ontario. Between 1984 and 1992, an average of 7.8 million fish (half of them Chinook salmon) were stocked every year.[27] Since commercial fishing had mostly disappeared on the Great Lakes – plus large salmon were not sellable because tests showed they were contaminated by pesticide chemicals associated with DDT – conservation officials hoped to create a sportfishery, and these charismatic fish were immediately popular with anglers.[28] They still are, as my fall drive around Lake Ontario demonstrated.

These salmon became a top predator in the aquatic food chain. Lake trout hatcheries were stocked and together with salmon they became the primary target of sportfishers. Rainbow smelt were also purposely introduced into Lake Ontario – my uncle told me that in the late 1960s they caught enough smelt in one day, just using nets from shore, to last the winter. White perch showed up in Lake Ontario about 1950, probably via the Oswego River. People did not complain, though, since these perch joined their yellow brethren as a desired catch.

There is a long history of foreign organisms entering the Great Lakes basin both before and after the creation of the St Lawrence Seaway. Despite knowing that the older alignments of the Welland Canal had allowed the intrusion of exotic organisms, the involved governments and agencies apparently did not consider the possibility, or did not care, that the Seaway could enable the infiltration of invasive species.[29] Since the 1950s, many accidentally introduced species have arrived via the ballast water of Seaway vessels; ocean freighters imported thirty-eight of the fifty-seven new species into the Great Lakes between 1973 and 2006. They hitch a ride in the ballast water of vessels originating in foreign waters, but when loosed in the Great Lakes–St Lawrence basin can create ecological domino effects.[30]

However, invasive species that came in after 1959 were not the inevitable result of the Seaway: if action had been taken earlier by the Canadian and American authorities to regulate the ballast water of foreign vessels, many of these interlopers might have been kept out. After all, government officials quickly realized that foreign invaders could come from other areas of the world via ballast water. The first in a long line of mistakes occurred in 1973 when the US Environmental Protection Agency exempted ballast water from the Clean Water Act (CWA), giving the responsibility to regulate this issue to the ill-equipped Coast Guard. Canada was not doing much better, and the shipping industry was not going to voluntarily police itself. But sadly it took several decades for either Canada or the US to create effective regulations.[31]

The most pernicious of these ballast water stowaways have been dreissenid mussels from Eastern Europe, native to the Caspian Sea. Zebra mussels were found in Lake St Clair in 1988, and quagga mussels appeared the next year. Over the following years, they both spread to Lake Ontario (if they were not there already). Though zebra mussels were first on the scene, after their period of dominance in the 1990s, they were mostly displaced by the quaggas. Both types of mussels attach to hard surfaces like docks, boat hulls, and breakwaters – up to 70,000 per square metre. They clog intake pipes for water supply, cooling, and irrigation, plus they foul beaches, all of which has cost billions to deal with.

The proliferation of these mussels unleashed a wave of unintended consequences. Mussels are filter feeders, and a trillion of them simultaneously doing so left the lake's water clearer but changed its chemical composition. From a recreational and aesthetic perspective, people like the transparent water that results. But the limpid water column had aquatic ripple effects, such as allowing sunlight to penetrate deeper, thus promoting aquatic vegetation growth.[32] Mussels shift the food web in other ways by absorbing the nutrients and food energy that would otherwise go to other species low on the food chain, thus depriving fish like sculpin and perch of food, since they cannot eat the mussels. Meanwhile, the few species that can consume the mussels benefit – such as the round goby, a foreign species that was first found in the lake in 1998. Mussel activity also shifts energy flows within the aquatic food web to deeper benthic zones: the mussels take nutrients out of the water column and deposit them at the bottom in their droppings. This also intensifies phosphorus concentrations, further prompting the growth of algae such as *Cladophora*. At the same time, the mussels spit out *Microcystis*, which is toxic blue-green algae; scientists believe this behaviour is one of the reasons there has been an increase in these types of algal blooms.

Colin Duncan, a history professor and sailing enthusiast who has spent most of his life close to Lake Ontario, told me that as a young man in the Cold War period he could not see more than a foot or two underwater, so thick with algae were the summer waters in Kingston harbour.[33] Then, after the foreign mussels spread, over just a couple of years the water became so clear that many shoals began to frighten local boaters who had no previous experience judging distance underwater on account of its murkiness. Objects retrieved from the water were caked many inches thick with mussels, alive and dead. Even Main Duck Island, which some people point to as the most unspoiled part of Lake Ontario, was not immune. A shallow limestone shelf extends several square miles from the island's southwest shore, and within a few decades mussel shells had accumulated here in windrows five feet deep and fifteen feet wide.

Other well-known Great Lakes invasive species include Eurasian ruffe, various types of water fleas, and different types of small shrimp. Non-native plant species include Eurasian watermilfoil and purple loosestrife. As previously mentioned, goby invaded Lake Ontario and can now readily be seen in small groups viciously feasting on the invasive mussels. These disruptors are small, the adult mussels in question not even attaining an inch in length, with the adult goby a little bigger. It and the invasive mussels appear to have achieved an equilibrium, as both abound and the water remains clear. That clarity bespeaks a collapse in the accessibility of food for countless fish species that were formerly abundant. It happens, moreover, to have roughly coincided with the rise in population of the double-crested cormorant.

These cormorants are actually native to the region, but they had been decimated a half-century ago. Their contemporary abundance likely speaks to a decline in the type of organochlorine contaminants that had led to their frequent reproductive failure in the past.[34] This large black bird breeds in huge colonies and eats large quantities of fish. Flocks flying in tight formation can be seen at the east end of Lake Ontario and down the St Lawrence River. They have crowded out formerly abundant gull species, partly with the help of Canada geese, mallard ducks, and the non-native mute swans. Cormorants are now year-round residents, seemingly benefitting from global warming and other causes of reduced nearshore ice formation. Many people consider these large birds a nuisance species because of their fish consumption and the vegetative depletion caused by their guano. But they are unfairly maligned, in my opinion, and it is good to see a native bird species rebounding and thriving at Lake Ontario.

Another type of large bird had also suffered reproductive problems from chemicals – and has also made a comeback. That would be the bald eagle. The heavy use of DDT in the Lake Ontario region and across the continent led to problems with thin eggshells and underdeveloped embryos. By the 1970s, these avian symbols of the United States found themselves on the endangered species list and on the verge of extinction. After DDT was banned, bald eagles slowly mounted a comeback. The first successful North American use of "hacking" towers – a technique to reintroduce raptors – for balds took place in the Lake Ontario watershed at Montezuma National Wildlife Refuge. But it would take until the twenty-first century before their numbers really started rebounding around Lake Ontario and they were taken off the US endangered species list.

The fish populations of Lake Ontario, particularly those that humans like to catch, have been stabilizing in recent years. Though it is difficult to quantify the amount of fish caught by recreational anglers, in the twenty-first century, sportfishing continues to dwarf commercial fishing in Lake Ontario. Nevertheless, both recreational and commercial fishing have markedly declined since the last decades of the twentieth century. The lake's remaining Indigenous fishery concentrates on walleye in the Bay of Quinte. Fish consumption advisories persist because of the toxicity levels in fish. Government stocking continues to put millions of salmon and trout into the lake and its tributaries every year, primarily for the benefit of the sportfishery.[35]

Between 1980 and 2000, the Canadian commercial catch was around one million pounds annually, but since the start of the new millennium the haul has generally stayed under half a million pounds. In 2019, just over 300,000 pounds of fish were commercially harvested in Canadian waters – whitefish, perch, walleye, and drum were respectively the top catches – with all commercial fishing licenses exercised in the area of the lake east of Brighton. In the American waters of eastern Lake Ontario the commercial catch – mainly perch – was just 55,000 pounds in 2019; in the early decades of the twenty-first century the US commercial harvest had dipped as low as about 4,000 pounds, though the average annual catch between 2010 and 2019 was 52,000 pounds. There have been calls to relax government quotas and change regulations that favour sportfishing over commercial fishing since fish offer a local protein source that is less carbon-intensive than other forms of meat. The wisdom of expanding Lake Ontario's commercial fisheries, however, is debatable, given the legacy of overfishing, scientific mismanagement of the fisheries, colonialism and Indigenous rights, the diminished levels of many species that humans like to eat, and the amount of pollutants and plastics in Lake Ontario fish.[36]

The twentieth century saw major changes to the composition and biodiversity of Lake Ontario's aquatic species. From overfishing to dramatically altering habitat, humans were undoubtedly the prime driver of these changes. Lake Ontario is now primarily occupied by invasive or introduced creatures – mussels, alewives, Pacific salmon – rather than other types of fish – for example, whitefish, Atlantic salmon, lake trout – that had previously characterized Lake Ontario's protein bonanza. Changing what lives in the lake so thoroughly is surely one of the most dramatic testaments to the extent of humanity's unsustainable relationship with Lake Ontario. The fact that it continues to support aquatic life of any kind, however, is a testament to its resilience.

Anthropogenic impacts are now being accentuated or exacerbated by human-caused climate change. Higher average temperatures have been slowly and almost imperceptibly warming the lake. Fish and many other lake species are very sensitive to changes in temperature gradients, as well as nutrient levels, and a slight bump can have outsized effects. Moreover, warmer waters can push the lake past critical thresholds associated with its seasonal turnover, or a lack of ice cover in the winter, which in turn can have even bigger impacts on the creatures and aquatic webs that dwell within. One of Lake Ontario's best defences against foreign species has always been the winter and cold waters. But in addition to making the lake less tolerable for certain native species, warming of the lake can make it more hospitable to potential future invaders. These can run the gamut from large creatures already on the public's radar, such as Asian carp, to microscopic creatures, such as viruses or invasive shrimp, that could be detrimental to the lake's ecology and human interests.[37]

𝕝𝕝

CHAPTER 7

𝕝𝕝

Pollution and Protection

As Canada celebrated its centennial and the United States waded deeper into the Vietnam quagmire, few were celebrating Lake Ontario or wading into it. Dead fish washed up on beaches. Smelly algae mats choked the water. Myriad chemicals lurked beneath the surface. Garbage and debris clogged harbours and bays. Lake Ontario in the 1960s, especially the western reach, was beset by pollution of many kinds, from industrial to agricultural to municipal. For decades, people had mostly looked the other way – a befouled lake was just the cost of progress.

Such was the irony: Lake Ontario was so dirty because people wanted to be clean. After all, much of the post-1945 pollution and eutrophication came from sewage and detergents. But long before the magic consumer products of the baby boom period appeared on store shelves, Lake Ontario had been treated as a garbage receptacle. This had not been too much of a problem for the lake, which could mostly dilute those inputs or at least keep them from becoming too great of a nuisance for humans. Nevertheless, as the population around Lake Ontario ballooned after the Second World War, so did the types and amounts of pollutants, running up against the limits of the lake's ability to disperse, degrade, or otherwise deal with them.

TRANSBORDER POLLUTION

The International Joint Commission, or IJC, was created by the 1909 Boundary Waters Treaty (BWT). This treaty was inked just as bacterial germ theory was on the verge of fully putting the miasmic theory of disease to bed.[1] There were nonetheless still prominent voices downplaying bacterial theory and promoting dilution as the only necessary safeguard. But the state of many waterbodies in the lower Great Lakes basin suggested otherwise. In 1906, the Government of Ontario promulgated a province-wide prohibition: "No garbage, excreta, manure, vegetable or animal matter or filth shall be discharged into or be deposited in any of the lakes, rivers, streams or other waters in Ontario, or on the shores or banks thereof." In 1909, New York governor Charles Evan Hughes averred that his state could "no longer afford to permit the sewage of our cities and our industrial wastes to be poured into our watercourses."[2] The BWT, signed the same year, explicitly stated that waters flowing across the international boundary should not be polluted on either side to the injury of health or property on the other. Globally this was the first comprehensive prohibition in international law against trans-border water pollution.

One of the IJC's earliest investigations involved crossborder water pollution in the Great Lakes connecting channels, namely the St Mary's, Detroit, Niagara, and St Lawrence Rivers. These investigations were in response to the local complaints about pollution. The commission's preliminary findings were ready by 1914. The researchers found all Great Lakes municipalities guilty of untreated sewage, which was the primary contributor to public health threats like typhoid. The Niagara River below the falls, for instance, was dangerously polluted – in their phrasing, it was "gross."[3] They argued that treating drinking water was even more important than treating effluent. The final report, issued in 1918, recommended that the IJC be given the authority to make appropriate rules and regulations.

The commission's recommendations were not heeded at the time, however. Inter- and intra-governmental jurisdictions jostled over who would pay for water or sewage treatment. During the decade following the 1918 report, there were diplomatic talks about a Canada–US agreement giving the IJC authority to unilaterally investigate, though not regulate, pollution. Canada and the US actually signed a Great Lakes pollution treaty in 1920, but it was never implemented. The Great Depression ended any hopes that further action might be taken. At least the IJC's pollution reference had stimulated discussion and improved the scientific approach to waterborne diseases: the widespread use of chlorine in public water systems had reduced some of the health threats of contaminated water.[4] Studies on water quality in the Great Lakes basin also put the involved experts on the cutting edge of the scientific study of large lakes limnology (limnology being the study of freshwater bodies). Much of the earliest formative limnological research took place in Europe, followed by North American researchers in the Great Lakes region.[5]

During the Depression and then the Second World War, water quality in the Great Lakes continued to worsen. Industrial effluent became a bigger problem than human waste, if it was not already. Measurable levels of dioxins were found in Lake Ontario as early as the 1930s. Concentrations of this persistent organic pollutant – POPs are toxic, take a long time to break down in the natural environment, and cause cancer, reproductive, or other developmental problems – only surged in the following decades. In 1946, Canada and the United States sent a reference to the IJC – a reference calls for a non-binding investigation – on pollution in Great Lakes connecting channels, with the Niagara River added to the study in 1948.[6] The following year, New York passed the Water Pollution Control Law, and created a control board, to maintain "reasonable" purity standards.

In the decade after the Second World War, Ontario's population grew by almost 50 per cent, while the personal income of its citizens doubled to an estimated total of $9.2 billion and the gross value of manufactured goods produced in Ontario surpassed $10.5 billion. But the byproducts of that growth included phenol, fly ash, and sundry pollutants, which were discharged directly into the water from the many industrial concerns around Lake Ontario: oil refineries, tar distilleries, starch factories, aluminum manufacturers, cement facilities, etc. The use of the lake as an approved place to dump garbage and refuse continued, though such activity became more tightly regulated by the 1970s. Accidental spills frequently discharged contaminants into the lake. Taking the summer of 1970 as a representative example, multiple oil and gas spills, some in the hundreds of thousands of gallons, occurred over the span of just a few months, along with releases of phosphates, different types of acids, and coal dust.[7] Moreover, those were just the spills that were reported or observed. The total volume of solid and chemical waste from both municipal and industrial sources that found its way into the lake was enormous. More and more, ordinary people began to notice and complain. At the same time, shifting baseline syndrome – which refers to the changes to an ecosystem over a long period of time that are so gradual and incremental that they keep people from accurately perceiving those changes – also meant that many did not realize how badly degraded the lake had become.

A large proportion of the toxic-spewing industry was concentrated near Niagara Falls, just upstream of Lake Ontario. Niagara Falls was the leading electrochemical and electrometallurgical centre in the United States, boasting a veritable who's who of American companies in those and other fields: Alcoa, Bethlehem Steel, Hooker Chemical, DuPont, Atlas, Carborundum Company, General Mills, International Paper, Union Carbide, Dunlop Tire and Rubber, and so on. All these industries, scores of them belching out toxic waste, had located in the Niagara region precisely because of the availability of cheap power and the Niagara River as a waste receptacle for their effluent. Given the types of products that these industries produced, and the lax standards of the time, the Niagara area – including the Canadian side, which also had substantial industry – had long been a dumpsite for hazardous waste.

The Niagara River was identified as the chief source of many of the pollutants entering Lake Ontario. This river, which at places was almost an open sewer, conveyed toxic pollution into Lake Ontario from not only the land abutting it but the upstream Great Lakes as well. An environmental study released in 1954 noted that "some 20 fish kills have been reported in the Buffalo-Tonawanda-Niagara Falls area during the past 17 years. Cyanides were implicated as the cause of 9 of the kills with phenols a contributing factor in two cases. A lethal dose of chlorine presumably was the cause of two of the kills."[8] Yet companies repeatedly claimed that their own discharges were benign while pointing fingers at their neighbours. By the 1970s, industrial operations were discharging over 250 million gallons of wastewater into the Niagara River every day.

Lake Ontario was also the recipient of some unique types of waste, such as those from nuclear installations. Model City, a sparsely populated hamlet four miles east of the Niagara River and about eight miles south of Lake Ontario, owed its origins to the ill-fated canal of William Love. It never became a city, despite its ambitious name, but the Lake Ontario Ordnance Works (LOOW) was established in this rural area during the Second World War to manufacture TNT. This became a disposal site for radioactive refuse from the Manhattan Project and then other Cold War–era nuclear endeavours, as well as a witches brew of industrial, toxic, and chemical waste.[9] (Despite its poor safety record, it is still operating today and proposals were recently made to expand it.) Around the City of Niagara Falls, at least thirteen local facilities received government nuclear contracts and secretly contributed to nuclear weapons development. But radioactive materials did not always end up in officially designated disposal zones – and the whole area ends up draining to Lake Ontario one way or another.

Other military-related disposals and discards took place in or near Lake Ontario. The town of Ajax, Ontario, arose during the Second World War to

host a huge TNT and shell-filling complex; shells were test-fired into the lake
from beside Duffins Creek. Military materiel, mostly defective shell-detonator
nosecones, was dumped in the lake near Rochester during the war.[10] Fort Niagara, at the mouth of the river of the same name, and Fort Ontario, at Oswego,
continued to operate in various capacities into the Cold War. In the late twentieth century, an assortment of discarded military ordnance and infrastructure
– mortars, fuses, grenade dischargers, lead ammunition, petroleum tanks –
were identified on the lakefront grounds of both forts.[11]

Prototypes of Canada's cancelled Avro Arrow plane were sent to the bottom of Lake Ontario in the 1950s. In 2018, one of the models was brought
up close to Point Petre, the southernmost part of Prince Edward County.
Elsewhere in the county, there was a Canadian Forces base just outside of
Picton for several decades, while Trenton has been the location of a Canadian
military installation going back to 1931. The latter was the largest site in the
British Commonwealth Air Training Plan during the Second World War,
and today it is Canada's largest Air Force base and the hub of the Armed
Forces' air transport operations. The surrounding area featured a number
of bombing ranges, meaning that countless rounds of practice ammunition
were lodged in Lake Ontario's sands and sediments. What is now the Wellers
Bay National Wildlife Area had been a bombing range from 1939 until 1953;
it was transferred to the Canadian Wildlife Service in 1969. But this area on
the northwestern banks of Prince Edward County, consisting of a long sand
spit and several islands that would otherwise make for excellent recreational
opportunities, remains full of unexploded ordnance and is therefore off
limits to the public. Practice bombing runs also occurred at other places
around the lake: near Toronto, for example, unemployed fishermen dove to
recover the lead.[12]

A range of energy-related industries have introduced contaminants into
Lake Ontario while withdrawing massive amounts of water for cooling.[13] In
the mid-twentieth century, pipelines began replacing the oil tankers con-
ducting interlake trade. The Interprovincial Pipe Line Company finished a
pipeline from Sarnia to Toronto in the 1950s; a spur line went to Port Credit's
oil refinery, built east of another hydrocarbons refinery complex on Mississauga's lakeshore, now run by Petro-Canada. Since the mid-1970s a pipeline,
Line 9, has traversed the north side of Lake Ontario on its way from Sarnia
to Montreal. This was built by the Interprovincial Pipe Line Company, now
Enbridge, to connect with its network of hydrocarbon lines throughout the
Great Lakes, which are fed by fossil fuels from Western Canada. Enbridge

also controls Line 7, extending from Sarnia to Oshawa, and Line 10, which starts near the head of the lake and heads to Buffalo, crossing the Niagara River in the process.

Though there are rich natural gas and oil deposits in the Lake Ontario watershed, relatively few are close to or under the lake. Most of the natural gas in the basin is in the Marcellus Shale formation. This formation is centred in Pennsylvania and West Virginia, with its northern extent roughly coinciding with the tips of the Finger Lakes. The first-ever commercial development of a natural gas deposit in the United States occurred in western New York in the early nineteenth century. Some natural gas fields opened close to Lake Ontario, such as in Oswego County, before the end of that century. Oil production was most active in the state around then, peaking during the 1880s at 6.7 million barrels.[14] Natural gas production in New York has gone through a number of cycles coinciding with new discoveries, including upswings during the Cold War. But most gas developments were in rural counties in western New York close to the Pennsylvania border. At any rate, after the end of the Cold War, New York State banned oil and gas plays under the waters of Lake Ontario and along the shoreline.

Even before Model City, uranium refinement for the nuclear industry was pursued elsewhere on Lake Ontario. In Port Hope, a refinery was built in the 1930s by Eldorado Gold Mining, a private firm.[15] At first, it processed radium – for luminescent paint and medical applications – and then, after being converted to a Crown corporation, uranium during the Second World War and then nuclear fuel for CANDU reactors. For a long time, the refinement facility's various waste sites drained directly to Lake Ontario. A long-term containment facility was built immediately west of Port Hope, beside the 401 freeway. This site leaked into a nearby creek in 1955 and a small pipeline was built to channel the effluent to Lake Ontario. But the containment site is not capped or lined, so runoff escapes into the local groundwater – and it turns out the separation between groundwater and waterbodies, such as Lake Ontario, is much more permeable than was previously believed. More recently, a remedial project has been underway to consolidate all the contaminated waste from the different disposal sites in the Port Hope municipality (which constitutes almost all the nuclear waste in Canada) into the long-term landfill by the freeway. So far, this has cost $1.8 billion, making it one of the most expensive remedial projects in the Great Lakes.[16]

Another nuclear waste site west of Port Hope, at Port Granby, was discharging 150 times the maximum radium concentration into Lake Ontario during the 1970s.[17] Investigations in the early twenty-first century demon-strated that toxic wastes from this dump site were still going into the lake, aided by a receding shoreline. Recently, 1.3 million tonnes of low-level nuclear waste were relocated 700 metres further away from the water in an above-ground engineered storage mound.[18]

After the Second World War, two Ontario Hydro nuclear power plants, Pickering and Darlington, were built close to Toronto. New York also built nuclear power plants: the James A. FitzPatrick and Nine Mile Point stations near Oswego, and the R.E. Ginna plant east of Rochester. Another, Sterling, was planned for the Sodus Bay area but never constructed. Other nuclear plants envisioned near Watertown and Waddington, which could have linked up with new high-tension power lines bringing electricity to New York State from northern Quebec, never materialized either. Nor did several other pros-pective Canadian nuclear-related sites not far from Lake Ontario: a waste disposal facility at Madoc, and a generating station between Prescott and Iro-quois on the St Lawrence.

In 1981, flooding caused 21,100 gallons of radioactively contaminated water from the Nine Mile Point station to spill into Lake Ontario.[19] The following year, a radiation venting incident occurred at Ginna, and this was not the only time.[20] In recent years, high lake levels have increased the possibility of similar accidents at these aging nuclear stations. For an extended period in the twenty-first century, the outdated cooling system at the Darlington nu-clear plant was blamed for annually killing millions of Lake Ontario fish.[21] Excessive levels of radioactive waste – uranium, tritium, thorium – are still found throughout the lake.

Coal plants, which draw massive amounts of water for cooling, were built all over the lake throughout the twentieth century. Up to the midpoint of the century, coal accounted for over half of Canada's annual energy consump-tion. This fossil fuel was primarily used for home heating, electricity gener-ation, and metallurgical production. Most of it was imported from the United States, primarily by Toronto, Hamilton, Kingston, and Montreal, with the coal coming across or around Lake Ontario.[22] Toronto alone imported over one million tons of US anthracite (domestic use) and bituminous (in-dustrial use) coal in 1903, and roughly double that amount by early in the Second World War. In 1950, the US exported 25,468,000 tons of the sooty stuff, and 90 per cent of that went to its northern neighbour.[23]

Power plants contribute pollution not just through their waste but via thermal pollution. Because power stations running on nuclear, coal, or natu-

Figure 7.1
Ginna Nuclear Power Plant in 2021. This nuclear plant is on the lakeshore just east of Rochester, New York. Fruit orchards are in the foreground, Lake Ontario in the background.

ral gas require massive amounts of water for cooling, they have usually been placed directly at the lake. The Ginna Nuclear Power Plant, for example, demanded 334,000 gallons per minute of cooling water from the lake when it opened; it drew water from the bottom of the lake and returned it to the surface. The nearby Russell coal-fired power station needed comparable volumes. The water sent back to the lake was 10 to 30 degrees Fahrenheit warmer; those higher temperatures were linked to multiple fish kills and other aquatic degradations.[24] In 2021, Canada and the United States collectively withdrew more than 39,000 million litres per day (mld) of water in the Lake Ontario basin for various purposes, the vast majority directly from the lake. Almost three-quarters of those water withdrawals were attributable to thermoelectric power generation, with public water supply responsible for less than 10 per cent (3,362 mld) of that total. Meanwhile, hydroelectric generation employed another 527,000 mld of water.[25]

GREAT LAKES WATER QUALITY AGREEMENTS

A good deal of the pollution the Niagara River disgorged into Lake Ontario came from Lake Erie. That lake was declared "dead" in the 1960s. But this was a mischaracterization. Lake Erie was definitely suffering from extreme cultural eutrophication, which refers to excessive human-caused nutrient overloads, primarily phosphates and nitrogen, which lead to plant growth, primarily algae and weeds. But that meant the problem was, in a way, too much life. That said, when all this algae decomposed, it used up the oxygen that other aquatic organisms needed. Given all the phosphorus and nitrogen coming in – from lawn fertilizers, sewage, and soaps and detergents used in dishwashers and clothes washers – from the many polluted tributaries, it is not surprising that Lake Ontario was experiencing problems.[26] Detroit's River Rouge, Cleveland's Cuyahoga River, and the Buffalo River all caught fire in the two decades after the Second World War, while the environmental organization Pollution Probe staged a mock funeral for Toronto's Don River in 1969 because it was so degraded.

In the United States, the Federal Water Pollution Control Act was passed in 1948 and then amended in 1956 and 1965. These changes established minimum water quality standards for the nation and provided some revolving funds for states to undertake pollution abatement. The federal government was also given oversight of water quality in all interstate waters. Further amendments in 1972, which became retroactively known as the Clean Water Act (cwa), constituted a new era in US water governance. This marked a shift from the cooperative pragmatism model, which relied on the voluntary regulation that had underpinned previous water laws, towards more robust command-and-control approaches. The 1972 act centralized authority in the federal government, which could delegate enforcement to the states, and funded the construction of water treatment plants to the tune of several billion dollars. It ambitiously aimed to eliminate all pollution discharges to navigable waters by 1985, while achieving "fishable, swimmable, and drinkable" waters. Unsurprisingly, the new regulations never came close to achieving such goals. Even so, the cwa was a laudable improvement over previous water pollution legislation. But by installing a system requiring all dischargers to secure a permit, the role of the recently created Environmental Protection Agency (epa) under the cwa essentially became permitting pollution up to predetermined amounts rather than preventing pollution.

The same was largely true for Environment Canada, as the 1970 Canada Water Act created a framework for federal–provincial actions to address water pollution. The year after the act was put in force, Ontario and the federal government signed an agreement that featured an accelerated program to fund the construction or upgrading of sewage treatment facilities for most urban centres on Lake Ontario. The province had created the Ontario Water Resources Commission in the mid-1950s, though it was frequently accused

of being too cozy with the industries it regulated, and in the early 1970s converted the provincial Department of the Environment into the Ministry of
the Environment and Water Resources. Under Governor Nelson Rockefeller,
the State of New York had already passed the Pure Waters Program in the
1960s, which helped create the regulatory momentum that led to the 1972
CWA. That New York program was partly financed by a $1 billion bond issue
and constituted one of the country's earliest and most aggressive state-level
water quality policy packages; in addition to tightening water laws, it provided funds to municipalities to build water treatment facilities.[27] Rochester,
as an example, benefitted from the Pure Waters Program and constructed a
range of water-related infrastructure in the 1970s.

As part of the 1940s reference about Great Lakes connecting channels, the
IJC had recommended a number of boundary waters objectives. Those responsible for pollution should be responsible for cleaning it up. The IJC established boards to continue studying and monitoring water health,
including one for Lake Ontario and the international section of the St Lawrence River. The Canadian and American federal governments had also
started their own separate studies. In 1956, on New York State's instigation,
the United States requested that Canada join it in sending a reference on pollution and lake levels to the IJC. Canada dragged its feet for some time, but
in 1964 the IJC was given a lower lakes pollution reference. This resulted in
detailed studies of pollution in Lakes Ontario and Erie, as well as the upper
St Lawrence River. In conjunction, the IJC held eight public hearings around
the lake in 1969 and 1970.[28]

The final report was released in 1970. It showed that industrial and municipal wastes, which had increased several-fold over the previous half-century, were the principal sources of pollution, and it recommended new water
quality objectives and regulations.[29] Stressing the need to address phosphates
from detergents, this report helped clear up much of the remaining scientific
uncertainty about the causes of eutrophication.

That report paved the way for the first Great Lakes Water Quality Agreement (GLWQA).[30] Many additional factors – local, regional, international –
coalesced to create the milieu in which the GLWQA was signed. Decaying
algae and alewife die-offs plagued Lake Ontario. Both washed up on shore,
fouling beaches. There were mercury, DDT, and PCB concerns not only in
the Great Lakes but across the globe, while crashing fisheries, eutrophication,
road salt runoff, dredging (which mobilized contaminated sediments), and
shoreline and wetland infilling bedevilled Lake Ontario specifically. Not far

upstream, in 1969 the Cuyahoga River famously caught fire, again, the same year the US Army Corps of Engineers dewatered Niagara's American Falls to investigate reconfiguring it. These, along with other events such as the publication of Rachel Carson's *Silent Spring*, the Santa Barbara oil spill, and the first Earth Day, heralded the environmental movement that was sweeping North America. In the past, river fires and dying lakes had usually been relegated to the back pages of newspapers, if they were mentioned at all. But the extent to which the media now prominently featured these issues spoke to how widespread environmental worries had become.

My colleague Steve Bertman, an organic chemist, grew up in Rochester. He remembers as a child going to the nearby Charlotte Beach on Lake Ontario in the late 1960s and early 1970s – but says that his parents did not allow him to go in the water for fear that it was too polluted.[31] The public input sessions the IJC offered throughout the basin made obvious that these sentiments were widespread among the 180 witnesses who appeared, with another 200 mailing in comments. What was striking was not only the number of people who turned out, but their composition. In addition to the usual industry and academic representatives, members of the League of Women Voters and Pollution Probe appeared, as well as many ordinary folks. Housewives and secondary school students lodged oral and written complaints about pollution and degradation: "Detergent manufacturers have mounted an intensive campaign to induce housewives to believe that 'whiter is better,'" said one, adding, "It is time they admit their corporate responsibility for the pollution which they are creating." Another relayed a similar sentiment: "The housewife believes phosphorous should be removed from the detergents – we don't care as much about snow white shirts as about cleaning up the Lakes."[32]

The 1970 Canada Water Act put limitations on the phosphorus percentage of detergents, and a few years later New York became one of the first states to ban phosphorus in laundry detergents. Both Canada and the US were moving toward sweeping improvements to their own environmental and water laws. In addition to the creation of the National Environmental Policy Act, the EPA, and the CWA south of the border, Ottawa proceeded with the Canada Water Act, a new Department of Environment, and an agreement with Ontario to address federal–provincial issues in preparation for a Canada–US water pollution agreement on the lower Great Lakes. Nevertheless, the process that produced the GLWQA likely would not have gained enough momentum without local activism. A half-century later, one of the involved

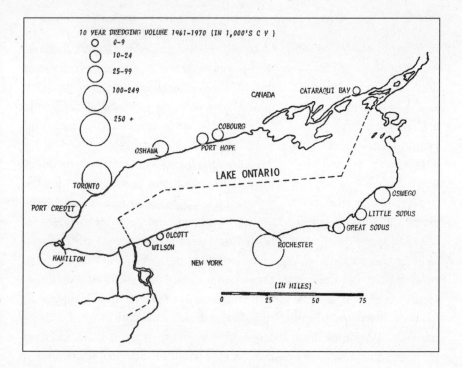

Figure 7.2
Average annual maintenance dredging volumes in Lake Ontario, 1961–1970.

scientist-policymakers, Henry Regier, points to the international scientific networks, particularly the emerging field of ecology, as an essential shaper of the evolution of the GLWQA. But he also contended that many, maybe most, of the key environmental victories in the Great Lakes basin were "won with leadership by women. Many of the women were unpaid volunteers or underpaid activists. Mostly it has been well paid men who then led with the implementation."[33]

Many chemicals and contaminants poured into the lake were then embedded in sediments at the bottom. Dredging became a way of removing them – but it also threatened to mobilize them. A great deal of lake dredging had already taken place for other purposes, such as achieving navigation depths to match those of the St Lawrence Seaway, and obtaining materials such as sand and gravel to use as fill or for other purposes like making concrete. Between 1951 and 1972, almost 8.7 million cubic yards of material was dredged in the US waters of Lake Ontario (see figure 7.2).[34] Of that total, 5.5 million cubic yards came from near Rochester, followed by Oswego at about 1.1 million cubic yards and the Sodus Bay area at a little less than 750,000

cubic yards. The Wilson and Olcott waterfronts received some limited dredging. Almost all of this – over 85 per cent – was classified as maintenance
dredging. During most of the 1960s, Canada undertook even more dredging
in Lake Ontario than the United States: between 1961 and 1972, Canada
brought up almost 5.5 million cubic yards, led by projects at Toronto and
Hamilton, as well as Oshawa, Port Credit, and Cobourg.[35]

Over 90 per cent of the material dredged from Lake Ontario in the 1960s
was polluted. Based on dredging samples, Rochester and Oswego were the
two New York harbours classified as "entirely polluted," while in Ontario the
Hamilton, Toronto, Whitby, Oshawa, Port Hope, and Cobourg harbours received the same designation. Phosphorous was the most commonly reported
pollutant. Recent legal changes required that polluted spoils be deposited in
confined disposal sites rather than open waters: a 1974 study estimated that
close to four million cubic yards would have to be placed in such landforms
in Lake Ontario over the following decade, drawing primarily from the major
harbours. Over time, local species would colonize many of these and treat
them as natural reefs or islands.[36] In fact, wildlife managers, realizing that
fish spawned on reefs that were the byproduct of industrial activities, are
now intentionally creating artificial reefs in Lake Ontario to serve as spawning habitat.

At the beginning of GLWQA negotiations, Canada had argued that each
country should be able to pollute up to half of the lake's assimilative capacity.
This was a self-interested position: since the larger US population across the
entire Great Lakes basin contributed more pollution, divvying up the allow-
able amounts this way would mean less onerous restrictions for Canada.[37]
But the US resisted that approach. It should be pointed out that, at the time,
Ontario accounted for almost two-thirds of the six million people living in
the Lake Ontario basin, a percentage which has since noticeably mush-
roomed. Thus, Canada's claims about the connections between population
and pollution levels did not hold up in the case of Lake Ontario specifically.

Besides, in addition to the fact that Lake Ontario's assimilative capacity
had probably already been reached when it came to certain pollutants, it
would later become apparent that assimilative capacity was a misnomer in
many regards because of flawed assumptions that pollutants would be
evenly distributed within the lake.[38] Lake Ontario experiences both vertical
and horizontal stratification. The latter means that nearshore waters stay
warmer for part of the year. Because the densities of water layers are affected

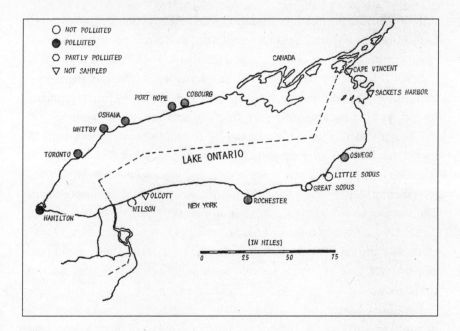

Figure 7.3
Pollution status of harbours in Lake Ontario.

by temperature, pollutants are held near the shoreline rather than spread, and thus diluted, throughout the lake. In much the same way, vertical strat-ification holds some pollutants at certain levels of the lake. Prevailing cur-rents and wind directions also concentrate pollutants in certain spots. In the summer, only water from the epilimnion – the upper layer of the lake – flows into the St Lawrence. Though the lake's retention time is about seven years, in some places it may take much longer for substances to leave, since bays and harbours trap polluted inflows. This gives those substances more time to lodge in sediments, suspend in the water column, and bioaccumulate in organisms.

After years of studies and negotiations, President Richard Nixon and Prime Minister Pierre Trudeau signed the GLWQA in April 1972.[39] Though its provisions were somewhat diminished – compared to what earlier IJC studies had called for – the GLWQA was a watershed moment not only for Great Lakes environmental protection but for large lakes globally. Noteworthy aspects included a nondegradation philosophy – though the meaning of "nondegradation" was unclear, considering all parts of the Great Lakes were suffering from ecosystemic degradation – and the establishment of common goals across the border. The agreement aimed at limiting phosphorus inputs, chiefly from detergents, soaps, and sewage, that led to hyper-eutrophication in Lakes Erie and Ontario, as well as the international stretch of the St Lawrence River. During the negotiations, Canada had pushed for an emphasis on phosphorus and upgrading sewage treatment, and the US agreed.

The agreement was made a "standing reference" under the BWT. This meant that the GLWQA was a good faith agreement, rather than a treaty, that could be terminated by one year's notice, and with no mechanisms for enforcement it would rely on the two countries living up to their commitments. The IJC was tasked with coordinating implementation by the two nations. The water quality and research boards, as well as a regional office at Windsor created by the agreement, also fell under the IJC's aegis. These would track and evaluate progress on the specific water quality objectives established by the GLWQA.

Measured against the initial objectives, the 1972 GLWQA was a success. To be sure, this success relied upon the billions of dollars of government funding, particularly through the CWA, to build sewage treatment plants. Phosphorus inputs from detergents, sewers, and agricultural fertilizer runoff were reduced. Within a few years, eutrophication and algae problems had mostly cleared up in Lake Ontario.

Since the water was clear, the public assumed the water was safe. But that was not necessarily the case. Stopping the point source loading of conventional nutrients would prove to be easier than dealing with persistent toxic and non-point source pollutants that did not originate from a discrete source. The 1972 GLWQA was therefore replaced by another bilateral agreement in 1978 that applied to all the Great Lakes basin, not just the lower lakes.[40]

The 1978 Great Lakes Water Quality Agreement went beyond just visible pollutants and called for the "virtual elimination" of toxics. This meant extinguishing any new discharge of hazardous contaminants as far as possible, while realizing that complete eradication was not always feasible because of the persistent and bioaccumulating behaviour of previously discharged persistent organic pollutants (POPS). For example, in 1973, mirex was discovered in Lake Ontario fish by a Canadian scientist.[41] This was just one of hundreds of contaminants found throughout the Great Lakes. The strange thing was that mirex, an organochloride used as a fire retardant and an ant pesticide, was not usually applied in the Great Lakes region. Mirex was getting into the lake because it had been manufactured by Hooker Chemical and Plastics Company – the company responsible for the toxic chemicals implicated in the Love Canal crisis – at its Niagara facilities. The mirex problem had been severe enough that eating Lake Ontario fish was prohibited from 1976 to 1978 in New York State.

The new GLWQA formally incorporated the "ecosystem approach," the first international agreement to ever do so. This approach meant restoring and maintaining the physical, biological, and chemical integrity of the Great Lakes by recognizing the interplay of water, land, and air. Ideas central to this approach had already been percolating amongst scientists in the Great Lakes basin before the Second World War. According to eminent ecologist Henry Regier, in the 1930s and 1940s there was a "large network of informed persons whose shared perspective of the 'conservation movement' was similar to what was called an 'ecosystem approach' to Great Lakes problems." They realized pollutants could, and did, come from the atmosphere, precipitation, and land. Granted, the precise meanings and applications of concepts such as "ecosystem management" and "virtual elimination" were debated at the time and continued to be subjects of contention.[42]

The dawning Love Canal crisis just upstream from Lake Ontario soon brought the toxic threat home in tragic fashion. William Love's aborted nineteenth-century project had been designed to take water from the Niagara River just upstream of the waterfall. The Hooker Company and the City of Niagara Falls dumped tons of chemical waste into this abandoned ditch for several decades. Such dumping was considered standard practice, as Hooker and myriad companies were discarding chemical waste at numerous other sites throughout the area. Hooker sold the Love Canal property in 1953 to the Niagara Falls school board for one dollar, advising them of what was lurking underneath. Soon the city began building homes and a school in the new suburb.

Fast forward to the later 1970s, and this working-class neighbourhood was beset by chronic illnesses and birth defects, which some residents suspected were caused by exposure to the buried waste. Complaints initially met with government apathy and dismissiveness, however, and it took several years, which saw standoffs and other pressure tactics, before those close to the contaminated site were evacuated. But Love Canal was only the tip of the toxic iceberg, not just in the Niagara frontier but around the country. This crisis helped spur on a grassroots environmental justice movement. It was a catalyst for the creation of Superfund in 1980, formally known as the Comprehensive Environmental Response, Compensation, and Liability Act (CERCLA), to address toxic contamination.

Love Canal was later "delisted" under CERCLA, meaning that remediation work was complete. The chemical cocktail is still entombed there, however, its location belied by a grass field topped with vents, enclosed by a chain-link fence in the middle of a residential neighbourhood. Hooker's Hyde Park dump, close to the Niagara River, Niagara University, and the Robert Moses hydroelectric station, actually contained four times more dioxin-laced toxic waste than Love Canal. It was delisted as a Superfund site in 2013, the 80,000 tons of poisons still buried there. Hooker, by this time owned by Occidental Chemical, has yet another toxic landfill – titled the S-Area – on the Niagara River, just upstream from the falls and the tourist zone, that is still today an active Superfund remediation site. Additionally, there are many other Superfund sites throughout the Lake Ontario basin, including some that have been delisted.

Pollution from all the industries that flocked to take advantage of Niagara's hydro power had long impaired the Niagara River. Municipal and industrial waste threatened the Niagara experience: the falls sometimes assumed an unnatural greenish hue, full of sewage effluent, and at times several feet of foam from detergents and chemicals formed at the base of the waterfall, spraying onto *Maid of the Mist* passengers. A study published in 1981 identified the Niagara River as "one of the most chemically contaminated bodies of water in America" and pointed to the thoroughly inadequate standards and permitting system for synthetic organic substances in New York State.[43]

Of course, whatever made its way to the Niagara River generally made its way to Lake Ontario. Studies in the early 1980s identified PCBs as the prevalent organic contaminant, followed by DDT, mirex, and chlordane, as well as lead, copper, and arsenic. Many of the identified chemicals were not even used anymore by industry in the Niagara region, having been banned in the 1970s, which indicated continuous leaching.[44] Further study showed that chloroflourinated compounds transported into Lake Ontario from the Niagara as suspended solids settled in lake sediments; then they were ingested by organisms and moved up the food chain, with concentrations of the contaminants getting larger because of biomagnification at higher trophic levels. And this did not just occur where the Niagara River gives its waters to Lake Ontario. Currents distributed contaminants to different parts of the lake: many of the chemicals and metals traceable to the

Niagara River were found at Kingston.[45] Of course, Kingston was the home of a Dow Chemical facility, as was Rochester. Chemical companies are spaced at regular intervals all around the lake. These and many other types of industrial concerns spew toxic waste, with the west end of Lake Ontario, Toronto, and Hamilton especially significant sources. Accordingly, chemicals abound all over Lake Ontario.[46]

AREAS OF CONCERN

Though the 1978 GLWQA made some important advances in treating pollution in the Great Lakes, it clearly was not enough. Most industries refused to curtail their discharges appreciably, and regulators were wary of cracking down on them. North American governments were often captured by the interests they were supposed to regulate, or let these industries police themselves. Unsurprisingly, the results were better for corporate bottom lines than for the lake ecosystem and public health. The human population in the Golden Horseshoe, and the amount of effluent that resulted, steadily climbed. Postwar agricultural practices increasingly sent chemicals to the lake as well. Though the amount of total agricultural land in the Lake Ontario basin declined, particularly on the west side of the lake where it was swallowed up by encroaching urban and suburban areas, what remained increasingly became more industrialized. Large-scale monocultures, such as corn and soybean, replaced smaller crop and fruit growers. Concentrated animal feeding operations (CAFOs, or factory farms) replaced small meat and dairy producers. The underregulated and overused synthetic crop fertilizers, pesticides, and herbicides, as well as the organic waste from CAFOs, sent constant pulses of nitrogen and phosphorous to the lake.[47]

Growing frustrated with the lack of compliance with the 1978 GLWQA, the IJC pushed to renegotiate it and include specific goals for the most degraded localities. The result was the 1987 Protocol. This added remedial action plans (RAPs) and lakewide management plans (LAMPs), and addressable issues expanded to include other subjects. Each Great Lake would get a LAMP, while the more than forty areas of concern (AOCs) throughout the Great Lakes would each receive their own RAP. AOCs are like Superfund sites for shoreline areas, most of them urban or industrial (some AOCs are also Superfund sites). Directly on Lake Ontario were seven AOCs: four in Canada and three in the United States (see figure 7.4). The Niagara and the international stretch of the St Lawrence River were also declared binational AOCs. Developing the action plan for each AOC, and identifying what are called beneficial use impairments (BUI), took considerable time and effort.[48] After that was accomplished, remediation work could begin. But progress on RAPs was extremely slow, mainly due to the challenging nature of remediation, the lack of adequate funding, and ongoing pollution.

In conjunction, Canada and the US signed the Great Lakes Toxic Substances Control Agreement in 1986, which created the Great Lakes Protection Fund. A Lake Ontario Toxics Committee was established and it released a management plan in 1989.[49] Then the Great Lakes Binational Toxics Strategy was signed in 1997, creating a binational framework to reduce or eliminate persistent toxic substances.

The political and economic context simultaneously underwent some noteworthy changes. The Canada–US Free Trade Agreement came into effect in 1988, superseded in 1994 by the North American Free Trade Agreement (NAFTA). But there were worries that rulings under this agreement could prevent either country from adequately protecting the freshwater resources of the Great Lakes. Great Lakes–focused NGOs, advocacy groups, and environmentalists became more involved in the GLWQA process as opportunities for public feedback became available. Government funding was meanwhile decreasing, deregulation increasing, neither country was paying much heed to the IJC's reports on Great Lakes water quality, and the commission itself was repeatedly sidelined by governments.

Canada and the United States inked a bilateral acid rain agreement in 1991. In the 1970s, acid rain had gone from a non-issue to among the most serious on the bilateral diplomatic agenda. What became popularly known in the 1980s as "acid rain" is a complex set of physical and chemical phenomena. Gases – especially sulphur dioxide (SO_2) and nitrogen oxide (NOx5) – are created and emitted, mostly by industrial processes and coal-fired power plants, and transported through the atmosphere, transformed into acidic compounds, and deposited on land and water. This has serious adverse effects on aquatic and terrestrial ecosystems. Lake and stream acidification kills fish and other aquatic species, for example. The impact is particularly strong during spring runoff, when melting snow produces an "acid shock" in streams. Acidification can cause long-term damage to some soils and has a deleterious effect on various crops and the growth of certain species of trees, particularly at higher altitudes.

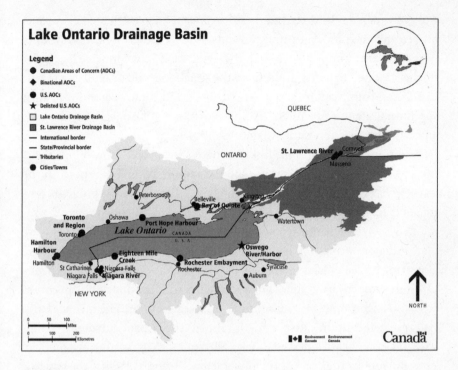

Lake Ontario Drainage Basin

Legend
- ● Canadian Areas of Concern (AOCs)
- ◆ Binational AOCs
- ● U.S. AOCs
- ★ Delisted U.S. AOCs
- ☐ Lake Ontario Drainage Basin
- ▦ St. Lawrence River Drainage Basin
- — International border
- — State/Provincial border
- — Tributaries
- ● Cities/Towns

QUEBEC

ONTARIO   St. Lawrence River   Cornwall
Massena

Peterborough   Belleville   Kingston
Bay of Quinte

Toronto   Oshawa   Port Hope Harbour   Watertown
and Region
Toronto   *Lake Ontario*   CANADA
U.S.A.
Hamilton
Harbour   Eighteen Mile   Oswego
Creek   River/Harbor
Hamilton   St Catharines   Rochester Embayment   Syracuse
Niagara Falls   Rochester
Niagara Falls   Niagara River   Auburn

NEW YORK

NORTH

0 50 100 Miles
0 100 200 Kilometres

Environment Environnement   Canada
Canada Canada

Figure 7.4
Map of AOCs and RAPs in the Lake Ontario basin.

In the Lake Ontario watershed, the problem was largely acid rain coming from the United States; Ontario certainly had its own sources, but prevailing winds tended to take the results away from the international border. The 1980s were characterized by negotiations, and stalling on the part of the Reagan Administration, for a transboundary air quality agreement. The eventual result was the 1991 Canada–United States Air Quality Agreement (AQA), which put caps on SO_2 emissions. Over the 1980 to 1995 period, Canadian emissions of SO_2 decreased by 43 per cent while emissions in the United States decreased by 26 per cent. But this had as much, probably more, to do with changed domestic regulations, practices, and technologies apart from the AQA.[50]

Despite the IJC's repeated and emphatic warnings, the Canadian and American governments and environmental agencies did not take the necessary steps to sufficiently address POPs. Rather than disallowing the emissions of persistent bioaccumulative toxics, both nations issued permits up to what were considered safe levels. But these levels were often calculated using out-moded and inappropriate principles and models. Furthermore, in some ways the ecosystem approach backfired: if everything is interconnected, calls for further research to better understand the situation could be used as a means of delay and obfuscation, and it became more difficult to take action against specific pollutants or polluters. In other words, scientific uncertainty became an excuse for inaction rather than precaution.[51]

Public displeasure with the lack of progress was vented at meetings about the GLWQA – enough so that in 1990 the required biennial report on the GLWQA was broken into two parts, the first dedicated to the public's comments.[52] Toxic chemicals were clearly the leading cause for concern and remained so through the 1990s. Levels of many conventional toxics were plateauing or decreasing. However, chemicals of "emerging concern" were appearing on the radar, as were new invasive species.[53] Many of these chemicals were endocrine disruptors that interfered with the body's hormones, as scientist Theo Colborn's groundbreaking research in the Great Lakes basin had revealed.[54] In the late twentieth century, the IJC and advocacy groups such as Great Lakes United routinely called out the Canadian and American governments for their lacklustre implementation efforts.[55] Since the two federal governments had ignored the IJC's calls to meaningfully regulate and prevent toxic waste, at the behest of polluting industries, the commission had largely given up on taking them to task by the early twenty-first century. The need for "increased accountability" euphemistically substituted for direct criticism.

Four Great Lakes AOCs have been delisted in the US since 1987, and three in Canada. Several others are in the recovery stage, and the actions have been completed at ten of them. Even when remediation activities are complete, we often need to wait for nature to finish the job, since further human intervention might be more damaging than letting natural processes take over. Consequently, there can be a long time lag between the completion of remediation activities and a safe declaration, even though there can be local pressure to delist AOCs before they are actually safe.[56]

Considerable progress has been made at the Niagara River AOC: two of the three RAP stages have been completed, and some "beneficial uses" have been restored. But the chief concern here remains toxic material. Much remains to be done, and chemicals buried long ago still leach into tributaries and groundwater heading to the Niagara River and then Lake Ontario. Though there are now only a few officially active Superfund sites in this community (i.e., on the National Priorities List), the area is still a checkerboard of toxic hotspots, with Love Canal the most infamous. A survey found 215 hazardous waste dumps in Erie and Niagara Counties. In Niagara Falls, even at some distance from Love Canal, soil samples contained high levels of benzene, groundwater samples contained pesticides such as heptachlor and aldrin, and the air contained tetrachloroethylene. Heavy metals were everywhere in the city. Radioactive soil was even recently detected close to the American Falls within the Niagara Falls State Park.

Eighteen Mile Creek in New York State flows from Lockport to Olcott, where it empties into Lake Ontario. Contamination from heavy metals and PCBS was the basis for its AOC designation. This site is still a long way away from delistment. There are two other AOCs in New York State: the Rochester Embayment and the Oswego River. The "Management Actions" have been completed at the former, where sewage was the big issue. The latter holds the distinction of being, in 2006, the second Great Lakes AOC that was delisted. Not only was Oswego the first site successfully remediated on Lake Ontario, it was the first in the United States. The Oswego River begins just downstream from Syracuse's Onondaga Lake. Historically, this city had a thriving chemicals industry and was once the world's largest producer of caustic soda chemicals and soda ash, leaving Onondaga one of the country's most polluted lakes because of sewage effluent and industrial waste. But because the population and industry had decreased in the Oswego watershed, this AOC had less challenging BUIS. Nevertheless, the Oswego, along with other New York tributaries such as Eighteen Mile Creek, the Genesee River, the Salmon River, and the Black River, contributed mercury and synthetic contaminants (PCBS, DDT, dioxin) to Lake Ontario. The levels of these contaminants was high enough that a decade into the twenty-first century the state government was still advising women of childbearing age and children under the age of fifteen not to eat fish from those waters.[57]

The Canadian AOCs are at Hamilton Harbour, Toronto, Port Hope, and the Bay of Quinte. Hamilton Harbour has received the most attention out of all the Lake Ontario AOCs and RAPS. The bay is a cherished recreational space, yet it is also one of Canada's most industrialized and polluted waterfronts – and one that is obvious to the millions of people who get a bird's-eye view as they drive over the Burlington Bay Skyway. Much work, maybe more than at any other Lake Ontario AOC, has been done in terms of remediating Hamilton Harbour. Well over $1 billion has been spent. But because it was so polluted it is likely the AOC furthest from delistment, since none of the identified BUIs have been removed.[58] Deindustrialization has helped reduce the influx of new pollutants, though Hamilton Harbour still remains one of the busier ports in the Great Lakes. The flight of industries has left orphaned brownfields but also opened up waterfront spaces for reclamation. A better balance between recreation and industry has been achieved in places: the western end of the bay and Cootes Paradise – now protected from invasive destructive European carp by a specially designed dam – sees more kayakers than ships.[59] But this is only part of the battle. The Randle Reef in Hamilton Harbour is considered one of the most contaminated sites in Canada. The resident coal tar blob at this reef slowly leeches carcinogens. Removing it was not considered viable, and hydrocarbon-eating microorganisms could not break it down. A gargantuan steel box the size of six city blocks was recently installed to contain the blob. It is better than nothing, but probably not good enough.

Toronto's area of concern is the recipient of one of the most intensely urbanized zones in the Great Lakes. This AOC encompasses the territory from Etobicoke Creek in the west to the Rouge River in the east, including the Humber and Don Rivers. As of 2007, numerous BUIs remained. The concentrations of many contaminants here – such as phosphorus – had declined since the 1970s but still exceeded target goals. Chloride levels, conversely, had risen appreciably because of the application of road salts; by the 1960s, if not earlier, scientists had recognized the negative effects that chloride burdens had on Lake Ontario and other waterbodies.[60] Since 2007, some of the original BUIs have been redesignated as "not impaired": pollution is not resulting in serious bird, animal, or fish deformities; effective restrictions have been placed on dredging; and neither pollution nor dredging is undermining the health of the organisms living in the harbour. Nevertheless, beach closures here remain common in the summer, particularly after large precipitation events overwhelm storm and combined sewers.

Continuing east, the Port Hope Harbour AOC was designated as such because of one problem. But it is a particularly nasty problem: sediment contaminated by radioactive waste from nuclear processing. Work is well advanced on cells meant to hold and contain the affected sediments, and I earlier discussed in more detail other nuclear waste challenges here. The Bay of Quinte AOC just to the east is on the verge of delisting. In this zig-zagging bay, whose tributaries include the Napanee, Salmon, Moira, and Trent Rivers, industrial and municipal sewage discharges have been the foremost pro-

Figure 7.5
Burlington Bay Canal, Skyway, and Hamilton Harbour in 2022. The canal is in the middle foreground. Note the steel industry buildings and smokestacks across the harbour.

ducers of cultural eutrophication and toxic pollution.[61] One of the palpable results of eutrophication is an abundance of *Cladophora*, a type of filamentous green algae that is unsightly and smells bad when it decomposes en masse. Heavy metals in sediments were the legacy of mining and logging operations upstream on the bay's tributaries. As far back as the end of the First World War, the Thurlow Fish Hatchery located at the mouth of the Moira River tested the water quality and found glaring pollution; the hatchery had to close within a few years because of the water impairment. Quinte's lucrative herring fishery went belly up in the 1940s, along with those of other fish communities. But there has been a partial rebound: more than half of the BUIS at this AOC have been restored, with all other BUIS except one no longer receiving the "impaired" designation.

The first stage of the LAMP for Lake Ontario was finalized in 1998.[62] It spotlighted four pan-lake problems: restrictions on fish and wildlife consumption, birds or animal deformities or reproductive problems, degradation of wildlife

populations, and loss of fish and wildlife habitat. The first three of these resulted from pollutants like PCBS, DDT, mirex, dioxins/furans, and mercury.
However, the LAMP has yet to progress beyond the first stage, indicating the
complexity and deep-rooted nature of the challenges. Following other funding
efforts that include the Great Lakes Legacy Act, since 2010 the Great Lakes
Restoration Initiative (GLRI) has provided billions in US federal funds, and
a good chunk of this has gone towards addressing AOCS.[63] The most recent
update to the GLWQA was in 2012.[64] This modernized the agreement: new annexes addressed issues such as climate change and invasive species, while improving accountability, engagement, and stakeholder involvement.

Congress has renewed the GLRI several times, most recently in 2021. The
cash infusion from the GLRI for restoration has been most welcome. These
funds have been used in the Lake Ontario basin in many ways: combatting
invasive species, reducing pollutants, restoring native salmon, enhancing lake
trout habitat, improving marshland health, etc. For example, at Braddock
Bay, just west of Rochester, a dwindling barrier beach was buttressed and expanded to protect and restore the habitat in the bay and the extensive wetlands complex.[65]

But for every gain made, a new obstacle seems to rear its head. In the
twenty-first century, another form of water pollution, plastic, has been recognized as an escalating problem. Indeed, plastics now account for 80 per
cent of the pollution by volume in the Great Lakes. Lake Ontario is saturated
by many different forms of plastic coming from tributaries, stormwater runoff, and wastewater treatment plants, especially near big cities.[66] Some you
can see, including bottles, bags, straws, and containers; others, the microplastics, are generally invisible to the naked eye but particularly pernicious.
Microplastics are less than five millimetres in size, while even smaller particles
between one nanometre and one micron are defined as nanoplastics. Microplastics can take different forms, including beads, foam, and fragments, but
plastic fibres constitute the majority in Lake Ontario and originate from diverse sources including clothing, debris, and building materials.

Both countries have banned microbeads, but most microplastics originate
from larger pieces of plastic broken down by natural processes. Some plastics
settle at the bottom of the lake in sediments, eventually compressing into a
plastic layer; others stay suspended in the water column. Freshwater biota,
such as fish, birds, and mammals, ingest plastics, which remain in their di-
gestive tracts and even in their body tissue. Within the lake, research suggests

that algae sticks to microplastics, making it look like food; aquatic organisms consume the algae and the plastics.[67] A belly full of plastic can cause creatures to starve to death or can poison them.[68] Microplastics also show up in drinking water and packaged drinks such as beer. And since we eat some of those fish and animals, and drink that water and beer, plastics are now found in the human body – including in the heart.

Once inside the body, microplastics leach chemicals and carcinogens, including POPs, causing health problems in humans and wild creatures alike. POPs biotransfer up the trophic chain from small fish to big fish and then to other fish-eating organisms, such as cormorants or humans. These chemicals cause a bevy of health complications, such as genetic problems, developmental abnormalities, reproductive issues, and cancer. PFAS chemicals, short for perfluoroalkyls and polyfluoroalkyls, have only recently been identified. But they are found in a wide array of Lake Ontario fishes, and there is evidence that these contaminants latch on to lacustrine plastic particles. Nicknamed "forever" chemicals because they do not break down in the natural environment like most other substances, PFAS have been used for decades throughout the Great Lakes basin. Sediment core samples show that perfluoroalkyl substances were getting into Lake Ontario as far back as the 1950s. These contaminants were used as flame retardants, among many other consumer uses such as nonstick coating for cookware and food packaging, or waterproofing for footwear. According to one study, the levels of flame retardants in Lake Ontario lake trout went up three-hundred fold in the last two decades of the twentieth century.[69]

Given these new and emerging contaminants, as well as the repercussions of treating the lake as a sink for so long, Lake Ontario may well be more polluted now than it was a half-century ago. At that time, new environmental regulations, such as the GLWQAS and the CWA, achieved impressive results in some areas such as reducing eutrophication and certain types of point source pollution. But the GLWQAS were ultimately unable to prevent Lake Ontario from becoming the most degraded of the five Great Lakes. Sewage contamination, despite all the treatment advances, is still a serious problem, both from storms that result in combined sewer overflows and ongoing leakage. Dealing with nuclear waste is still a perplexing challenge; yet nuclear power creates more than half of Ontario's electricity and a quarter of New York State's, and does so without carbon emissions. And for every toxic problem we address, such as DDT or PCBS, new ones like microplastics or PFAS emerge. Through the Great Lakes Water Quality Agreement we have the regulatory architecture in place that, if adequately funded and supported, might allow us to make big strides in cleaning up the lake. But that would require not only a stronger transnational commitment to the GLWQA, but a societal prioritization of environmental and human health over economic growth. Unfortunately, we seem far from doing any of that.

CHAPTER 8

Levels and Regulation

Stop the Disaster – #repealPlan2014
IJC Plan 2014 stinks
IJC stop flooding our homes – rescind Plan 2014 now!

These were just some of the slogans I saw plastered on placards and yard signs near Lake Ontario, especially on the New York side, in the late 2010s. Lake Ontario had hit its highest recorded levels, and properties and homes along the water were being threatened (see figure 8.1). The problem was most pronounced on the New York shore, since geology and zoning laws left property owners there more exposed than in Ontario. Many people blamed the dams in the St Lawrence River and the new method of regulation that had recently come into effect. They were partly right that humans bore some responsibility. But it was not so much the method of regulation and dams; rather, it was through humanity's impact on the climate and the corresponding increase in regional precipitation.

Debates about dams versus climate change speak to the human inclination to control, or believe that we can control, large natural systems like Lake Ontario. The lake has always fluctuated naturally.[1] Within the past century, during which recorded observations of lake levels are more reliable, these fluctuations usually stayed within general high and low parameters, even if these cycles were not entirely predictable. Since the First World War, the lake's surface has almost always been between about 242 feet and 247 feet above sea level (see figure 8.3). After the creation of the St Lawrence Seaway and

Figure 8.1
Flooding along the Lake Ontario shoreline in New York State.

Power Project, Lake Ontario levels became even more compressed and usually stayed within a three-foot range.[2] However, climate change has seemingly scrambled the normal range, and record high levels have occurred in recent years.

Modifying Lake Ontario's levels is a contested and politicized process. That is the case today. It was also the case a half-century earlier, as I will show in this chapter, which explores the modern history of attempting to regulate and control Lake Ontario. I first delve into the process of establishing Lake Ontario levels as part of the St Lawrence Seaway and Power Project. The dams and infrastructure constructed in conjunction with this megaproject meant that Lake Ontario became the Great Lake most affected by human-built control works. Later in the twentieth century, once it had become apparent that regulating the St Lawrence and Lake Ontario had detrimental impacts, though there were different perspectives about which impacts were the main problem, officials and experts began exploring new methods of regulation. This resulted in the unveiling of a new regulation plan in 2017, albeit amidst much controversy. Wrapped up in all this was an evolving expert understanding of the causes of changing water levels, which frequently conflicted with the beliefs of locals and other stakeholders about the efficacy and purpose of trying to regulate the lake.

METHOD OF REGULATION

The dams of the St Lawrence Seaway and Power Project, discussed in an earlier chapter, were built to not only control the water flows of the eponymous river but also those of Lake Ontario. The Moses-Saunders power dam blocks the St Lawrence River between the Canadian mainland at Cornwall, Ontario, and Barnhart Island, New York (see figure 8.2). The biggest transborder power dam in the world for several decades, it works in conjunction with two other dams in the upper St Lawrence to regulate levels: the nearby Long Sault Control Dam, which can act as a release spillway, and the Iroquois Dam much further upstream.

To proceed with planning the St Lawrence Seaway and Power Project, the engineers needed to develop a "method of regulation." The method of regulation, or regulation plan, referred to the levels between which water elevations would be maintained by the dams and control works. The engineering goal was to improve on nature by removing the extremes of high and low levels, creating a predictable and orderly aquatic environment. All plans and specifications had to be approved by the binational St Lawrence Joint Board of Engineers; after construction of the project was finished, the International St Lawrence River Board of Control took over supervision of water levels and related issues. The main users of the St Lawrence Seaway and Power Project as well as those affected by it – hydroelectric production, navigation and shipping, shorefront property owners, and various interests downstream in Quebec – wanted different minimum and maximum water levels or varying ranges of stages (i.e., differences between high and low levels). Pleasing everyone seemed impossible.[3]

To begin, engineers sought to use natural flows as a baseline. "Natural" was defined as that which had existed in the nineteenth century before the first human alterations to water levels – that is, the state of things before Canada installed the Gut Dam in the St Lawrence River in the early twentieth century. This dam, a 500-foot-long submerged structure, was placed under

Figure 8.2
Moses-Saunders Powerhouse today. The border runs through the middle of the powerhouse;
the left side is American and the right side is Canadian.

water only part of the way across the river, between the Galop and Adams
Islands. Canada built this dam to improve navigation by raising the water
level at the entrance to the Galop Canal and blocking off a crosscurrent that
interfered with vessels. In 1903, the United States had consented to the dam's
construction with a few conditions concerning compensation if it led to damages from high water levels. Canada requested to raise the dam higher the
next year, which the US again agreed to with similar caveats.

But what, exactly, constituted the "natural" state of the water levels? That
question was problematic for experts in the 1950s. Not only did representatives of the two countries disagree upon the historical impact of the Gut
Dam, partly for partisan and political reasons, but it was also difficult to find
information regarding past levels to use as a baseline. There were concerns
that historical measurements were unreliable. Indeed, engineering studies
indicated that natural factors must be playing a much larger role than man-
made factors (i.e., diversions into the Great Lakes basin) in the higher Lake
Ontario levels that were happening at that very time. But engineers were trying to ascertain the historical conditions on which they were basing their ar-
guments – even though they admitted they could not know these historical
conditions with much certainty – while simultaneously drafting their sche-
matics and plans. Thus, they kept couching their pronouncements on precise
water levels with the caveat "as nearly as may be."

In the early 1950s, Lake Ontario reached record high levels. In certain low-
lying parts, a lacustrine rise of just a few inches could submerge or affect a

significant stretch of the littoral zone (the region of the waterbody near to, and including parts of, the shore). Shore dwellers on Lake Ontario and in the Thousand Islands section of the St Lawrence complained about the water damaging their property. Complaints came from the Toronto and Bay of Quinte regions. But the damage was particularly bad for south shore owners in the vicinity of Rochester and Sodus Bay, where those affected formed the Lake Ontario Land Development and Beach Protection Association. By the postwar period, more people had the time, money, and mobility to buy or rent a vacation property on the water or to commute to work from a water-front home. Enough lakefront properties had been snapped up that the public began complaining about the lack of easy access to the lake near certain urban areas.

Many blamed the Gut Dam for the high levels, attributing to it a lake rise of almost a foot during high water cycles. They also called for a temporary reduction of the diversions from Ogoki–Long Lac into Lake Superior, citing the downstream effects for Lake Ontario, which Ontario Hydro obliged. Shore owners in New York agitated for compensation, congressional action, or an IJC investigation. The Lake Ontario Land Development and Beach Protection Association opened direct negotiations with Canada. Before hitting an impasse, they even arrived at a draft arbitration agreement to form an international tribunal. Soon the issue of whether Lake Ontario levels could be regulated to protect property owners was given its own IJC docket (#67), separate from the St Lawrence project (docket #68).[4] The IJC formed an International Lake Ontario Board of Engineers and tasked it with reducing water level fluctuations and protecting the various interests from injury. The recommendations would be incorporated into the water regulation plan for the Seaway and Power Project. The Gut Dam was already slated for removal as part of Seaway construction and Canada agreed to do so ahead of schedule in January 1953.

The Canadian and American sections of the International Lake Ontario Board of Engineers initially disagreed about the desirable maximum level of Lake Ontario and the impact of the Gut Dam on water levels.[5] The engineers knew that their provisional regulation plans would need to evolve with the construction of the St Lawrence megaproject because of unknown conditions in the field and the inability to predict all future aspects. Of course, when speaking to the public or politicians they projected an aura of infallibility, keeping with the societal and professional expectations of experts in this era.

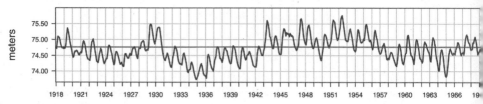

Figure 8.3
Graph of Lake Ontario water levels from 1918 to 2023.

In March 1955, the IJC told the Canadian and American governments that it was possible to regulate both the St Lawrence and Lake Ontario in such a way as to balance the disparate demands. They replaced the existing method of regulation with a regulation plan called 12-A-9. But there were still problems with that approach: for example, tests showed that this regulation plan might inordinately constrict the river channel at Montreal. Indeed, making sure shorelines downstream in Quebec would not experience problems any worse than pre-project conditions was a prime consideration. The chief goals were obviating floods during the spring – Montreal is susceptible to seasonal flooding since it is at the confluence of the St Lawrence and the Ottawa Rivers – and sufficiently limiting the river flow during the ice-forming season. A chief design element of the St Lawrence works was in fact to control the ways ice did and did not form in the waterways and at power station intakes. The aforementioned control dams, and the configuration of their gates and sluices, were therefore intended to alter ice formation processes as well as water levels.[6]

Lacustrine property owners, and municipalities such as Hamilton and Toronto, requested that the maximum lake elevation be lowered another foot or two lest inundation problems occur. The recent experience of Hurricane Hazel left this area particularly wary of flooding. In the wake of that hurricane, prohibitions against building too close to Lake Ontario's edge were put in place in Ontario. Several Congressmen and the US section of the IJC formally suggested a revised method of regulation that topped out at 247 feet. The IJC planners decreased the upper limit marginally, from 248.3 to 248.0. Bringing the maximum stage down all the way to 247 feet, however, would cost the power utilities and shipping companies millions of dollars because

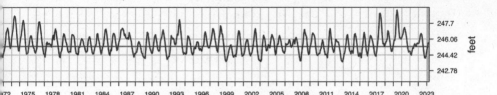

of the lost dam head or the need to dredge deeper navigation channels to compensate. Doing so would also lower the available depths of Lake Ontario harbours and delay the opening of the Seaway, perhaps by a year, because of the extra work that would be required. An Army Corps of Engineers study concluded that lowering the range of levels by one foot "would unduly delay the overall project and does not appear to be justified on an economic basis."[7] The US Federal Power Commission concurred. The two federal governments accepted the IJC's recommendation that the levels be set between 244 and 248 feet, again with the caveat "as nearly as may be."

The flexibility offered by that caveat allowed planners to progressively adapt to real-world conditions. In other words, engineering uncertainty was beneficial to a certain extent since it required them to incorporate room for adaptation, thus avoiding some negative path dependencies, unfavourable technological lock-in, and likely additional expenses. But it was also an implicit admission that they could not fully control the natural environment, including water levels. Nevertheless, the experts sought to bracket out or ignore these limitations, and proceeded with a high degree of hubris. Indeed, the St Lawrence Seaway and Power Project was the North American epitome of what has been called high modernism, which at base is a belief in the infallible ability of experts to use science, engineering, and technology to control and reorder environments and societies on a very large scale. The reliance on hydraulic scale models was indicative of a high modernist mindset. Ontario Hydro built nine power project models, while the Canadian federal government built models for the navigation aspect. Meanwhile, the US Army Corps of Engineers had hydraulic scale model studies underway in Mississippi and Minnesota. The governmental agencies bragged that models saved millions of dollars by solving problems in advance of construction and avoiding mistakes in the field. The use of models for this project was heralded as a major advance in global hydraulic modelling.[8]

But blueprints and models inevitably require abstraction, simplification, and obfuscation. The types of materials used to mimic nature, while innovative, sometimes were not accurate enough. When extrapolated onto the real world, minuscule model mistakes could have large ramifications. Even after years of using the models, there was still much disagreement about how to calibrate them properly.[9] The chair of the Canadian section of the IJC, General McNaughton, emphasized "that the balance of conditions on Lake Ontario is so delicate that he could not feel assurance that the engineers could in fact keep the levels within the [specified] range."[10] To accommodate such uncertainties, the "as nearly as may be" rider remained an indispensable variable within the planners' iterative attempts to identify a water level range that could best balance the competing demands.

In 1956 the IJC issued a supplementary order, amending its original October 1952 order, that laid out the future operation of the water regime, incorporating Method of Regulation 12-A-9.[11] This was intended as a best guess, based on hydraulic models, to get the St Lawrence project off the ground. The experts expected they would change and update the plan based on actual operational experience once the Seaway and Power Project was open, and that was indeed the case. The IJC replaced 12-A-9 with Method of Regulation 1958-A in 1960. That was superseded by Plan 1958-C at the beginning of 1962, which in turn was replaced in October 1963 by Plan 1958-D. In 1961, the Board of Control was granted "discretionary authority" to depart temporarily from the flow plan when a deviation of limited magnitude and duration would provide beneficial effects or relief from adverse effects, without appreciably harming any other interests. Put simply, the Board of Control could authorize frequent alterations to the outflows of the dams in the St Lawrence when faced with changing conditions – so as long as that did not endanger meeting the criteria and other requirements of the order of approval.

There were conspicuous problems with low water levels in Lake Ontario in the 1960s and then high water levels in the 1970s. These were attributed to natural supplies of greater variance than had occurred in the historical period upon which the engineers had based the methods of regulation – likely some of the early manifestations of climate change.[12] Fluctuating levels required the Board of Control to tweak its methodology for dealing with deviations. The board kept account of the deviations and, except in rare circumstances, each divergence required subsequent offsetting deviations from the plan to return Lake Ontario to the Plan 1958-D level.[13] Because the actual Lake Ontario outflow was different from the specified Plan 1958-D outflow on a fairly consistent basis, this approach to regulation was called "Plan 1958-D with deviations" or Plan 1958-DD. This would remain in place, albeit in modified form, until the twenty-first century, when it was replaced by Plan 2014.

LITIGATING LEVELS

While discussions about the method of regulation were still ongoing in the mid-1950s, Lake Ontario property owners sought legal indemnification for any future problems with high water levels. But exactly who would be held legally culpable? That was unclear, since the St Lawrence power project was a joint New York and Ontario undertaking. The head of the Power Authority of the State of New York (PASNY), notorious NYC planner Robert Moses, had brushed off local apprehension with his characteristic brusqueness. In a public speech, he referred to "assorted characters who are steaming up distant owners on the Great Lakes shorefronts to sue us for the rise and fall of tides."[14] Canadian and American representatives disagreed about how to handle potential damages. They did not want this issue to delay progress on the St Lawrence project. Plus officials felt an international lawsuit would create other potentially difficult jurisdictional legal problems. Lacustrine property owners were nonetheless assured that PASNY and Ontario Hydro could likely be held responsible in the event of damages.

Lake Ontario shore owners in New York continued to seek compensation for past injuries from the high 1951 to 1952 waters. The claimants went to the American courts to try to sue Canada over the impact of the Gut Dam. Canada did acknowledge that it was responsible for any proven damages caused by the dam, but countered that the record high levels in the early 1950s were chiefly the result of natural causes or other artificial changes to Great Lakes levels upstream. Furthermore, the Canadian government argued that it had immunity from such lawsuits; really, they were worried that US courts would favour American plaintiffs and be more likely to assess high damages, or drag the matter out for too long.[15] The US State Department retorted that in the diplomatic notes from 1903 and 1904, which constituted American consent for the raising of the Gut Dam, Canada agreed to be under the jurisdiction of American courts.

Government officials debated the legal precedents and niceties with an eye to setting up some sort of international adjudication body. Technical experts meanwhile wrestled with the pivotal question: how much had the Gut Dam actually raised water levels? On that score, there was considerable uncertainty. In 1956, a US federal court dismissed the court charges for lack of jurisdiction, a decision upheld by the Supreme Court in 1957. An investigation by the IJC's International Lake Ontario Board of Engineers concluded that the Gut Dam raised Lake Ontario levels by four inches at most.[16] Granted, that amount was mostly counteracted by other infrastructural works prior to the Seaway, such as dredging and canals that lowered water levels by about the same amount. And even if the Gut Dam was responsible for a four-inch increase of the water level, that amount accounted for merely one-quarter of the lake's damaging rise during the early 1950s.

Momentum for a Gut Dam settlement slowed down for a while. The Lake Ontario Land Development and Beach Protection Association reduced its claims before the courts, which initially totalled $50 million, to $18 million, and then $2.5 million. In 1959, the association's lawyer said his clients would settle with Canada for $850,000. But the Canadian Department of External Affairs declined, since, in its view, the claims were likely invalid. Plus, any settlement might set a dangerous precedent about the ability of US citizens to make transborder claims against the Canadian government. Behind the scenes, Canadian officials showed some willingness to settle but ultimately prevaricated. Ottawa seemed to hope the problem would just eventually fade away. Dealing with other delicate Cold War issues, the United States, for its part, did not want to strain relations with a key ally and trade partner by pressing for a decision about such a minor matter.[17]

The shore owners turned to the US Foreign Claims Settlement Commission, submitting 542 claims adding up to almost $8.5 million. This brought Canada back to the table. But the possibility of the commission finding Canada culpable, especially if the damages were large, still raised a host of prickly transborder legal and political questions. With the support of the two federal governments, the matter was moved to a bilateral Lake Ontario Claims Tribunal. More than two hundred claims were submitted to the tribunal totalling about $650,000. The claims records show that a considerable number of those affected were unable to remain at their lakeside residences during 1951 to 1952 because of the high water. Significant damage was done to the built infrastructure, such as residences, rental cottages, piers, and boathouses; natural features, such as beaches, lawns, and trees, also eroded away.

The costs of new breakwaters or riprapping built to withstand flooding were submitted for consideration. In their claims, many asked to be compensated for the lost property appraisal value because of the decrease in overall aesthetics or water access.

Martha King, who resided at the lake in Monroe County, New York, attested in an affidavit that during the high waters, "[t]he beach was flooded. In addition, extensive erosion took place washing away parts of the bluff and lawn area. The retaining wall that existed prior to 1951 was virtually destroyed. The area surrounding the house and cottage was inundated by water making the property unusable for portions of spring and summer ... The flooding of the property caused the foundation of the house to loosen." As many others did, she included written testimony, receipts, photos, and other evidence. Hilda Mauer, who owned property in Hilton, New York, experienced similar destruction, and "in order to ensure that further damage would be held to a minimum" she hired a company to spread heavy stone fill across fifty feet of lake frontage. The resulting "rip rap stone wall was built at a cost of $837.97," but it also "reduced the value of the property, because ready access to the water was made difficult." One owner on an island in Sodus Bay, a district prone to inundation, claimed about $4,000 in damages; another outside of Pultneyville claimed $12,000. A couple down the St Lawrence near Alexandria Bay asked for $20,000 in compensation.[18]

The Lake Ontario Claims Tribunal found that Canada was liable for damages. But it suggested that the two nations work out a compromise solution. In 1968, Canada agreed to pay a token US$350,000 as final settlement for the alleged damages. A settlement also allowed both sides to maintain their "factual positions," which meant that this did not set an international legal precedent. Thus ended the protracted Gut Dam problem. However, high water would soon rear its head again – in the early 1970s, the 1990s, and then in the twenty-first century.[19]

UNDERSTANDING LEVELS

The Gut Dam controversy speaks to the historical challenges of ascertaining the nature of Great Lakes level changes. The Great Lakes normally fluctuate under the influence of natural forces: chiefly precipitation and evaporation, but also glacial (or isostatic) rebound. Precipitation and evaporation are seasonal. Both colder and warmer weather can lead to higher lake levels,

depending on the season in which they occur: for example, greater precipitation during the spring or summer puts more water into the system,
while colder winters result in more extensive ice cover, which reduces evaporation. There are other seasonal and short-term fluctuations from storms,
winds, barometric pressure changes, seiches (standing waves), and aquatic
plants (which can cumulatively displace a significant volume of water). But
for much of the twentieth century, only some of this was well understood
by experts. Even today, there is still scientific uncertainty about certain
aspects of the lake's processes.[20]

Further complicating things, humanity has repeatedly altered the natural
regime of the Great Lakes water system. It is impossible to accurately quantify
the total amount of dredging done in Lake Ontario. Also, human activity
continuously affected sediment deposition patterns. Was a dredging contract
just restoring a harbour to the depth it had before mill sediments, soil erosion, or sewage runoff covered the bottom? Prior to the later twentieth century, most dredged material seems to have been deposited in the lake with
the location rarely recorded. No one was keeping precise track of how much
the stonehookers had collectively removed either. Greater sediment loads
from erosion and tributary streams also changed the shoreline and nearshore
areas over time. Some shoreline features, like bluffs and spits, retreated, while
others expanded. Going back some two centuries, many breakwaters, riprapping, revetments, and groins were put up to stop erosion, protect harbours
and wharves, and encourage beach nourishment. Based as they often were
on an incomplete comprehension or understanding of cause and effect, these
sometimes proved counterproductive.

Some installations, such as piers and breakwaters, became prime public
vantage points, while others blocked off access to the lake. In both the State
of New York and the Province of Ontario, governments control and grant
public access to Lake Ontario.[21] Courts have used the public trust doctrine
– the legal principle that the government manages or protects certain natural
resources for the benefit of the general public – to uphold the contention
that the state controls up to the "ordinary high water mark." This means that
the public has access to any shore or beach between that mark and the water's
edge, which private owners cannot cordon off without governmental consent. That said, there are many, many cases in which Ontario and New York
gave permission to install, or installed themselves, a range of infrastructure,
from railways to marinas to breakwaters, in this zone. The right of public access below the "ordinary high water mark" has been legally adopted in some

Great Lakes states. The same is mostly true in Ontario, aside from some grandfathered-in water lot rights that can prohibit public access to the water-line.[22] But in New York State, such a right of public access has not yet been legally enshrined and is still open to court challenges and interpretation. Nevertheless, the public can access most of Lake Ontario's littoral zone below the ordinary high water mark.

Dredging, diversions, control structures, and consumptive uses can all affect lake levels in different ways. Picture the lake as a bathtub. Some of these anthropogenic interventions are like turning the faucet, thus changing the amount, temperature, and speed of the water coming in. Human-caused climate change is turning up the hot water knob. A diversion out of the lake is akin to puncturing a very small hole in the side of the bathtub. Other anthropogenic interventions, like dredging, adjust the depth of the bathtub – even if the amount of water does not change, the volume declines relative to the rim of the tub (i.e., the shoreline). Reclaimed land has the opposite effect, shrinking the width of the bathtub: cities such as Toronto and Hamilton extended their shorelines hundreds of metres out into the water, while backshore wetlands were covered with infill. Continuing with the bathtub metaphor, the St Lawrence River is the drainpipe leading from the tub, with the dams constituting partial stoppers or clogs in the drain. While it might seem intuitively obvious that the St Lawrence's three dams raised lake levels, that is not really the case. The reason is this: creating the Seaway and Power Project also involved making the St Lawrence River bigger and deeper. This increased the outflow of Lake Ontario, equivalent to enlarging the size of a bathtub's drainpipe. In short, the new dams and methods of regulation essentially brought the lake's levels back to what it would have been before the St Lawrence project, albeit with more ability to compress those levels within a certain range.

Lake Ontario is the only Great Lake, aside from Lake Superior, that has control dams in its outlet river.[23] And since this lowest of the Great Lakes has just a fraction of the water volume of the uppermost Great Lake, Lake Ontario is therefore the Great Lake that humans can most directly control. However, that control is only limited to a few feet – and once natural supply outstrips the variance in the method of regulation, humans and their infrastructure cannot do much to adjust the lake levels.

Over the second half of the twentieth century, it was becoming clearer and clearer that, even if attempts to control water levels passed cost–benefit muster, when it came to determining water levels, human works paled in efficacy compared to those of nature. Such were the findings of several IJC reference studies on Great Lakes water levels in the decades after the completion of the Seaway and Power Project.[24] In addition to natural precipitation as the paramount driver, the IJC recognized the temporary impacts of prolonged wind or seiches, and the slow but steady isostatic, or glacial, rebound that was elevating the west end of the lake about a foot every century.[25] They found that changes to the Chicago or Ogoki–Long Lac diversions would not be noticeable in Lake Ontario for well over a decade. According to a mid-1980s IJC report, the Chicago Diversion reduced the mean level of Lake Ontario by 3 centimetres (0.10 feet).[26] Out of the various man-made diversions and ways that humanity utilizes Great Lakes water, the IJC also pointed out that consumptive uses – in which the water is not returned to its source – might have the largest cumulative effect. All in all, by the 1980s the IJC was recommending that governments not consider the manipulation of existing diversions to either raise low levels or decrease high levels in the Great Lakes.[27]

Meanwhile, momentum was building for legal arrangements to prevent new diversions out of the Great Lakes basin. The megaprojects of the 1950s had led to plans for even more hubristic large-scale water control schemes, such as the monumental Great Recycling and Northern Development (GRAND) canal concept and North American Water and Power Alliance (NAWAPA). While these were rightfully dismissed, other water transfer schemes were, and still are, more likely. Most involved sending Great Lakes water elsewhere in the United States. Water management in the Great Lakes–St Lawrence basin is governed by a network of legal regimes, including international instruments such as the Boundary Waters Treaty (BWT) and IJC, federal laws and regulations in both Canada and the United States, the laws of the eight Great Lakes states and Ontario and Quebec, and the treaties and rights of Indigenous peoples. But in the 1980s it appeared that there were either loopholes or no sure-fire way of saying "no" if the dry Great Plains or Southwest came calling for Great Lakes water with the support of the US federal government. With the population of the Sun Belt exploding, to some it seemed easier to move water to people than people to water. That was what California had done, after all. The Great Lakes states and provinces therefore sought out governance and regulatory mechanisms to prevent such an occurrence.[28]

In 1985, the eight states and two provinces bordering the Great Lakes–St Lawrence basin adopted the Great Lakes Charter. Any plan proposed in any

Great Lakes state or province that involved major consumptive water use or diversion had to give prior notice to, and seek the approval of, all other states and provinces. However, the Charter was a nonbinding, good faith agreement, and holes soon appeared. For example, the possibility of bulk exports out of the Great Lakes basin surfaced (e.g., in 1998 the Nova Group of Sault Ste. Marie proposed sending Great Lakes water by tanker to Asia), as did the transfer of water to smaller communities in the US straddling, or just outside of, the Great Lakes watershed. When it came to Lake Ontario, not all of these flashpoints were outside the basin, however. The village of Webster, close to Rochester, explored bottling and selling its groundwater. In 1997, the Haldimand diversion from the Lake Ontario basin to the Lake Erie basin became operational. This involved the City of Hamilton, which draws its municipal supply from Lake Ontario, sending a tiny volume of its treated water (two cfs) to three small communities in the neighbouring municipality of Haldimand. From there, the water flows to the Grand River, which discharges into Lake Erie.

The 2001 Annex to the Great Lakes Charter committed the parties to develop binding regulations to ensure no net water loss through diversion or consumption – or through adverse impacts on water quality, since polluting water is essentially losing it in key respects – with a commitment to ensuring public input. In 2005 the Great Lakes–St Lawrence River Basin Water Resources Compact was forged amongst the Great Lakes states and the US federal government, coming into effect in 2008. The Great Lakes–St Lawrence River Basin Sustainable Water Resources Agreement, which added Ontario and Quebec, was also inked. Though this companion agreement involving the two Canadian provinces is non-binding, the American compact has the force of law.

These agreements banned new or increased water diversions out of the Great Lakes–St Lawrence basin, with some strictly controlled exceptions.[29] The states and provinces party to the accords also pledged to use a consistent standard to review proposed uses of water and withdrawals, including consumptive uses within the basin, as well as develop and implement water conservation and efficiency programs. This was a significant improvement. But concerns remain. For example, there are legitimate worries that under international trade accords, such as the 2020 United States–Mexico–Canada Agreement (the successor to NAFTA), efforts by governments to protect and conserve their water resources might be ruled as discriminatory practices.

That the 2008 compact might contribute to the commodification of water is a legitimate concern, as is the fact that the compact does not limit exports out of the Great Lakes basin of packaged water or beverages (bottled water, juice, beer, etc.) in containers smaller than the average office water cooler.

REVISITING REGULATION

For decades, the regulation of Lake Ontario outflows provided benefits to hydro power production and shipping, as well as to shoreline property owners, by reducing naturally occurring episodes of extreme high water levels on Lake Ontario. Though the method of regulation dampened the highs and lows, along with a changing climate it did shift the seasonal range and cycles of Lake Ontario's levels.[30] The 1972 to 1973 period was unusually wet in the Great Lakes basin, resulting in unprecedented high water supplies to Lake Ontario. Although the peak level set a record high for the lake, the regulation plan held the level of Lake Ontario more than 0.3 feet lower than it would have been otherwise.[31] Regulation provided similar reductions to Lake Ontario flood levels in the later 1970s, the 1980s, and the 1990s. Simultaneously, the occurrence of damaging high water levels in the Montreal region was reduced by compensating for high flows on the Ottawa River during the spring runoff.

Nonetheless, during the 1980s dissatisfaction with the regulation plan and the ijc order of approval grew among some stakeholders: property owners on the south shore of Lake Ontario, recreational boaters and marina owners along the St Lawrence, and environmental groups throughout the system concerned with wetland and habitat loss.[32] The expectations of shorefront landowners, especially in New York, was that regulation would reduce extreme high water levels and raise extreme low levels such that erosion of the shoreline immediately in front of their properties would be better off than had there been no regulation. While there was a measurable reduction in waterline erosion, it was not as much as property-owners had hoped – probably unrealistically – and these citizens put pressure on their political leaders and the ijc.

Environmentalists were concerned about the ecological impacts. The ijc's initial methods of procedure gave precedence to navigation, riparian, and hydroelectric generation rights on the St Lawrence over ecological and recreational factors. Peaking operations involving water level fluctuations are hazardous for aquatic ecosystems – they were not allowed under the initial IJC order but the commission and power interests quickly reversed this.[33] Regulating a river or lake at too uniform a level, and therefore not allowing for natural and seasonal variability, is ecologically detrimental, especially for shoreline wetlands. For example, the marshlands at Presqu'ile Provincial Park are immediately and noticeably affected when lake levels drop or rise.

The IJC committed to reviewing the method of regulation to address the needs of recreational boating and the environment. The International St Lawrence River Board of Control recommended a new approach, Plan 1998. But this faced a general lack of support, and outright opposition, at six public meetings.[34] In January 1999, the commission decided not to implement Plan 1998 because there was insufficient information about the environmental impacts, and the proposed plan would not result in enough of an improvement over Plan 1958-D with deviations.

Concerns about climate change had already motivated studies about a warmer climate's impact on Great Lakes levels. Different scientific models produced different results. As the models became more refined moving into the twenty-first century, the projections still varied widely: most predicted higher water levels, some lower. Of course, making predictions about water levels was, and remains, exceedingly complex. Within the range of different model results, however, it was becoming evident that more frequent level fluctuations would likely become the norm, which has proven to be the case.[35]

The IJC recognized that a more comprehensive study of the regulation of Lake Ontario flows was necessary. It appointed the International Lake Ontario–St Lawrence River Study Board in 2000, which included stakeholders on the Study Board itself and all its technical working groups. Additionally, efforts were made to better incorporate Indigenous perspectives: Akwesasne/St Regis Mohawk members were added to the Study Board, and an Akwesasne Task Force on the Environment was created. Out of all the variants the Study Board investigated, two plans emerged. Plan 2007 was named for the year in which it was developed. Another variant, Plan B+, provided more environmental benefits than Plan 2007 but had more adverse consequences for waterfront property unless mitigation was undertaken. Most navigation, shoreline, and downstream interests found Plan 2007 unacceptable. For their part, environmental interests wanted to implement Plan B+ as soon as possible. After further consultation with stakeholders, public input sessions, deliberation, and refinement, the IJC then developed another proposal, which came to be called Plan 2014.

Plan 2014 provided for a more natural hydrological regime that would better mimic natural changes while still helping to moderate extreme highs and lows, as well as balance the requirements of upstream and downstream users and interests. This method of regulation, which allows for more seasonal variations than its predecessors, was better for the health of the lake ecosystem, particularly shoreline wetlands. It incorporated an adaptive management strategy to allow short-term deviations, necessitating less frequent need for major deviations from the plan; a set of high and low lake levels were added to trigger special actions to better protect hydro power intakes, navigation, boating, and shore interests.

The IJC invited public comment and convened public hearings on the proposed Plan 2014.[36] More than 5,500 comments were received. The responses were polarized, ranging from short endorsements or rejections of Plan 2014 to formal responses from various levels of government and non-governmental organizations.[37] Most south shore property owners in New York State who participated in the hearings, and their local governments, opposed Plan 2014. Save Our Sodus, a non-profit group, presented a petition with more than four hundred comments that either rejected Plan 2014 or documented past flooding and erosion problems that had occurred under the existing regulation rules. This group feared that the higher maximum water levels under Plan 2014 would cause more shoreline and property damage and that the lower levels would make boating more difficult.

The US Department of Transportation raised concerns that the priority given to environmental objectives in Plan 2014 violated the Boundary Waters Treaty. That reflected similar statements by several other respondents involved with commercial navigation on the Seaway, including the St Lawrence Seaway Management Corporation, the Canadian Shipowners Association, and the Shipping Federation of Canada. Commercial navigation worried that Plan 2014 would hinder their operations: it could potentially create significantly lower levels on Lake Ontario in a few years out of a hundred, thus forcing ships to reduce loads and lose profits. Ultimately, it was the commercial navigation concerns that had to be overcome by the IJC before the governments consented. Only after a serious effort was made to resolve this issue by altering some of the limits in the plan did the navigation interests assent. Interestingly, though the political demarcations drawn through and downstream from Lake Ontario made the regulation debates a diplomatic issue, the shared perspectives within the different stakeholder groups transcended borders in much the same way as the water they were arguing over.

A sufficient range of stakeholders now supported Plan 2014, with the notable exception of the group of shoreline property owners based in New York State and their local political representatives. After more than fourteen years of intensive analysis and extensive consultation with governments, experts, industry, Lake Ontario and St Lawrence River interests, and the public, the IJC concluded that Plan 2014 should be implemented immediately. In June 2014, the IJC formally recommended the plan, and both governments concurred in December 2016. The IJC appointed a new International Lake Ontario–St Lawrence River Board and charged it with implementing the new regulation plan, which took effect in the first month of 2017.[38]

Unfortunately, the initiation of Plan 2014 coincided with high precipitation throughout the Lake Ontario–St Lawrence basin in 2017 and then again in 2019. The result was record flooding at Lake Ontario, the St Lawrence River, and the Ottawa River. Residents on the south shore of Lake Ontario were outspoken in their criticism of the new regulation plan, to which the signs and slogans at the beginning of this chapter attest. They complained about eroding shorelines, crumbling buildings, and sinking property values. The owners of a marina at Irondequoit Bay, for example, said rising water levels put their livelihood at risk, and "[i]nstead of fixing our docks, we're filling sandbags because we've got land that's covered in water, a gas dock covered in water, and it's coming up on our sea walls and into our yards."[39]

Many of the complaints disregarded the natural causes. But some of those affected made more nuanced critiques. For example, New York State homeowner and engineer Bernard Gigas contended that Plan 2014 was balanced unfairly in favour of the region downstream of the Moses-Saunders dam: "Montreal can say, 'We don't give a shit. We have a hard limit. You can't release any water.' That's hard coded into the plan. I'd call it an oversight, but it wasn't an oversight. It was put in there on purpose and the Americans must have been asleep at the wheel when it happened. But fair's fair. We shouldn't suffer just because they have more people." A member of the St Regis Mohawk Tribe, located immediately downriver from the Moses-Saunders dam, countered that during the 2017 flooding "over 6,000 people were displaced from Quebec, 1,000 houses were unsalvageable. It was a forced managed retreat. Does that sound like they're being favored by the plan?"[40]

The IJC may have been guilty of framing the method of regulation as primarily a technical issue in its public relations. Nevertheless, many of the criticisms of Plan 2014 are misplaced, since during instances of extreme natural supply any method of regulation would only have a minimal ability to restrict

Lake Ontario water levels. In short, high levels and flooding would have taken place regardless, including under the old regulation plan. But it is true that navigation and power interests, particularly the former, have since the Seaway's creation been given too much sway within the process of determining the method of regulation. And the question of how to balance the protection of Quebec property owners with those along Lake Ontario is a tricky one that requires trade-offs. Furthermore, legitimate questions can be raised about whether humanity should even attempt to control levels on enormous waterbodies such as this Great Lake.

It is easy to understand why people want to live beside this glorious lake. But building too close to Lake Ontario, especially on the south shore, signifies a failure to heed nature's past warnings. Regulating the lake primarily to benefit property also prioritizes private interests over the wider public good, not to mention the even wider ecological good. Despite repeated high-water events since the middle of the twentieth century demonstrating that it is risky to do so, people continue to reside in low-lying topographies along the lake, some building on land reclaimed since the post-1950 flooding events. For decades, authorities have allowed lakeside construction with insufficient restrictions, safeguards, and requirements, while grandfathering in many homes. Imprecise, outdated, or missing maps and information have contributed to the problem.[41] Perhaps the main culpability is attributable to those governments, contractors, and realtors who zoned, built, and sold properties in areas they knew, or should have known, were vulnerable.

Ultimately, Plan 2014 is an improvement over its predecessor, though further tweaks might be beneficial.[42] The primary cause of recent high levels is natural forces, including climate change. The recent yo-yoing of water levels is likely becoming the new normal; by early summer 2021, just two years after the record highs of 2019, Lake Ontario was back down to low water conditions. Whether a changing climate will ultimately result in lower or higher lake levels remains up in the air, literally and metaphorically. Likely it will be both, since what does seem certain is that climate change introduces uncertainty – in this case, water levels that change much more frequently. Of course, uncertainty had always been a part of the long history of regulating Lake Ontario. The question of how to respond to fluctuating water levels was, and likely will remain, hotly contested – not only because of different conceptions of the role of climate change but because choosing a regulation plan means choosing some uses and interests over others.

CONCLUSION

Listen to the Lake

Lake Ontario is both remarkably resilient and incredibly fragile. Given enough time, it can deal with many of the abuses humanity heaps on it. But in the shorter term – that is, on human timescales – it is clearly vulnerable. We have changed the amount of water in the lake, the quality of that water, and what lives in that water. In many fundamental respects, the lowest Great Lake is now very different than it was a few hundred years ago.

Lake Ontario and human societies have imposed themselves on each other. Up until the nineteenth century, Lake Ontario did more of the imposing. By the time of the US Civil War and Canadian Confederation, that scenario was reversing, a trend that only accelerated in the following century. Lake Ontario materially enabled the modes of human life that crowded its edges and used its resources, from fertile agriculture landscapes to energy production systems and sprawling cities. Providing food, drinking water, energy, waste disposal, industry, transportation, and more, this lacustrine environment influenced not only the nation-states that emerged but the types of political economies – capitalist, liberal, and democratic – that they became. The lake conceptually empowered the human communities that grew up around it, its plentiful resources instilling expectations of abundance. The governmental involvement that went into managing those resources conditioned societal attitudes toward a more interventionist role for the state, particularly in the Province of Ontario.[1]

The Great Lakes–St Lawrence system is central to the Canadian national imaginary, but far more peripheral to the historical narrative of the United States. In many ways, Lake Ontario is now the most ignored of all the Great

Lakes, especially in the United States. Yet it is also arguably the most important of the Great Lakes, particularly north of the border, when measured by
political and economic significance. Lake Ontario barely registers a mention
in most histories of the United States or New York State; conversely, Lake
Ontario is the Great Lake most intrinsically tied to Canadian nation building.
This inland sea looms equally large in the history of the province that bears
the same name. The political and economic centres of power in English-
speaking Canada had huddled by this lake since the time of European settlement. Lake Ontario provided not only a fluid link to other parts of the
territory that became Canada, as well as back to the mother country, but a
permeable filter between Canada and the American republic.

Canada would have looked very different without Lake Ontario. In fact,
without it, the nation might not exist at all, considering that Confederation
was, at its core, the consolidation of power along the Lake Ontario–St Lawrence corridor. The lake underwrote the initial viability of the Dominion of
Canada as an independent entity, and was indispensable to its continued
growth and success. The lake still hosts Canada's largest and most powerful
province, and its largest and leading city. The majority of the provincial inhabitants of Ontario, and a quarter of the entire country's population, live
by this lake.

Public access to Lake Ontario has been increasingly controlled over the
last two centuries through zoning, infrastructure, and governmental
measures to regulate fishing, recreation, transportation, industry, and pollution. Some of this benefitted the lake, particularly those regulations aimed
at protecting it, such as the Great Lakes Water Quality Agreements (GLWQAS)
or domestic water pollution and water treatment measures. But some of this
– restricting Indigenous fishing practices, reserving waterfronts for private
profits and industrial activities, polluting the lake for economic development
– was also about controlling people and their access to amenities and resources. Humanity sought to regulate Lake Ontario, but the lake also became
a means of regulating people.

Over the last century and a half, human impacts have changed Lake Ontario so much that it is almost impossible to keep track of, let alone fully
catalogue, each and every modification. In the nineteenth century, we cut
down forests, dammed tributaries, dug canals, and obliterated fish species.
In the twentieth century, our impacts only expanded: pollution, toxics, invasives, urban sprawl, larger canals, hydroelectric dams, and climate change.
Those impacts truly intensified in the middle of the twentieth century. The

period since then, or perhaps starting even earlier, has been called the Anthropocene, in reference to humanity's role as the primary driver of changes to earth systems.[2] (Incidentally, the sediments of Crawford Lake, a small but deep waterbody near the head of Lake Ontario, has been proposed as the official "golden spike" marking the onset of the Anthropocene.) The period since the Second World War has also been dubbed the Great Acceleration because of the dramatic and simultaneous surge in many human trends and activities – population growth, consumption rates, energy use, greenhouse gas emissions, etc. – and the resulting impacts on planetary biogeochemical systems.[3] Both concepts appear valid when viewed through the prism of Lake Ontario's modern history.

Even seemingly minor or imperceptible alterations to lake environments can cumulatively lead to cascading changes across trophic levels, making it difficult to tease out cause and effect. Sometimes these changes are not so slow: tipping points are reached, and suddenly the lake is coated with green algae, while the beach is littered with dead fish. The state of the nearshore area improves for a few years while the deep water zones decline; then it flips. One fish species disappears; another thrives. Then we introduce a new chemical or pollutant to the mix, allow in a foreign species, or stock a new fish, and everything shifts again.

It bears repeating: we are lucky that Lake Ontario is so resilient and adaptive. But there are nonetheless limits and repercussions. The health of this sweetwater sea has improved in recent decades. But that does not mean it is healthy, considering how bad of a state it had been in previously. Even though the first dramatic regulatory steps to address pollution were taken during the 1970 to 1990 period, the lake's ecosystem health was nevertheless still degraded by half during this era, according to one scientific study.[4] The 2022 *State of the Great Lakes* report gives Lake Ontario's overall status a rating of "fair" and "unchanging to improving." Drilling down into the specific indicators that constitute Lake Ontario's ranking, most are "fair" while a number – such as coastal wetland plants, *Cladophora* frequency, hardened shorelines, and impacts of invasive species – garner a "poor" rating.[5] Even "fair" is not necessarily a safe enough state for human or ecological health, and only small pushes are needed to move the lake into clearly unsafe status. Plus one wonders how relative these rankings are – is Lake Ontario only in "fair" condition when compared to the 1960s? Perhaps the best that can be said nowadays about Lake Ontario is that, for the most part, it does not seem to be getting too much worse.

Figure 9.1
A contemporary view across Lake Ontario. This image was taken near the mouth of the Niagara River from the New York State side looking north across the lake. In the distance the skyline of Toronto is faintly visible.

RECENT TRENDS

Yet in recent years the lower Great Lakes have shown signs of reverting to some of the problems that instigated the first GLWQA. For example, Lake Ontario has seen a rise in toxic algal blooms. Some of the causes or amplifiers are new, such as climate change. Human waste remains a contributor: sewage overflows from storms as well as chronic undetected leaks. For example, in Hamilton two recently discovered sewage leaks are estimated to have released a combined 400 million litres of wastewater into Lake Ontario since 1996.[6] In addition to sewage discharges from a climbing urban population, leaking septic systems in rural regions are a widespread but often unrecognized problem.

All that said, when it comes to aquatic nutrient loading, agricultural runoff, which adds excessive nitrogen, is now the bigger culprit than urban waste, which primarily adds phosphorous. Phosphate levels in Lake Ontario have gone down since the 1980s, while nitrate levels have gone up. This despite the fact that suburbs in Lake Ontario's Canadian watershed have replaced much of the top-tier agricultural land. The remaining agriculture has mostly become industrialized and large-scale monocultures, with corn and soybean replacing smaller crop and fruit growers throughout the basin while concentrated animal feeding operations (CAFOs or factory farms) have been replacing smaller dairy, beef, fowl, and swine producers. The overapplication of crop fertilizers results in nitrogen and phosphorous finding their way into tributaries and then to Lake Ontario; higher inputs of chemicals from pesticides and herbicides also result.[7] Among a host of other challenges linked to agricultural runoff, factory farms are a pernicious problem. The gross volume of waste and manure they produce is, well, gross – one 3,000-head dairy operation not far from the lake in New York reportedly produces four times as much organic waste as the entire city of Syracuse.[8] Toxic accumulation – "chemicals of mutual concern" in IJC terminology – remains a colossal danger, but one largely unappreciated by the general population, since these contaminants do not always present obvious and immediate sensory cues like green water, dead fish, or smelly beaches. And new chemicals keep appearing on the horizon.

Both the Biden and Trudeau governments pledged to increase spending on Great Lakes water quality. But such spending pulses only look sufficient when compared to the efforts of the Trump administration to gut environmental protections in general and for the Great Lakes specifically. Even hundreds of millions of dollars more in funding for Great Lakes cleanup will not be enough, especially when those same governments simultaneously promote the types of economic growth, consumption, and fossil fuel use that threaten the lakes to begin with. The end results of the two nations' efforts are not so different. Both countries, and Ontario and New York, are failing Lake Ontario.

We are victims of our own success in some ways – many of the wicked environmental problems we now have to deal with were not even recognized a half-century ago. The populations of both countries, and thus their environmental footprints, are now much larger. We have gone further down a neoliberal and deregulation road in which profits and growth trump all else. It was much easier to reach a transborder agreement about a particular waterbody in the 1970s when relatively few stakeholders were consulted and the onus was put on the public, rather than companies and corporations, to reduce their individual pollution. Environmental knowledge, and thus expectations and beliefs about what constitutes sustainability, are also quite different now. Even though uncertainty still defines many problems, we know far more scientifically than did past decision-makers. But as environmental requirements and responsibilities pile up, along with the legacy of past pollution, biodiversity impoverishment, and other mistakes, managing them becomes that much more difficult and complex.

The life of Lake Ontario, and the many forms of life that depend on it, are in jeopardy. Lake Ontario is the most anthropogenically altered, and stressed, of the Great Lakes. Priority issues remain toxic, nutrient, and bacterial contamination, and the loss of native species habitat along with the introduction of foreign species.[9] According to recent assessments by the Great Lakes Fishery Commission, most fish populations have recently been stable, though many are well below historical norms, as is fish diversity. The future of the predator–prey balance is uncertain, in part because the trout and salmon populations remain stable only because of heavy stocking and restoration efforts by both countries (that is, these fish have not achieved self-sustaining populations).[10] Trawling studies of the lake in the spring of 2021 found that alewife made up a worrying 89 per cent of the prey fish biomass.[11] Diporeia, a tiny shrimp-like zooplankton that was a major energy source in the aquatic food chain, are almost gone from the lake, potentially because of quagga mussels. These mussels replaced zebra mussels as the dominant type in the lake around the turn of the millennium. But they seem to have fallen off the public radar for the most part, which may have more to do with our growing accustomed to them or the fact that we do not see them as much as zebra mussels, since quaggas prefer deeper waters. When dreissenid mussels gather at nearshore areas they do so in greater numbers in the northern part of the lake, likely because of the greater availability of the hard surfaces they prefer latching on to. Localized *Cladophora* blooms, cyanobacteria blooms, and botulism outbreaks have increased, doubtless connected to the mussels' filtering activities. But mussels are also responsible for clearer lake waters.[12]

In the 2012 addition to the GLWQA, new annexes addressed aquatic invasive species and other contemporary concerns such as climate change. As of late, a new non-native species has infiltrated the Great Lakes on average about once every four years, when all vectors are taken into account. But, through a concatenation of regulations, technologies, and luck, since 2006 evidently only one foreign species has arrived through ballast water. Exotic species have made it to the Great Lakes in other ways: from discarded aquarium store purchases or recreational boats travelling between different North American watersheds. Ironically, the Great Lakes have shifted from being a victim of the introduction of zebra and quagga mussels to the perpetrator, as these Eurasian mollusks have spread from the Great Lakes basin to much of the rest of the continent.

The Chicago Diversion is a means for non-native species to get in and out of Lake Michigan. Many fear that it will be the vector by which Asian carp enter the Great Lakes. Asian carp is a catch-all name for several different types of foreign carp, with bighead and silver carp the most worrisome. These carp devour plankton or plant material, out-competing native fish species and catalyzing critical repercussions along the food chain. Their intrusion could be disastrous for Great Lakes ecosystems and human interests such as tourism and recreational fishing.[13]

It is not all bad news. The open part of Lake Ontario is much cleaner than it was a few decades ago. Granted, the metrics for establishing what exactly constitutes "clean" are unclear, especially if we take into account the likelihood of shifting baseline syndrome, which distorts our sense of how much we have harmed an ecosystem over time. The lake is certainly more oligotrophic, meaning it is not experiencing the almost hyper-eutrophic conditions that afflicted it in the 1960s and 1970s. However, embayments and nearshore areas close to urban sectors are not doing so well in this regard. Sturgeon and deepwater sculpin are rebounding in the lake; some piping plovers are again nesting in the sand. The American eel population, while still extremely low, no longer seems on the verge of extirpation. Large muskies have recently been caught in Toronto's harbour. Salmon and trout stocking continue, and people continue to fish for these species. Fewer foreign species are being introduced than in the past. No longer is coal used locally to produce electricity, and smog is much less common. Drinking water quality has improved. The 2008 compact and the companion agreement with Canada have given some legal teeth to efforts to resist schemes to divert Great Lakes water to the US Great Plains or Southwest.

Integrated and coordinated environmental planning and monitoring at the wider watershed level – that is, not just Lake Ontario, but its tributaries and their watersheds – have increased, though there is certainly much room for improvement. We have restored some shoreline wetlands – though what exists is still just a fragment of what once was – and protected more parkland. Realistically, since pre-colonial times, much of the basin's land cover has been radically altered.

Some progress has been made in addressing Toronto's sewage overflows, which happen every time there is a large precipitation event. But there is still a long way to go. The Coxwell Bypass Tunnel, which the city has been building, will help. This enormous tunnel runs over ten kilometres to Ashbridges Bay. It is intended to be part of an even larger system, named the Don River and Central Waterfront Wet Weather Flow System, to intercept, hold, and treat combined sewer overflows.[14] However, the many new condo towers on the waterfront were short-sightedly put onto combined sewer systems. Toronto's Deep Lake Water Cooling System, opened in 2004, utilizes Lake Ontario to provide an alternative source of air conditioning. This system uses three five-kilometre-long pipelines to draw water from the bottom of the lake, where the water remains close to freezing throughout the year, replenished by the seasonal turnover from top (epilimnion) to bottom (hypolimnion). The naturally chilled liquid passes through heat exchangers to capture and transfer the energy into a closed circuit, which is then transferred through the cooling towers and on to buildings in downtown Toronto, including Scotiabank Arena and City Hall. Since the water also passes through a filtration plant, it is added to the city's potable water system.[15] A $100 million expansion of this system is expected to be complete in 2024. Granted, sending warm and nutrient-rich water back to the lake could have ecological repercussions, akin to the discharge of power plants, when done on a large enough scale.[16]

One of the recent changes in the Lake Ontario saga, and a positive one that bodes well for the future, has been people turning toward the lake and embracing it. Lake Ontario is losing its stigma as a dirty waterbody. The number of people who care about Lake Ontario, who love this lake, is on the rise. The organization Lake Ontario Waterkeeper (LOW), part of the Swim Drink Fish network, is surely an indispensable player in this process. LOW's goals are to stop pollution, protect human health, and restore habitat through advocacy, awareness, and fundraising. This organization's most well-known activity may be its crowd-sourced Swim Guide app to check water quality at Lake Ontario's beaches. In the summer of 2021, I interviewed environmental lawyer Mark Mattson, the founder and director of LOW. Sitting on a marina patio near Kingston, Mattson told me that he was most proud of the way that this organization had been instrumental in changing people's perspectives about Lake Ontario. It has fostered a community of people and citizen scientists who care about the lake, who want to engage with it and protect it.[17]

Through a collaboration between LOW and the City of Kingston, that city has reputedly created the world's best stormwater/sewage alert system, providing real-time monitoring and notifications about overflows into Lake Ontario. LOW was also instrumental in the creation of the Gord Downie Pier at Kingston in 2018. This, the first urban deep water swimming pier anywhere on Lake Ontario, honoured the deceased Tragically Hip frontman, who had been a prominent supporter of LOW. In 2021, authorities announced that Ontario Place in Toronto's harbour would be reimagined and would include public swimming facilities. Later in the year, Mississauga announced that it intended to construct the longest pier in Lake Ontario. These types of community-building initiatives reconnect people to the lake in tangible ways. Fostering this personal connection to the water underpins environmental protection laws and regulations with moral purpose, making them more effective and enforceable.

When asked about the future of Lake Ontario, Mattson stressed several problems that need to be addressed: governance and Indigenous reconciliation, sewage and waste, and climate change.[18] Mattson is very concerned about Port Hope's nuclear waste. The long-term containment landfill will eventually be thirty storeys tall and hold 1.2 million cubic metres of low-level radioactive waste. Meanwhile, the high-level nuclear waste is stored in pools at the refining plant at the lakefront, its long-term destination uncertain. Nuclear plants such as those at Pickering and Darlington, and the other nuclear waste storage site at Port Granby, emit over one hundred chemicals on top of the radioactivity danger. Attempts to monitor or even assess the threat of nuclear refinement and power generation on Lake Ontario are complicated by the nuclear industry's lack of public transparency.[19]

In the last decade or so, more areas of concern (AOCs) were delisted than in all the previous decades combined. We are directly inputting less of some conventional pollutants, such as mercury, than in the past. But we have created all sorts of synthetic products, like the plastics and microplastics that permeate the water and living bodies. In addition to measures to stop microplastics from getting into Lake Ontario and its tributaries, a general societal decline in plastic use will be necessary to fully combat the problem at its source. That will be difficult because of society's dependence on plastics, petrochemicals, and fossil fuels, not to mention the political power of the fossil fuel industry. Plus we have to deal with the legacy of toxic chemicals, like the chemical family of perfluoroalkyls and polyfluoroalkyls (PFAS). Fish advisories still remain in effect for many species – because of PCBs in fish in Hamilton Harbour, dioxins and furans in fish in the Bay of Quinte, and mercury in fish in the upper St Lawrence River. It was much simpler to address point source pollution, as the 1972 GLWQA did, than to address non-point source pollution, which was a goal of the 1978 GLWQA and subsequent additions. The majority of contaminants in Lake Ontario still come in through the Niagara River, which underlines the fact that protecting Lake Ontario also requires protecting the rest of the Great Lakes basin. Given that the lake remains so impaired in many ways, even though 2022 marked the fiftieth anniversary of the first GLWQA, we still have a lot of work to do. Now would be an opportune time for Canada and the United States to recommit to protecting these magnificent waterbodies.

CLIMATE PAST, CLIMATE FUTURE

Since the deep past, the climate of the Lake Ontario region has noticeably shifted at least several times. Such shifts presented both challenges and opportunities for different human societies. The various Indigenous groups that occupied the Lake Ontario basin, and their resource and food acquisition strategies, needed to be attuned to climatic realities. For those groups, and the Euro-Americans who later arrived, an especially frigid winter or a particularly dry summer could determine if a community starved. Yet, as I noted earlier in this book, seasonal unpredictability was likely the biggest obstacle introduced by the climatic downturn of the Little Ice Age, at least in the Lake Ontario region.

By limiting when and where certain human activities were possible, climate and environmental factors helped direct the course of empires in North America, both Indigenous and Euro-American. During conflicts that involved Lake Ontario, such as the Seven Years' War, the American Revolution, or the War of 1812, big weather events or the timing of the spring ice break-up could decide the outcome of a military campaign or handicap a lake fleet. The harsher conditions of the Little Ice Age encouraged the fur trade, but for a time dissuaded Europeans from migrating to northern North America on a larger scale; milder weather in the nineteenth century went hand in glove with the expansion of permanent colonization efforts. Those living in these settlements still remained vulnerable to the weather and needed to adapt their subsistence strategies to the climate they encountered in the Lake Ontario watershed. Such adaptations had social, political, and economic ramifications: a society based on trading furs, which requires constant mobility, organizes itself quite differently than one reliant on agriculture and grain, which requires a sedentary population.

Thus, the geopolitical organization that prevailed at various times around Lake Ontario – Indigenous nations, the French and British empires, the Canadian and American nation-states – hinged to at least some extent on the shifting climate of the region. The warming that took place in the nineteenth century led to conditions that were generally stable and favoured societal and agricultural flourishing. Prolonged economic and population growth characterizes Lake Ontario's modern era. Technological innovations and rising living standards meant that human societies were more sheltered, literally and metaphorically, from harsh weather; but technology and progress also fostered societal hubris about our ability to control nature. The shifting range of lake levels experienced in the second half of the twentieth century, and the severity of pollution and invasive species, reflected, even if indirectly, the impact of pumping more and more greenhouse gases into the atmosphere.

In July 2020, Lake Ontario's average surface water temperature was the warmest ever recorded. Since 1995, Lake Ontario has warmed on average over two degrees Celsius, which is more than any other Great Lake. Two degrees Celsius may not sound like much, but these averages can be misleading. The difference in the human body between a normal temperature and a fever is a little more than half a degree Celsius, after all. In terms of the lake, a one degree Celsius increase in water temperature decreased the survival rate of lake trout hatchlings by 150 per cent.[20] Global warming threatens to undo past solutions, exacerbate current challenges, and create new problems. But when, how, and how much remain uncertain. Make no mistake: we are already in a climate crisis. But it is on track to get much worse. The two countries that share Lake Ontario are two of the biggest climate villains in terms of emissions per capita. And neither is remotely on pace to sufficiently reduce its carbon emissions within the short time frames this climate emergency requires.

Warmer air holds more moisture, which has repercussions for Lake Ontario's water regime. In addition to altered precipitation and ice patterns, climate change alters the heat exchange between the atmosphere and the lake. The region will probably experience wetter springs and winters, though with more rain and less snow in the latter, and drier summers.[21] As early as 2001, scientists contended that Lake Ontario's annual rise and fall were taking place one month earlier.[22] Greater precipitation and inflow will likely occur in some years, leading to higher water levels; in other years, lack of precipitation or ice cover (which results in more winter evaporation) might prevail, which would lower lake levels. We have recently seen both highs and lows in the alarming span of just two years. What all this means for lake levels is hard to predict. Almost all the Great Lakes, including Lake Ontario, have seen record high levels and summer temperatures in the last few years. Some recent projections do predict that levels across the Great Lakes are more likely to experience small drops. But such prognostications are difficult, since climate change is throwing off the standard predictors and inputs, and models are just informed guesses. Uncertainty remains the name of the game.

In most cases, shoreline resiliency measures and related infrastructural changes (e.g., storm walls, riprap, raising homes) will not suffice. No future construction should be allowed too close to the lake, at least not without a great deal of study. Properties affected by high water levels should be bought out, or buildings moved back – with generous terms offered, since it was governments that authorized or grandfathered in homes and buildings in the affected areas.

Considering the countless toxics, chemicals, nutrients, and other things we have poured into Lake Ontario, we are lucky that it is resilient and has a high assimilative capacity. But we are pushing the lake to its limits, plus human actions combined with climate breakdown are also potentially lowering those limits. In other words, we may be undercutting the very resilience and adaptability that has allowed Lake Ontario to cope with our many abuses. Human-caused ecological stressors can be worse than the sum of their parts when combined with climate change. Lake Ontario's water temperature will likely keep getting warmer into the foreseeable future.[23] Warmer water can affect oxygen concentrations, nutrient cycling, eutrophication, and aquatic species distribution. Winter is one of the best deterrents against invasives, but accidentally introduced species will be more likely to survive in warmer waters. A hotter lake can exacerbate existing problems, pushing some issues from minor nuisances to major challenges or undoing past improvements and remediations. A hotter lake could cause tipping points associated with the thermocline, the band of water between the warmer upper epilimnion and the colder lower hypolimnion, which is crucial to stratification, seasonal overturn, and the mixing of dissolved oxygen and warmer/colder water. If this broke down, there would be unknown repercussions for the distribution and availability of nutrients, as well as the distribution and location of pollutants. Such changes could alter the entire food web, with the ripple effects for species composition, energy flows, and biodiversity in the lake extremely hard to predict.

Heavy ice cover has been decreasing since the mid-nineteenth century. For the last few decades, studies have shown that ice formation has declined as a result of climate change.[24] Lake Ontario's deepest parts rarely ice over, so any substantial reduction will be nearer to the shore. By the middle of our current century, heavy ice seasons may be gone entirely, with very light ice seasons becoming the norm.[25] Less ice cover would have knock-on effects for the lake, potentially affecting fish populations and drinking water quality, though researchers are still unsure about the implications.[26] In fact, scientists still know relatively little about the winter ecology of the Great Lakes compared to other seasons, when it is easier to conduct research.[27] Reduced ice cover could also increase lake effect snow, resulting in larger snow and precipitation events. Ice storms could become more prevalent. A higher frequency and greater intensity of storms in other seasons seems likely too.

Physical changes to Lake Ontario will have economic and cultural repercussions. Given that the southern periphery of the lake is a preeminent North American snow belt, and big snowfalls are woven into the cultural fabric of the region, how might altered winter patterns change society in Upstate New York? As a result of hotter growing seasons, agriculture and crop yields in the basin over the next few decades will suffer in some ways, but maybe benefit in others. A changed climate regime could have appreciable repercussions for Lake Ontario's fruit and wine belts, though in what ways remains a matter of conjecture. Cottaging, recreation, and tourism will be impacted. Boating is obviously a prime activity in the Great Lakes, and the boating season might shift or look different. At parks such as Chimney Bluffs and Sandbanks, will the picturesque sand landforms change? Beaches disappear when there are high water levels. Lack of sufficient ice cover, especially near the shore, will eliminate winter activities like ice fishing and iceboating. At the Bay of Quinte, for example, ice was sometimes thirty inches thick in the 1950s; in the twenty-first century, it is less than half of that.[28] Embodied understandings of when it is safe to cross ice will be impaired or nullified, with potentially tragic consequences. In addition to direct economic impacts, degraded environments have negative psychological and spiritual effects; conversely, studies abound demonstrating the mental health and happiness benefits of interacting with water.

Toronto's average summer air temperature swelled over the last half-century.[29] This rise was doubtless more pronounced at Toronto because of deforestation, urban development, and the urban heat island effect. As the number of hot days climbs, residents will want to go into the lake to cool off, especially those without air conditioning or other options. At the same time, beaches will be less safe because of hotter weather. Warmer lake temperatures lead to a greater frequency of E. coli, cyanobacteria, and algal blooms, including the toxic kind, which will thwart beaches, swimming, and boating opportunities. Public water supplies for the millions of people who rely on Lake Ontario for drinking water will be threatened. This was foreshadowed in 2014 when Toledo had to shut down its public water supply, drawn from Lake Erie, for three days because of toxic algal blooms. The greater frequency of extreme weather events will result in more flooding that stresses infrastructure: sudden precipitation swells urban runoff and causes combined sewer system overflows. Continued population growth will likely decrease land cover and amplify the spread of impermeable surfaces – buildings, parking lots, roads, etc. – in the Lake Ontario watershed. It is all too easy to forget that the health of Lake Ontario is tightly linked to what we do with the land, tributaries, and groundwater throughout the basin.

Higher water levels have been eroding shorelines along with houses and infrastructure, threatening septic systems, nuclear power stations, and fuel refineries. We too often respond with engineered solutions, rather than respecting the lake and being patient, moving back or out of the way. Those trying to protect their property resort to installing riprap, retaining walls, and other water protections below the lake's high water mark – in some cases, this constitutes the appropriation and privatization of public bottom lands. Armouring shorelines generally does not work in the long run anyway, but just pushes the erosive force of the water to the next unprotected section. Those property owners, in turn, are tempted to take similar measures, which merely passes the problem along.

Some littoral infrastructure like marinas and docks, which obviously require water of sufficient depth, are threatened by fluctuating water levels, both low and high. Less ice cover would help extend the commercial shipping season, but might result in more winter evaporation and thus lower water levels for deep-draft vessels. There are definitely limits to how much we can, and should, try to alter Lake Ontario and St Lawrence levels to benefit shipping. The Seaway typically stops operating for a few months in winter, normally around New Year's Day. This is a later end date than in the past, as warmer water temperatures have delayed or reduced ice cover, as have inno-vations such as icebreakers and ice bubblers. Over the last few decades there have been serious calls to open the Seaway to winter shipping. Changes to water levels also have implications for hydro power stations: lower levels mean less electricity is generated. Yet it has also become apparent that hydro-electricity is not near as "green" as it is often touted, so removing dams may well be an appropriate response. That said, we do need to remember that Lake Ontario and the upper St Lawrence are ecosystems that have adapted to the dams and water regime instituted in the 1950s. Moreover, even though the Seaway had many negative ecological impacts and deepening it or ship-ping certain products on it such as oil would be unwise, moving goods by water generally requires less energy than alternative forms of transport.

Figure 9.2
Mouth of Genesee River in late November. On the left a pier extends out into Lake Ontario; in the middle a ship heads north out of the Rochester Harbor.

Out of the five Great Lakes, Lake Ontario is the foremost power producer. It boasts the most hydroelectric capacity: in addition to the large hydroelectric plants on the two rivers entering and leaving Lake Ontario, there are many other hydro stations in the basin. Lake Ontario also has the most nuclear reactors out of any of the Great Lakes. These power plants rely on lake water for cooling, as did the formerly numerous coal-fired electricity stations. Fuel storage tanks, pipelines, and refining facilities are all over. This speaks to the water–energy nexus, which is the relationship between water used for energy production and the energy employed to make water available to humans. In the United States, more energy is used to heat, treat, and pump water than for lighting. The power production sector is also the country's largest total user of water, even above agriculture (though the latter has a higher consumptive use of water, which refers to water not returned to its source). The point is that since energy production and consumption are leading contributors to North America's greenhouse gas emissions, how we use water directly impacts those emissions.

The Somerset coal-fired power plant on Lake Ontario in Niagara County closed in early 2020 – it was the last of New York's coal-fired plants, not only on the lake but in the entire state. The Oswego coal-fired power station was recently converted to oil, and the new generating station near Napanee runs on natural gas. There are currently fewer nuclear generators along the water than a few decades ago. The Pickering station is scheduled to close in the next few years. The FitzPatrick nuclear station almost closed in 2016 but has remained open under new ownership. Ontario Power Generation announced in late 2021 that it would build a small modular reactor at Darlington. Wind power installations have gone up around Lake Ontario, such as the Wolfe Island Wind Farm, visible from Kingston. The Lake Ontario region offers plenty of untapped opportunities for wind and solar power.

New technologies, ample domestic supplies, and the touting of natural gas as a "bridge fuel" – even though the resulting methane is a more potent greenhouse gas than carbon dioxide – spurred a three-fold increase in New York State's gas production in the early twenty-first century.[30] High-volume hydraulic fracturing, or fracking, became a common way to access oil and gas deposits in North America. This technique involves copious amounts of water mixed with undisclosed chemicals that pollute local waterways and aquifers, but fracking was exempted from the US Safe Drinking Water Act. However, in 2008, New York instituted a moratorium on high-volume fracking throughout the state and in 2015 this became an outright ban. Though there is no indication that natural gas developments or fracking have directly contaminated Lake Ontario, since most deposits are concentrated in the southern part of the watershed, these preemptive regulations should hopefully keep it that way.

Enbridge's network of fossil fuel pipelines in the Great Lakes includes several near Lake Ontario: Line 7 from Sarnia to near the head of Lake Ontario, Line 9 traversing the entire north shore of Lake Ontario, and Line 10 near the southwest shore. Given this company's poor safety record and the many Lake Ontario tributaries these pipelines cross, Lines 9 and 10 in particular, a spill into the lake or its tributaries could be catastrophic. Between 1999 and 2008, there were 610 oil and gas spills on Enbridge's vast pipeline network, which does not inspire confidence.[31] One also hears rumblings about increased shipping of crude and tar sands oil on Lake Ontario and the Great Lakes.

Climate change in other parts of North America could have repercussions for Lake Ontario. Drought and water shortages in the western United States will increase calls to divert water from the Great Lakes. Along with all the potential problems I have identified above that a rapidly warming climate might introduce to the Lake Ontario basin, it and the general Great Lakes region are also predicted to become a climate haven as other regions of North America become uninhabitable due to heat, water shortages, crop failures, extreme weather, etc. At least to a certain extent, or for a while, growing seasons in Upstate New York and southern Ontario might get longer. Winters could well be shorter and milder. The downside is that this could mean even larger populations at Lake Ontario and even greater anthropogenic stresses on the lake and its environs.

We should be doing everything we can to limit further anthropogenic climate change. But it is too late to stave off all climate change impacts: even if we magically cut off all greenhouse emissions tomorrow, we have already started feedback loops that will continue to warm the Earth for some time. Nevertheless, there is still a small window to prevent the worst impacts. As the environmental history of Lake Ontario suggests, we are capable of adapting in multiple ways. But will those adaptations be appropriate? Will they be just and equally shared? After all, the historical adaptations to changing environments in the Lake Ontario context created winners and losers, a tendency the deeply unequal and stratified contemporary American and Canadian societies would likely accentuate.

LISTEN TO THE LAKE

The Lake Ontario ecosystem has been heavily influenced by human activities for centuries. Some argue that we will affect the lake whether or not we mean to, so we might as well do so with purpose and intentionality grounded in ecological science. I am sympathetic to this line of thought. But our attempts to scientifically manage the lake and the species therein, or to rely on tech-nofixes, have frequently been as much a problem as a solution. We are not near as wise as we think, and nature and its interconnections are exceedingly complex. There is, or should be, a rule of unintended consequences when it comes to environmental manipulation. After all, who would have thought that burning coal, or building hydro power reservoirs, would release green-house gases that would lead to global warming? Or, invoking the Jevons para-dox, who would have predicted that improving the efficiency of appliances, devices, and vehicles would lead us to consume more, not less, energy? I can-not help but wonder whether the purposeful introduction of foreign species into Lake Ontario or the annual poisoning of certain nuisance species rep-resent attempts to solve problems that nature could have taken care of itself if we only gave it time or backed off.

Do not get me wrong. We need science-driven policies. But we also need to recognize the limits and blinders that are a part of the Western scientific and engineering approach: framing humanity as entirely separate from na-ture and being overly reductionist, mechanistic, and hubristic in approaching ecological problems. Science needs to be joined with empathetic and rela-tional ways of knowing the more-than-human world, with ways of seeing nature that do not reduce it to a commodity to be quantified and exploited. The union of modern scientific techniques with Indigenous perspectives, such as "two-eyed seeing" and traditional ecological knowledge (TEK), offers alternative approaches.[32] Researchers keep finding evidence of the ecological interconnections that First Nations have traditionally espoused. We have much to learn from the wisdom and humility of cultures that lived harmoni-ously with the Great Lakes for so many generations. They are willing to bear witness and share their knowledge – Water Walkers such as Josephine Man-damin and Autumn Peltier are prominent Great Lakes examples.

However, we should not lose sight of the fact that Indigenous ways of knowing are deeply embedded in specific places and cultures. This means that there are limits to the ways that their beliefs and practices can be incor-

porated by non-Indigenous peoples into the governance of contemporary
capitalist societies that value nature very differently. Indigenous beliefs were
developed by and intended for their cultures, not to be selectively mobilized
as instrumental knowledge by the very societies that colonized them. Settler
learning can easily verge into appropriation, tokenism, or different forms of
colonization if not lead by First Nations themselves.[33] For Indigenous
peoples to guide this process, they need the freedom to practice their traditional lifeways. The reconciliation process should be led by the First Nations
that have suffered centuries of settler colonialism, land theft, and genocide;
reconciliation will require returning land and resources, including those
around Lake Ontario.

Recognizing tribal and treaty rights that both countries have disregarded
potentially furnishes legal grounds for resisting destructive environmental
practices and infrastructure, provided this is done in consultation and cooperation with those who hold such rights. Another way of working within
our legal systems to protect Lake Ontario, and which draws on Indigenous
ethics, involves efforts to grant legal personhood to waterbodies, which have
been undertaken in North America and around the world. For example, in
2019 Toledo residents voted in favour of a Lake Erie Bill of Rights (though
this was subsequently invalidated by a court decision) and in 2022 a New
York State assemblyman attempted to introduce a Great Lakes Bill of Rights.[34]
The public trust doctrine, which holds that resources such as navigable waters
should be preserved for the benefit of the public, offers another legal avenue
for protecting the Great Lakes.

Ultimately, the greatest obstacle when it comes to the future of Lake Ontario is not a lack of scientific understanding. We know enough about what
we technically need to do. Rather, the biggest obstacles are political, economic, and cultural. We do not seem collectively willing to make the necessary
sacrifices or systemic changes to our unsustainable lifestyles, political economies, and ways of thinking. We need to see the lake as a gift, not as a mere
resource or commodity. We need to escape our reliance on fossil fuels and
we need to do so immediately. This energy shift needs to involve a just transition that does not leave people behind. The two countries surrounding
Lake Ontario are addicted to overconsumption and perpetual growth. The
need to always have more and the belief that we should control and dominate
nature drives so many of our unsustainable patterns. Doing right by this
Great Lake will require changing both those specific actions that directly

harm the lake and the general attitudes that encourage unsustainable behaviour. The good news is that, just as Lake Ontario is highly adaptable, so too does the human species have a capacity for change. And Lake Ontario is telling us we need to change – will we listen to the lake?

Notes

INTRODUCTION

1 Anna Jameson, *Winter Studies and Summer Rambles in Canada*.
2 Heasley and Macfarlane, "Negotiating Abundance and Scarcity: Introduction to a Fluid Border."
3 Heasley, *The Accidental Reef and other Ecology Odysseys in the Great Lakes*.
4 In 1945 Arthur Pound published a book on the history of Lake Ontario, which focused primarily on the political and social history of the lake, as part of a larger series in which each Great Lake received a volume. Pound, *Lake Ontario*. John L. Riley's 2013 *The Once and Future Great Lakes Country* offers an ecological history, as its subtitle suggests, though as the "country" in the main title indicates, the book is more about the land around the Great Lakes, especially southern Ontario, than the Great Lakes themselves. Nancy Bouchier and Ken Cruikshank published an environmental history of Hamilton Harbour, titled *The People and the Bay*. Other academic environmental history books that focus on one Great Lake, or look at more than one of these freshwater repositories through the lens of a particular resource or theme (fishing, pollution, invasives, etc.), include: Campbell, *Shaped by the West Wind*; Langston, *Sustaining Lake Superior*; and Margaret Beattie Bogue, *Fishing the Great Lakes*. The fact that all the Great Lakes except Michigan (though it might rightfully be considered one lake with Huron) are shared between two countries has likely accounted to some degree for the relative lack of studies. There are also a number of environmental studies of the Great Lakes basin aimed at a general audience: Egan, *The Death and Life of the Great Lakes*; Dempsey, *On the Brink*; Ashworth, *The Late, Great Lakes*;

Swan, ed., *Fresh Water*; Grady, *The Great Lakes*; Alexander, *Pandora's Locks*; and Annin, *Great Lakes Water Wars.*

5   Gateley, *A Natural History of Lake Ontario*; Gateley, *Saving The Beautiful Lake*. On the heritage history of the Canadian side of the lake, see works such as Brown, *From Queenston to Kingston*. A partially fictionalized account is offered in McFadden, *A Trip Around Lake Ontario*. Given that the first Great Lakes Water Quality Agreement (GLWQA) applied to only the two lower Great Lakes, a fair bit has been written about Lake Ontario in the context of pollution. Likewise, as the closest to the Atlantic, Lake Ontario has loomed large in Great Lakes fishing and invasive species literature. And because Canada's largest city is on Lake Ontario, the copious work on Toronto's history and waterfront often deals with Lake Ontario, at least indirectly. Some of the larger rivers connected to Lake Ontario have received academic treatment – for example, Bonnell, *Reclaiming the Don*; Macfarlane, *Negotiating a River*; Macfarlane, *Fixing Niagara Falls* – while some of the smaller rivers and harbours on the Canadian side have also received monographs (albeit mostly for a local audience).

6   Indigenous oral histories that involve Lake Ontario are discussed in more detail in chapter 2. In terms of archaeological studies on the Indigenous nations that frequented Lake Ontario, a recent book, Ford's *The Shore Is a Bridge*, focuses on the lake. Ford also emphasizes the materiality of the premodern period, including the Indigenous use of resources, making it useful from an environmental history perspective.

7   These cross-lake swims traditionally traverse from near the mouth of the Niagara River to Toronto, a distance of a little over fifty kilometres.

8   Lake Ontario Partnership, *Lake Ontario: Lakewide Action and Management Plan, 2018–2022.*

9   Colin Duncan, personal correspondence with Daniel Macfarlane, 20 March 2020.

10 French, *Wind, Water, Barley and Wine.*

11 Kennard, *Shipwrecks of Lake Ontario*. In 2021 the National Oceanic and Atmospheric Administration (NOAA) released a draft proposal for a national marine sanctuary for the New York waters of eastern Lake Ontario and the Thousand Islands and its sixty-four identified shipwrecks: https://sanctu aries.noaa.gov/lake-ontario. The most visible "shipwreck" is the La Grande Hermine, which has been stranded in the Jordan Harbour for decades, visible from the Queen Elizabeth Way (QEW) highway. However, after regulators deemed it an environmental risk in 2021, the government put out a call

for bids for a buyer. It is still in place as of this writing, but its future
is uncertain.

12 This area has been called the Marysburgh Vortex because of the high
number of shipwrecks and other strange incidents: Max Hartshorn, "Strange
Things Out There"; Cochrane, *Gateway to Oblivion*. Incidentally, the earth-
quake history in and around Lake Ontario is far less exciting. Hough, *The
Geology of the Great Lakes*.

13 The Lake Erie basin is the most heavily populated out of all five of the Great
Lakes basins, once cities such as Buffalo and Detroit are also included. However, Lake Ontario and Lake Michigan have larger populations directly on
the water. Fergen et al., "Updated census in the Laurentian Great Lakes
Watershed."

CHAPTER ONE

1 Flannery, *The Eternal Frontier*.

2 Pielou, *After the Ice Age*.

3 Steeves, *The Indigenous Paleolithic of the Western Hemisphere*; Johnson, "The
Indigenous Environmental History of Toronto, 'The Meeting Place'"; Bobi-
wash, "The History of Native People in the Toronto Area, An Overview";
Bolduc et al., eds., *Indigenous Toronto*.

4 Ford, *The Shore Is a Bridge*.

5 Jackson with Burtniak and Stein, *The Mighty Niagara*.

6 Examples include: Kimmerer, *Braiding Sweetgrass*; Simpson, *As We Have
Always Done*; Whyte, "Settler Colonialism, Ecology, and Environmental
Justice."

7 Smith, *Sacred Feathers*, 13.

8 Ibid., 35; Nelson, "The Hydromythology of the Anishinaabeg."

9 Recht, "The Role of Fishing in the Iroquois Economy 1600–1792"; Pound,
Lake Ontario, 48.

10 Parmenter, *Edge of the Woods*; Pritchard, "For the Glory of God: The Quinte
Mission, 1668–1680"; Parsons, *A Not-So-New-World*.

11 Ford, *The Shore Is a Bridge*, 48.

12 "Toronto" or "Tkaronto" likely referred to the narrows between Lakes Sim-
coe and Couchiching, rather than the location of the city of Toronto. Smith,
"The Dispossession of the Mississauga Indians"; Fletcher, *Humber*; Lizars,
Valley of the Humber, 1615–1913.

13 Some of the most extreme cold swings, such as the infamous 1816 "year
without a summer," were the result of volcanic explosions.

208   NOTES TO PAGES 29–41

14 Zilberstein, *A Temperate Empire*; White, *A Cold Welcome*; Brooke, *Climate Change and the Course of Global History*; Degroot, *The Frigid Golden Age*; Coates and Degroot, "'Les bois engendrent les frimas et les gelées.'"
15 Koch et al., "Earth System Impacts of the European Arrival and Great Dying in the Americas after 1492."
16 Riley, *Once and Future Great Lakes Country*, 146; Harris, *The Reluctant Land*.
17 Parmenter, *The Edge of the Woods*; Richter, *Ordeal of the Longhouse*; Brandão, *"Your Fyre Shall Burn No More"*; Konrad, "An Iroquois Frontier"; Williamson and von Bitter, *The History and Archaeology of the Iroquois du Nord*.
18 Utley and Scott, *Fort Niagara*.
19 Hill, *The Clay We Are Made Of*; Williams, *Kayanerenkó:wa*; Migizi (Williams), *Michi Saagiig Nishnaabeg*.
20 Blackhawk, *The Rediscovery of America*, 110–12.
21 On the political and diplomatic history of the Iroquois League, see Parmenter, *The Edge of the Woods*; Rice, *Rotinonshonni*; Fenton, *The Great Law and the Longhouse*; Aquila, *The Iroquois Restoration*; Shannon, *Iroquois Diplomacy on the Early American Frontier*; Preston, *Texture of Contact*; MacLeitch, *Imperial Entanglements*.
22 Ford, *The Shore Is a Bridge*, 57.
23 McDonnell, *Masters of Empire*; Hamalainen, *Indigenous Continent*; Englebert and Wegmann, eds., *French Connections*; Hele, ed., *Lines Drawn upon the Water*; Hele, ed., *Nature of Empire and the Empires of Nature*. Heidi Bohaker cautions against assuming that Indigenous conceptions of alliance were the same as Europeans in *Doodem and Council Fire*.
24 Desbarats and Greer, "North America from the Top Down."
25 Snyder, *Oswego*.

CHAPTER TWO

1 Thomas, *Pioneer History of Orleans County, New York*, 29–32.
2 Zeller, *Inventing Canada*, 2nd ed.; Slonosky, *Climate in the Age of Empire*.
3 Whyte, Caldwell, and Schaefer define settler colonialism as "a form of oppression in which settlers *permanently* and *ecologically* inscribe homelands of their own onto Indigenous homelands," in "Indigenous Lessons about Sustainability Are Not Just for 'All Humanity,'" 158.
4 Hauptman, *Conspiracy of Interests*.
5 Oberg, *Peacemakers*.
6 Parmenter, *The Edge of the Woods*, xlix.
7 Ford, *The Shore Is a Bridge*, 67.

8   Joan Holmes and Associates, "Aboriginal Title Claim to Water," 12.

9   Lytwyn, "Waterworld"; Bohaker, *Doodem and Council Fire*, chapter 4: Cities and Growth.

10 Much of this paragraph draws from Smith, *Mississauga Portraits*.

11 Ripmeester, "'It Is Scarcely to Be Believed ...'"

12 Whetung-Derrick, *History of the Ojibwa of the Curve Lake Reserve and Surrounding Area*; Whetung-Derrick, "Oshkigmong"; Hoggarth, *Waashkiigmaang Nbi Wi - Nagamo*; Shpuniarsky, *Village of Hiawatha*.

13 Blair, *Lament for a First Nation*; Whetung, "(En)gendering Shoreline Law."

14 Broyld, *Borderland Blacks*.

15 Robertson, *Diary of Mrs. John Graves Simcoe*, 154.

16 Taylor, *Civil War of 1812*.

17 Malcomson, *Lords of the Lake*.

18 Ibid.

19 On the Great Lakes, including Lake Ontario, as a "permeable border" see also Bukowczyk et al., *Permeable Border*.

20 Bartram, *Observations on the Inhabitants ...*; Rannie, *Lincoln*, 62; Carnochan, *Niagara*.

21 Robertson, *Diary of Mrs. John Graves Simcoe*, 118–19.

22 Moodie, *Roughing It in the Bush*, 251.

23 Agassiz and Cabot, *Lake Superior*, 20. My thanks to Lynne Heasley for pointing out this quote.

24 Canniff, *History of the Settlement of Upper Canada (Ontario)*, 201; Russell, *How Agriculture Made Canada*.

25 Duncan, *The Centrality of Agriculture*.

26 Phenological studies suggest that the region was warming up in the latter half of the nineteenth century. Futter, "Patterns and Trends in Southern Ontario Lake Ice Phenology"; Clark, "Climate and Indian Effects on Southern Ontario Forests."

27 Tiro, "A Sorry Tale," 1005.

28 In a 2019 paper, Henry Regier postulated that the usual cluster of five complexities interacting in complex ways (taxon, habitat, capture, market, administration) had self-organized as a loose ecogeny with a focus on Atlantic salmon by late in the eighteenth century in Lake Ontario. Indigenous fishers participated in it. Regier, "A Candidate Hypothesis about Ecogenic Science Applied to Fish and Fisheries within the Great Laurentian Basin during the 19th and 20th Centuries."

29 McCullough, *Commercial Fishery of the Canadian Great Lakes*, 15.

30   Tiro, "A Sorry Tale."
31   The Kerr sources are available online: https://archive.org/details/kerrfamily
     fonds
32   Ellsworth, "Eastern Lake Ontario Commercial Fishery, 1673–1900"; Milner,
     "Report on the Fisheries of the Great Lakes." See Heasley's *The Accidental
     Reef* for a unique take on sturgeon in the St Clair River region, and also on
     sturgeon see Langston, *Climate Ghosts*.
33   Ketola et al., "Effects of Thiamine on Reproduction."
34   McNaught, Buzzard, and Levine, "Zooplankton Production in Lake Ontario."
35   Smith, "Early Changes in the Fish Community of Lake Ontario"; Morrison,
     "Chronology of Lake Ontario Ecosystem and Fisheries," 299.
36   Thwaites, ed., *Jesuit Relations and Allied Documents*.
37   Eyles et al., "Geophysical and Sedimentological Assessment"; Eyles, Meriano,
     and Chow-Fraser, "Impacts of European Settlement."
38   Bogue, *Fishing the Great Lakes*, 22.
39   Wood, *Making Ontario*; McCalla, *Planting the Province*; McCalla, *Consumers
     in the Bush*.
40   Guiry et al., "Deforestation Caused Abrupt Shift."
41   Minns, Hurley, and Nicholls, eds., *Project Quinte*; C.K. Minns, M. Munawar,
     and M.A. Koops, *Ecology of the Bay of Quinte*.

CHAPTER THREE
1   Cooper, *The Pathfinder*, 114.
2   Ibid.
3   Ibid.
4   White, *The Middle Ground*.
5   Even as the Seaway was being built in the 1950s, some American interests
    feared that the Welland Canal would be a bottleneck and pushed for an
    American canal from the Niagara River to Lake Ontario. New York State
    Archives (hereafter NYSA), "St. Lawrence Seaway-Welland Canal Subject
    File," B1415-94, D482/1.
6   Though the Black River Canal was never very successful, efforts to improve
    it continued into the twentieth century, as were studies that looked at con-
    necting this canal to Lake Ontario by building a new channel from Carthage
    to Sackets Harbor: NYSA, "Resident Engineer's Report on Work Done under
    Chapter 190, Laws of 1911, Known as the Black River Survey for the Exten-
    sion of the Black River Canal from Carthage to Sacketts Harbor on Lake

Ontario," New York State Engineer and Surveyor histories of various canal projects on Western Division of the Erie Canal, B0681-85.

7 Attempts were also made to create a canal that ran from the Erie Canal to Lake Ontario at Sodus Bay.

8 Drescher, *Engineers for the Public Good*, 108–9.

9 Additionally, the Chemung Canal connected the southern end of Seneca Lake to the Chemung River. Shaw, *Canals for a Nation*.

10 Snyder, *Oswego*, 116–17; O'Connor, "A History of the First Fresh Water Port."

11 Shaw, *Canals for a Nation*, 49; Styran and Taylor, *This Great National Object*.

12 Gateley, *A Natural History of Lake Ontario*, 33.

13 Larkin, *Overcoming Niagara*, 111.

14 Nelson, *Oceans of Grain*, 55.

15 Widdis, "'Across the Boundary in a Hundred Torrents.'"

16 Bouchier and Cruikshank, *The People and the Bay*, 35.

17 Passfield, *Military Paternalism, Labour, and the Rideau Canal Project*; Watson, *Engineered Landscapes*.

18 Fort Henry was expanded in the 1830s and several Martello towers were added around Kingston in the 1840s in response to fears about American intentions during the Oregon boundary dispute.

19 Quoted in Simpson, *A Short History of the Blockade*, 20, and drawn from Whetung, "(En)gendering Shoreline Law"; see also Gidgaa Migizi, *Michi Saagiig Nishnaabeg*.

20 Angus, *A Respectable Ditch*; Forkey, *Shaping the Upper Canadian Frontier*; Boyce, *Belleville*; Mike and Mika, *Mosaic of Belleville*.

21 This mean level was in reference to mean tide at New York City. Woodford, *Charting the Inland Seas*, 63–4.

22 An Army Corps of Engineers report found that the benefits did not justify the cost, however. State of New York Archives, Army Corps of Engineers, "Deeper Waterway – Great Lakes to the Hudson – Notice of Adverse Report" (25 February 1926), File: All American Canal and St Lawrence Ship Canal and Power Project, D260/5, B0746-85.

23 Archives of Ontario (hereafter AO), "Report of the Huron and Ontario Ship Canal Company to the President of the Board of Directors," (1867), B415279, F 4498.

24 Christie and Smol, "Ecological Effects of 19th Century Canal Construction and other Disturbances on the Trophic State History of Upper Rideau Lake, Ontario."

25 Stradling, *The Nature of New York*, 46.

26 Langston, *Sustaining Lake Superior*, 45; Benidickson, "Private Rights and Public Purposes in the Lakes, Rivers and Streams of Ontario, 1870–1930."

27 Water diverted out of the Lake Ontario basin via the Erie Barge Canal and the public water supply for Rome, New York, totaled 41 million gallons per day (154 million litres per day) in 2021. Great Lakes Commission, *Annual Report of the Great Lakes Regional Water Use Database*, 29.

28 Ibid.

29 Weightman, *The Frozen Water Trade*.

30 Gateley, *Sweet Water Stories of Lake Ontario*, 28.

31 Brimacombe, *The Story of Oakville Harbour*. In addition to Brimacombe, for more information on stonehooking see Turcotte, *Places and People on Bronte Creek*; Snider, *Tales From the Great Lakes*; AO, RG 4-32, "A.W. Porte, J.P., Oakville; Query whether stone-hookers have the right to remove stones from beaches on Lake Ontario, 1909," container B803228.

32 Colin Duncan, interview with Daniel Macfarlane, 22 April 2020.

33 Ibid.

34 Ibid.; Banks, *Warriors and Warships*.

35 Berger, *Lighthouses of the Great Lakes*; Seguin, *For Want of a Lighthouse*.

36 Karamanski, *Mastering the Inland Seas*; Woodford, *Charting the Inland Seas*.

37 Babian, *Setting Course*, 69. On shipping in general and related infrastructure, see also Pierre Camu's two monumental volumes, *Saint-Laurent et les grands lacs au temps de la voile 1608-1850* and *Le Saint-Laurent et les Grands Lacs au temps de la vapeur, 1850-1950*.

38 On the history of Canada–US environmental and energy relations, see Macfarlane, *Natural Allies*.

39 Ozone, a highly toxic gas, was considered to have health benefits to the extent that some resorts-cum-sanatoriums were constructed on lakes renamed to advertise the advantage: for example, Lake Ozonia in the Adirondack Park. My thanks to Michael Twiss for pointing this out to me.

40 Colin Duncan, interview with Daniel Macfarlane, 22 April 2020.

CHAPTER FOUR

1 Moir, "Planning for Change," 29.

2 Nelles, "The Islands." See also Bain, "Recreation on Toronto Island"; Freeman, *A Magical Place*; Gibson, *More than an Island*; Fairburn, *Along the Shore*.

3 Barbour, *Undressed Toronto*.

4 Jackson, *The Welland Canals and Their Communities*.

5 Bouchier and Cruikshank, *The People and the Bay*.

6 Tomkiewicz and Husted, *Eight Miles Along the Shore*.

7 McKelvey, *Rochester*, 83.

8 Ibid.

9 Ibid.

10 Lyon-Jenness, *For Shade and for Comfort*, 91; Burd, *The Roots of Flower City*.

11 McKelvey, *Rochester*; O'Reilly, *Sketches of Rochester*.

12 Green, *History, Reminiscences, Anecdotes, and Legends*; Cook, *Pioneer History of Sodus Point, N.Y.* Many of the Lake Ontario communities in New York State have been the subjects of books in Arcadia Publishing's Images of America series.

13 Somerville, "This Is Where I Love to Go."

14 Monmonier, *Lake Effect*; McKelvey, *Snow in the Cities*.

15 Royal Ontario Museum, John W. Kerr diaries, 25 July 1881; 16 April 1883: https://archive.org/details/kerrfamilyfonds.

16 Baskerville, *Sites of Power*, 169.

17 See Bonnell, *Reclaiming the Don*. For more on the social and cultural history of the communities that would come to comprise the GTA, see Fairburn, *Along the Shore*.

18 Jackson, "From Liability to Profitability"; Conway, "Boundaries and Connectivity."

19 Whillans, "Changes in Marsh Area Along the Canadian Shore of Lake Ontario."

20 Incidentally, Harris himself thought a sewage treatment plant should have been farther east. McMahon, "Toronto's Urban Organic Machines."

21 Moir, "Planning for Change," 39–40.

22 On the Toronto waterfront as an energy hub, see Prudham, Gad, and Anderson, "Networks of Power."

23 Adam, *Toronto, Old and New*, 168–9. Taken from MacFadyen, "These Well-Wooded Towns."

24 Bonnell, *Reclaiming the Don*.

25 Barbour, *Undressed Toronto*.

26 Ibid.

27 Niagara-on-the-Lake Museum, "Niagara-on-the-Lake's Black History," Google Arts and Culture, accessed 26 January 2024, https://artsandculture. google.com/story/niagara-on-the-lake-s-black-history-niagara-historical-

society-museum/-QXR3nRTdnmqJw?hl=en; Jacqueline Scott, "Uncovering the Black History of 10 Ontario Rivers," *The Narwhal*, 22 February 2023, https://thenarwhal.ca/ontario-rivers-black-history.

28 Du Bois, *City of Frederick Douglass.*

29 Robinson and Cruikshank, "Hurricane Hazel"; Jim Gifford, *Hurricane Hazel.*

30 Lu and Desfor, "Cleaning Up the Waterfront."

31 For more on the Leslie Street Spit and the Tommy Thompson Park, see Foster, "Toronto's Leslie Street Spit"; Foster and Fraser, "Predators, Prey and the Dynamics of Change at the Leslie Street Spit"; Conway, "Boundaries and Connectivity"; Kehm, *Accidental Wilderness.*

32 In March 1857, one of Canada's worst train disasters took place when a passenger train went off the rails at a bridge here, plunging into the frozen canal and killing fifty-nine people.

33 Bouchier and Cruikshank, *The People and the Bay.*

34 Chapman, "Agriculture in Niagara,"; Gayler, "Urban Development and Planning in Niagara."

35 Hill, "A Serpent in the Garden."

36 Morgan, *Creating Colonial Pasts.*

37 Shawn Micallef, interview with Daniel Macfarlane, 14 July 2021. On perceptions of Toronto, and Lake Ontario to an extent, in literature, see Harris, *Imagining Toronto*, 58–74.

38 Crombie, "Interim Report, Royal Commission on the Future of the Toronto Waterfront," 124.

39 See chapter 7, "Remembering the Don," in Bonnell, *Reclaiming the Don.*

40 Shawn Micallef, interview with Daniel Macfarlane, 14 July 2021.

41 Jacqueline L. Scott, "Swimming at Ashbridge's Bay Park," *Black Outdoors* (blog), 8 July 2022, https://blackoutdoors.wordpress.com/2022/07/08/swimming-at-ashbridges-bay-park.

42 Alghoul, "Beauty of One of North America's Oldest."

43 Meach, *Illustrated Historical Atlas.*

44 Smithson, "Coal Merchants of Kingston," 77; Wevers, "When Coal Was King," 125.

45 MacNaughton, "More than a Drop in the Bucket."

46 On the history of Kingston, see Osborne and Swainson, *Kingston.* Anna Young provides an intimate case study of the Gildersleeves, a family based out of the Kingston area that played a prominent role in Great Lakes shipping between 1816 and 1931, in her *Great Lakes' Saga.* On Wolfe Island, see La Rocque, *Wolfe Island.*

47 Moore, "LaSalle Causeway."

48 Manion, Campbell, and Rutter, "Historic Brownfields and Industrial Activity"; Crowder et al., "Rates of Natural and Anthropogenic Change"; Patterson, "Why Kingston Did Not Become a Major Industrial Centre."

49 Killan, *Protected Places*, 74.

50 Summers, "'Coldest Sport in the World'"; Leveridge, *Fair Sport.*

51 Duncan and Marcille, "Meditations on Ice"; Boynce, *Belleville*, 160.

52 Brant, *I'll Sing 'Til the Day I Die.*

53 Joan Holmes and Associates, and Konrad, "Mohawks of Bay of Quinte Resource Harvesting Activities," 125–34.

54 Ibid., 145.

55 Backhouse, *Colour-Coded*, 104.

56 Pasternak, Collis, and Dafnos, "Criminalization at Tyendinaga"; Simpson, *Mohawk Interruptus.*

57 On Tyendinaga Mohawk cosmology and philosophy, see Rustige, *Tyendinaga Tales*. On the concept of blockades from a Lake Ontario watershed Ojibwe perspective, see Simpson, *A Short History of the Blockade.*

58 Bockner, "On Tyendinaga Mohawk Territory."

59 Hauptman, *Iroquois Struggle for Survival*; Hauptman, *In the Shadow of Kinzua.*

60 These statistics are taken from "Indigenous People of Toronto," City of Toronto website, accessed 26 January 2024, https://www.toronto.ca/city-government/accessibility-human-rights/indigenous-affairs-office/torontos-indigenous-peoples. See also Bolduc et al., eds., *Indigenous Toronto.*

61 McKelvey, *Rochester.*

62 Rafuse, *Coal to Canada*. Around 1980, Oswego had been considered as the US terminal for a prospective cargo truck ferry across the lake. Early in the twenty-first century, a fast ferry briefly ran from Rochester to Toronto.

63 McKelvey, "Port of Rochester," 24.

64 Charlotte was annexed by Rochester in 1916. Somerville, "This Is Where I Love to Go"; McKelvey, *Rochester.*

65 Snyder, *Oswego*, 199; Drescher, "Modernization."

66 In the late 1970s and 1980s, proposals were still being made for new bulk storage facilities, including cement silos and potash, at the Port of Oswego. Many of these were contested by local groups, including environmental and historical preservation groups. State Archives of New York, "81-01-1: Port Authority of Oswego Bulk Storage Building – City of Oswego – Oswego Co.," Box 16, 13405-95, St Lawrence-Eastern Ontario Commission.

CHAPTER FIVE

1 Macfarlane and Watson, "Hydro Democracy."

2 Macfarlane, *Fixing Niagara Falls*.

3 The first electrical power was generated on the Ontario side of the Niagara Peninsula in 1886, when the St Catharines Electric Light and Power Company built a small direct current (DC) station at a lock on the second Welland Canal. Other small electricity generation took place at another lock on the canal and in Merriton. Jackson et al., *Mighty Niagara*, 206–7.

4 Water is taken from the river about a mile above the crest of the Horseshoe Falls and just above the rim of the first cascade of the upper rapids. From thence three pipelines, each about 6,300 feet long, lead to the power station situated at the base of the cliff below the Horseshoe Falls. The plant operated at an average head of 180 feet and featured a total installed capacity of 208,200 horsepower.

5 The term "intermittent waterfall" was used by Thomas H. Norton in a 1916 paper read to the American Electro-Chemical Society. See Dow, *Anthology and Bibliography of Niagara Falls*, vol. 2, 1,051.

6 Macfarlane and Heasley, "Water, Oil, and Fish."

7 Styran and Taylor, *This Colossal Project*.

8 Ontario Hydro was also allowed to divert 2,500 cfs from the Welland Ship Canal (technically allotting it to the Albany River diversion contributions). On the technical aspects of the DeCew plants, see Biggar, *Ontario Hydro's History*.

9 See the National Inventory of Dams: https://nid.sec.usace.army.mil/#/.

10 NARA II, RG 59, box 4047, file 711.42157 SA 29/1288-1/2: Memorandum (by Hickerson), 23 June 1934; President Franklin D. Roosevelt's Office Files, 1933–1945, pt. 4, Subject File, "Memorandum (no author), February 22, 1934."

11 NARA II, The Minister in Canada (Armour) to the Secretary of State, No. 441, 26 February 1936, file 711.4216 NI/339, Box 4051, RG 59; NARA II, From Ottawa Legation to Sec of State, Despatch 443, Subject: St Lawrence Waterways and Niagara Falls Treaties, 29 February 1936, file 711.4216 NI/339, box 4051, RG 59.

12 Evenden, *Allied Power*.

13 The Long Lac diversion, completed in 1941, connects the headwaters of the Kenogami River with the Aguasabon River, which naturally discharges into Lake Superior about 250 kilometres east of Thunder Bay, Ontario. The Ogoki diversion, completed in 1943, connects the upper portion of the Ogoki River to Lake Nipigon, and from there flows into Lake Superior

96 kilometres east of Thunder Bay. The 14 October 1940 note was followed by supplementary notes on 31 October and 7 November, and then additional notes on 20 May 1941, and 27 October 1941. Library and Archives Canada (hereafter LAC), RG 25, vol. 3650, file 1268-D-40C: St Lawrence River–Niagara River Treaty Proposals (General Correspondence), Part 7, June 1/47–Jan 16/48: Letter from Adolf Berle (for the Sec of State) to Christie, 14 October 1940.

14 These two diversions together increase the mean level of each of the Great Lakes as follows: Lake Superior by 6.4 cm (0.21 feet), Lakes Michigan and Huron by 11.3 cm (0.37 feet), Lake Erie by 7.6 cm (0.25 feet), and Lake Ontario by 6.7 cm (0.22 feet).

15 IJC, *Great Lakes Diversions and Consumptive Uses.*

16 LAC, RG 25, vol. 3560, file 1268-K-40C: St Lawrence–Niagara River Treaty between Canada and United States – Additional Diversion of Water at Niagara Falls, pt. 1 (April 24/41 to Dec 8/41): Letter from Wrong to Robertson, 24 April 1941.

17 See Macfarlane, "'A Completely Man-Made and Artificial Cataract.'"

18 IJC, Docket 64, "Specifications for Preservation & Enhancement of Niagara Falls, U.S. Flank of Horseshoe Falls, U.S. Corps of Engineers: Preservation & Enhancement of Niagara Falls, International Niagara Falls Engineering Board, 1 March 1953, Niagara Falls Reference, Box 107, 64-4-2:2.

19 HEPCO, Niagara Remedial Works, Minutes of a Meeting of Working Committee Held at Buffalo on 31 January 1952.

20 IJC, Docket 64, INBC – Final Report of Construction of Niagara River Remedial Works – 1960/09/30: Construction of Niagara River Remedial Works, Final Report by the International Niagara Board of Control, 30 September 1960, Niagara Falls Reference, Box 110, 64-7-3:3 (3).

21 Ibid.

22 Macfarlane, "Nature Empowered."

23 SUL, Robert Moses Papers, Box 6: PASNY, "Niagara Power and Local Taxes," 2 December 1957; PASNY, Meeting Minutes – 9 February 1961: Niagara Power Project – Increased Costs for Contract N-10 – Construction of Tuscarora Power Plant, 9 February 1961.

24 Macfarlane, *Negotiating a River*; LAC, RG 25, Memorandum: An All-Canadian St Lawrence Waterway, 17 May 1949, file 1268-Q-40, St Lawrence Waterway Project-Interdepartmental Committee – General File, pt. 1.2, 6184.

25 Bryce, *Hydraulic Engineering History of the St. Lawrence Power Project*; St Lawrence University Archives, St Lawrence Seaway Series, box 66, Power

Authority of the State of New York, "Land Acquisition on the American
Side of the St. Lawrence Seaway and Power Projects," 18 July 1955.

26 See Macfarlane, *Negotiating a River*; Osborne, "Canadian 'Riverscape,'
National 'Inscape.'"

27 Brief consideration was given to fishways at the beginning of the planning
for the power project but they were soon abandoned. Eel ladders were added
to the Canadian portion of the Moses-Saunders dam in 1974 (and the
American part in 2006) and the Beauharnois dam in 1998.

28 IJC, Canadian Section, 68-5-6, St Lawrence Power Application, General
Memorandum 1955, a Report to the International Joint Commission on
Concerns of the St Regis Band Regarding Impacts from the St Lawrence
Seaway and Power Development, March 1982.

CHAPTER SIX

1 Quote in Bogue, *Fishing the Great Lakes*, 27.

2 Knight, "Samuel Wilmot."

3 Morrison, "Chronology of Lake Ontario Ecosystem and Fisheries," 298–9.

4 Government of Canada, Department of Marine and Fisheries, *First Annual
Report*.

5 Kerr's diaries are accessible online and in person at the Royal Ontario
Museum: https://archive.org/details/kerrfamilyfonds.

6 Forkey, "Maintaining a Great Lakes Fishery."

7 NYSL, W.J. Christie, "Review of the Changes in the Fish Species Composition
of Lake Ontario," Technical Report No. 23, Great Lakes Fishery Commission,
Ann Arbor, Michigan (January 1973), 2, WAT 110-4 TWOLO 215-2764.

8 NARA II, RG 0022 – US Fish and Wildlife Service. Office of the Commissioner of Fish and Fisheries. Entry #P44: Records of the Joint Fisheries Commission Relative to the Preservation of the Fisheries in Waters Contiguous
to Canada and the United States: 1893–95, Folder: Lake Ontario and St
Lawrence River. Dr F.S. Law, Pulaski, New York. Interviewed by R.R. Gurley,
23 July 1894.

9 NARA II, RG 0022 – US Fish and Wildlife Service. Office of the Commissioner of Fish and Fisheries. Entry #P44: Records of the Joint Fisheries Commission Relative to the Preservation of the Fisheries in Waters Contiguous to
Canada and the United States: 1893–95, Folder: Lake Ontario & St Lawrence
River. Mr. Fitzgerald, Grenadier Island, New York. Interviewed by Evermann
and Bean, 27 June 1894.

10 NARA II, RG 0022 – US Fish and Wildlife Service. Office of the Commis-
    sioner of Fish and Fisheries. Entry #P44: Records of the Joint Fisheries Com-
    mission Relative to the Preservation of the Fisheries in Waters Contiguous to
    Canada and the United States: 1893–95, Folder: Lake Ontario & St Lawrence
    River. W.W. Brodie & O. Luff, Stony Island, New York. Interviewed by Ever-
    mann and Bean, 2 July 1894.

11 NARA II, RG 0022 – US Fish and Wildlife Service. Office of the Commis-
    sioner of Fish and Fisheries. Entry #P44: Records of the Joint Fisheries Com-
    mission Relative to the Preservation of the Fisheries in Waters Contiguous to
    Canada and the United States: 1893–95, Folder: Lake Ontario & St Lawrence
    River. C.M. Clark, Cape Vincent, New York. Interviewed by Evermann and
    Bean, 26 June 1894.

12 NARA II, RG 0022 – US Fish and Wildlife Service. Office of the Commis-
    sioner of Fish and Fisheries. Entry #P44: Records of the Joint Fisheries Com-
    mission Relative to the Preservation of the Fisheries in Waters Contiguous to
    Canada and the United States: 1893–95, Folder: Lake Ontario and St Law-
    rence River. Container #6. Interview with Chas. McFarland, Nine Mile Point,
    NY. Interviewed by R.R. Gurley, 10 August 1894.

13 In 1908, the United States and Great Britain (acting for Canada) signed the
    1908 Inland Fisheries Treaty. The accord called for an Inland Fisheries Com-
    mission, composed of one expert from each of Canada and the US, which
    would recommend regulations. If implemented, the treaty would apply to
    various boundary waters across the continent and address key areas such
    as open seasons, net types, and fishing stocking. The Canadian Parliament
    adopted the treaty. But the United States never ratified it because of lack
    of support from the public and key constituencies.

14 This paragraph is paraphrasing from a conversation I had with fish ecologist
    Dr Henry Regier. In addition to his academic position at the University of
    Toronto, Regier served in a variety of important domestic and international
    governmental roles concerning natural resource and environmental issues:
    Canadian commissioner on the Great Lakes Fishery Commission; advisor
    for the International Commission for the Northwest Atlantic Fisheries
    (ICNAF); chief of the Stock Assessment Branch of the Fisheries Department
    of the UN Food and Agriculture Organization; advisor on the UN Conven-
    tion on the Law of the Sea; member of the Science Advisory Board of the
    IJC's Great Lakes Water Quality Agreement (GLWQA); lead author in a
    chapter included in the 1995 report of the Intergovernmental Panel on

Climate Change (IPCC), and others. Henry Regier, personal correspondence with Daniel Macfarlane, 11 June 2021. See also: Meisner et al., "An Assessment of the Effects"; Regier et al., "Likely Responses to Climate Change."

15 McCullough, *Commercial Fishery of the Canadian Great Lakes*; Brenden et al., "Great Lakes Commercial Fisheries," 381.

16 Henry Regier, personal correspondence with Daniel Macfarlane, 7 June 2021.

17 One of those voices was Henry Regier. Henry Regier, personal correspondence with Daniel Macfarlane, 11 June 2020; Bocking, "Fishing the Inland Seas."

18 Christie, "Review of the Changes"; Mills et al. "A Synthesis of Ecological and Fish-Community Changes."

19 US Fish and Wildlife Service, "Report to Congress: Great Lakes Fishery Resources Restoration Study."

20 Kerr, "Historical Review of Fish Culture"; Szylvian, "Transforming Lake Michigan."

21 Lake Ontario Waterkeeper, "Bringing Back the American Eel," Swim Drink Fish Canada, accessed 26 January 2024, https://www.swimdrinkfish.ca/lake-ontario-waterkeeper/case/american-eel; Busch and Braun, "A Case for Accelerated Reestablishment."

22 MacGregor et al., "Declines of American Eel"; Casselman et al., "Status of Upper St. Lawrence."

23 Great Lakes Fishery Commission, "Fish Community Objectives," 5, 16; Patch and Busch, "Fisheries in the St. Lawrence River"; Casselman and Scott, "Fish-Community Dynamics of Lake Ontario."

24 Brant, *Great Lakes Sea Lamprey*; Knight and Bocking, "Fisheries, Invasive Species."

25 This is based on Regier's reading of the diaries of fishery overseers John W. Kerr and Frederick W. Kerr. Henry Regier, personal correspondence with Daniel Macfarlane, 9 October 2021.

26 Great Lakes Fishery Commission, "Limnological Survey of Lake Ontario, 1964 (Technical Report No. 14)."

27 Eshenroder and Lantry, "Recent Changes in Successional State," 146.

28 Tanner, *Something Spectacular*.

29 On invasive species, also see Willoughby, *Joint Organizations of Canada and the United States*; Dorsey, *Dawn of Conservation Diplomacy*; Bogue, *Fishing the Great Lakes*; Scarpino, "Great Lakes Fisheries."

30 Alexander, *Pandora's Locks*, xix.

31 In the US the Nonindigenous Aquatic Nuisance Prevention and Control Act

(NANPCA) of 1990 required ships to exchange ballast water at sea, but the Coast Guard did not apply it to ships without ballast water, which was a major loophole because of organisms in residual ballast water and sediment (No Ballast on Board, or NOBOB). The National Invasive Species Act of 1996 amended the 1990 NANPCA but still did not give it teeth. In 2006, a federal court ordered the EPA to remove the ballast water exemption under the Clean Water Act. The US and Canadian St Lawrence Seaway agencies enacted saltwater flushing requirements for NOBOB vessels. But there are still debates about how to regulate this, and debates about the most effective technological means of treating ballast water. New York State generated tougher regulations, but these were dropped in 2012 in the face of Canadian opposition to this unilateral approach. Canada proposed new ballast regulations – which the US Lake Carriers' Association argued constitutes discrimination against US flag vessel operators. Alexander, *Pandora's Locks*.

32 Bin Zhu et al., "Quantification of Historical Changes"; NYSL, R. Warren Flint and Robert J.J. Stevens, *Lake Ontario: A Great Lake in Transition*; Heasley, *The Accidental Reef*.

33 Colin Duncan, interview with Daniel Macfarlane, 6 April 2020.

34 Stewart et al., "Pond Sediments on Nesting Islands."

35 Stewart, Todd, and Lepan, "Fish Community Objectives for Lake Ontario."

36 New York State Department of Environmental Conservation, "2019 Annual Report"; Ontario Ministry of Natural Resources and Forestry, "Lake Ontario Fish Communities and Fisheries."

37 Ruhland, Paterson, and Smol, "Lake Diatom Responses to Warming."

CHAPTER SEVEN

1 Benidickson, "The IJC and Water Quality in the Bacterial Age," 122–5; Benidickson, *The Culture of Flushing*; Melosi, *Sanitary City*; Tarr, *The Search for the Ultimate Sink*.

2 Benidickson, "The IJC and Water Quality in the Bacterial Age," 122–5.

3 IJC, Progress Report, 1914, 45, quoted in Benidickson, "The IJC and Water Quality in the Bacterial Age."

4 Chlorine can also join with some sewage compounds to form halogenated hydrocarbons harmful to humans.

5 Egerton, "History of Ecological Sciences, Part 50"; Egerton, "History of Ecological Sciences, Part 57"; Bocking, *Ecologists and Environmental Politics*.

6 Read, "Origins of the *Great Lakes Water Quality Agreements*"; Read, "Addressing 'A Quiet Horror'"; Kehoe, *Cleaning Up the Great Lakes*; Hartig,

Burning Rivers; McGucken, *Lake Erie Rehabilitated*; Visser, *Cold, Clear, and Deadly*.

7   For a detailed catalogue of discharges into Lake Ontario see AO, "Table 5: Municipal Waste Discharges Direct to Lake Ontario and St. Lawrence River 1966–67 (short tons/year)" and "Table 6: Principal Industrial Discharges into Lake Ontario and St. Lawrence River 1966–67 (short tons/year)," RG 84-1, container b228913 Commissions: IJC – Pollution Control Board – Lake Ontario 1969.

8   NARA II, RG 59, Decimal File, 1945–49, box 3306, files 711.4216 N 1/1-145 to 7.114216 N 1/12-3149: "Industrial Waste Summary Reports: International Joint Commission Boundary Waters Pollution Investigation, Lake Erie-Lake Ontario Section," 1949.

9   Chemical Waste Management continues to run the LOOW, which was the government's designation for the Model City discard complex. See Jenks, "Model City USA."

10 NYSL, Gregory Kennedy and William Kappel, "Survey of Lake Ontario Bottom Sediment off Rochester, New York, to Define the Extent of Jettisoned World War Materiel and its Potential for Sediment Contamination" (NYS-DEC/USGS, 2000), SAI 045-4 SURIT 219-1168.

11 US Army Corps of Engineers, "Fort Niagara"; US Army Corps of Engineers, "Fort Ontario." My thanks to Alex Souchen and Elodie Charrière for pointing me to information about unexploded ordnance (UXO) in and near Lake Ontario. On a related military note, a secret spy-training school named "Camp X" was opened during the Second World War on the Lake Ontario shore near Whitby, while Fort Niagara was a prisoner-of-war camp and Fort Ontario at Oswego was from 1944 to 1946 the only shelter in the United States for Jewish refugees fleeing the Holocaust.

12 Fairburn, *Along the Shore*, 377.

13 Syracuse was doing the same into Lake Onondaga.

14 Martin, "Oil and Gas Industry in the Empire State."

15 Sanger, *Blind Faith*; Pitkanen, "Hot Commodity."

16 Mark Mattson, interview with Daniel Macfarlane, 23 July 2021.

17 Sanger, *Blind Faith*, chapter 5.

18 O'Meara, "Port Granby low-level radioactive waste mound safely closed."

19 Dave Lochbaum, "Flooding at Nine Mile Point," *The Equation*, 25 June 2018, https://blog.ucsusa.org/dlochbaum/flooding-at-nine-mile-point/.

20 Gateley, *Sweet Waters Stories of Lake Ontario*, 51–2; see also several chapters about nuclear power in Gateley, *Saving the Beautiful Lake*.

21 "Waterkeeper Submits Request to Intervene: Darlington Nuclear Refurbish-
    ment," Swim Drink Fish, accessed 26 January 2024, https://www.swimdrink
    fish.ca/lake-ontario-waterkeeper/blog/24348.

22 Watson, "Coal in Canada."

23 Ibid.

24 Genesee/Finger Lakes Regional Planning Board, *Lake Ontario Shoreline*,
    42–4; Wyman and Dischel, "Factors Influencing Impingement."

25 However, public water withdrawals had a higher consumptive rate, since
    most of the water used for power generation was returned to its source.
    Great Lakes Commission, *Annual Report of the Great Lakes Regional Water
    Use Database*, 29.

26 Hartig, *Burning Rivers*; O'Connor, *First Green Wave*.

27 Kehoe, *Cleaning Up the Great Lakes*, 83–5; Gargan, "Politics of Water Pollu-
    tion in New York State"; Martin, *Water for New York*.

28 International Lake Erie Water Pollution Board and the International Lake
    Ontario–St Lawrence River Water Pollution Board, *Pollution of Lake Erie,
    Lake Ontario and the International Section of the St. Lawrence River*; AO,
    "Report to the Lake Erie and Lake Ontario International Joint Commission
    Advisory Board on Water Pollution of the Niagara River, 1971," B335702,
    RG 12-88.

29 IJC, *Pollution of Lake Erie, Lake Ontario and the International Section of the
    St. Lawrence River*.

30 Read, "Origins of the *Great Lakes Water Quality Agreements*."

31 Steve Bertman, personal correspondence with Daniel Macfarlane, 11 Novem-
    ber 2021.

32 IJC, *Pollution of Lake Erie, Lake Ontario and the International Section of the
    St. Lawrence River*. For a sampling of public complaints, see: AO, "Pollution
    Complaints – Lake Ontario, 1969," container B281661, RG 12-88-52; AO, "Pol-
    lution Complaints – Lake Ontario, 1970," container B245034, RG 12-88-0-260.

33 Henry Regier, personal correspondence with Daniel Macfarlane, 15 Novem-
    ber 2021.

34 Raphael et al., *Future Dredging Quantities in the Great Lakes*. For fine-
    grained details on the politics, and quantities, of dredging in Ontario in the
    early Cold War period, see various files in: AO, RG 1-339, containers B287594
    and B287595, Lake Ontario General.

35 Raphael et al., *Future Dredging Quantities in the Great Lakes*.

36 Ibid.; NYSL, Roger Banerman et al., "Phosphorous Uptake and Release by
    Lake Ontario Sediments" (EPA, February 1975), LEG 733.1-4 ONFPL 75-10176;

NYSA, "Dredging of Oswego Harbor and Open-Lake Discharge of Dredged Materials, Oswego County York," in "USACE Oswego Harbor Dredging," Box 17, 13405-95, St Lawrence–Eastern Ontario Commission.

37 Botts and Muldoon, *Evolution of the Great Lakes Water Quality Agreements.*

38 This critique of assimilative capacity in the Great Lakes draws from Langston, *Sustaining Lake Superior.*

39 Canada and the United States, "Great Lakes Water Quality Agreement" (15 April 1972).

40 Canada and the United States, "Great Lakes Water Quality Agreement of 1978" (22 November 1978).

41 Kaiser, "Mirex."

42 Henry Regier, personal communication with Daniel Macfarlane, 11 June 2021. On the development of mid-twentieth-century fisheries ecology in Ontario, see Bocking, "Fishing the Inland Seas."

43 Hang and Salvo, *Ravaged River*, 1.

44 Warry and Chan, "Organic Contaminants"; Thomas, "Lake Ontario Sediments"; Durham and Oliver, "History of Lake Ontario Contamination"; NYSL, Haile et al., *Chlorinated Hydrocarbons in the Lake Ontario Ecosystem (IFYGL).*

45 Kaminsky et al., "Fates of Organic Compounds"; Whittle and Fitzsimons, "Influence of the Niagara River"; Sly, "Sedimentology and Geochemistry"; NYSL, Neilson, "Trace Metals in Lake Ontario."

46 Nriagu and Wong, "Historical Records of Metal Pollution."

47 DeBues et al., "Stream Nutrient and Agricultural Land-Use"; Liu et al., "Agricultural Intensification."

48 Rang et al., "Impairment of Beneficial Uses in Lake Ontario."

49 AO, RG 12-156, "Toxics Management Plan. A Report by the Lake Ontario Toxics Committee, February 1989," container B441881, Lake Ontario Toxic Management Plan (LOTMP).

50 On the AQA and the IJC, see Munton and Temby, "International Joint Commission and Air Pollution."

51 Langston, *Sustaining Lake Superior*, 193–4; 197–9.

52 IJC, *Fifth Biennial Report under the Great Lakes Water Quality Agreement of 1978.*

53 IJC, *Status of Restoration Activities in Great Lakes Areas of Concern.*

54 Colborn, *Great Lakes, Great Legacy?*; Colborn, Dumanoski, and Myers, *Our Stolen Future.* See also Langston, *Toxic Bodies.*

55 Great Lakes United, *Great Lakes Green Book.*

56 Hartig and Zarull, *Under RAPs*; Hartig and Munawar, *Ecosystem-Based Management of Laurentian Great Lakes Areas of Concern*; Krantzberg, "Great Lakes Remedial Action Plan Program."

57 Wooster, *Living Waters*; NYSL, Litten, "Toxic Chemicals in NYS."

58 O'Connor and McLaughlin, "Economic Benefits of Remediating."

59 On the Hamilton AOC and RAP, see chapter 8 in Bouchier and Cruikshank, *The People and the Bay*, and several of the chapters in Grover and Krantzberg, eds., *Great Lakes*.

60 Chloride inputs into Lake Ontario from road salt (sodium chloride) had been recognized by scientists as having a potential impact on water quality by the 1960s, if not earlier. A 1978 study from the Province of Ontario's Water Resources Branch identified these road salts (almost 300,000 tonnes of rock salt were applied in lakeshore communities within Ontario during 1976 to 1977, with much more coming from New York tributaries, particularly the Oswego River, which was discharging over a million tonnes per year) as the largest single source of lake chloride but discounted them as a significant impediment to water quality compared to the chloride load carried by the Niagara River. AO, RG 12-88, container B370263, J.G. Ralston and F. Hamilton, "Chloride Inputs to Lake Ontario and the Significance of Deicing Salts," Ontario Water Resources Branch, Ontario Ministry of the Environment (April 1978).

61 Wong et al., "Monitoring Toxicity."

62 NYSL, US EPA and NYS Department of Environmental Conservation, "Lakewide Impacts of Critical Pollutants."

63 These federal funding initiatives were helped along by the Council of Great Lakes Governors' Great Lakes Priority Initiative, the Lake Ontario Coast Initiative Action, and other efforts. Makarewicz et al., "Lake Ontario Coastal Initiative Action Agenda."

64 VanNijnatten and Johns, "International Joint Commission."

65 Gateley, *A Natural History of Lake Ontario*, 76–7. During the twentieth century, the barrier beach at Braddock Bay dwindled, since erosion and sand movement patterns had changed because of both natural and human-induced causes. This intervention cost $9 million.

66 Grbic et al., "Microplastics Entering Northwestern Lake Ontario"; Krantzberg et al., *Plastic Pollution*.

67 Thompson, "Combining Algae, Plastic."

68 Corcoran et al., "Hidden Plastics of Lake Ontario."

69 Langston, *Sustaining Lake Superior*, 211.

CHAPTER EIGHT

1 Older water level records are not as accurate as current observations. Some of the earliest reliable gauges were in the Niagara River, giving us some idea of historical Lake Ontario inflows. But neither county developed a wide network of level gauges until the early twentieth century. These gauges were mainly intended to benefit navigation. The limited dispersal of gauges as well as their technological limitations meant that knowledge about water levels was still subject to a great deal of uncertainty. O.M. Meehan, "Canadian Hydrographic Service."

2 See NOAA-GLERL: https://www.glerl.noaa.gov/data/wlevels.

3 On the politicization of the process, see Macfarlane, *Negotiating a River*; IJC, "Further Regulation of the Great Lakes."

4 IJC, *Water Levels of Lake Ontario*.

5 The regulation criteria outlined that the water level of Montreal Harbour should be no lower than what would have occurred if the power project had not been built. Bryce, *Hydraulic Engineering History*, 94; LAC, RG 25, 6778, file 1268-D-40, pt. 43.2, St. Lawrence Seaway and Power Project – General File, DEA Memorandum: Lake Ontario Levels, 26 April 1955.

6 On the history of controlling ice in rivers of the lower Great Lakes–St Lawrence basin, see Macfarlane, "'As Nearly as May Be.'"

7 NARA II, RG 59 – Office of the Legal Advisor, Assistant Legal Advisor for European Affairs. Lot 67D271. Records Relating to the US–Canada International Joint Commission and International Boundary Waters, 1948–1966. Alaska: Int'l Rail and Hwy Commission to Lake Ontario: Correspondence, 1956, Box 1. NN3-059-96-010. File: Lake Ontario – Correspondence, etc., 1955. Summary of Corps of Engineers Analysis of Lake Ontario Land Development and Beach Protection Association Comments on Lake Ontario Regulation Plan NO. 12-A-9.

8 Macfarlane, "Nature Empowered."

9 IJC, Canadian Section, Assoc. Committee on St Lawrence River Model Studies, Progress Memorandum No. 2, National Research Council, 15 January 1958, Docket 64.

10 IJC, Canadian Section, Correspondence from 1954/01/01 to 1954/12/21, 68-3-V2, Memorandum of Meeting, 3 July 1954, St Lawrence Power Application.

11 IJC, *Water Levels of Lake Ontario*.

12 Bryce, *Hydraulic Engineering History*, 108.

13 IJC, "History of the Lake Ontario–St. Lawrence River Order of Approval and the Regulation Plan and Related Studies," 3.

14 NARA II, RG 59 – Office of the Legal Advisor. Assistant Legal Advisor for
    European Affairs. Lot 67D271. Records Relating to the US–Canada Interna-
    tional Joint Commission and International Boundary Waters, 1948–1966.
    Alaska: Int'l Rail and Hwy Commission to Lake Ontario: Correspondence,
    1956. Box 1. NN3-059-96-010. File: Lake Ontario – Correspondence, etc., 1955.
    Department of State Memorandum of Conversation. Claims of Property
    Owners on the South Shore of Lake Ontario and Lake Ontario Reference
    to International Joint Commission. 5 January 1955.

15 NARA II, RG 59 – Office of the Legal Advisor. Assistant Legal Advisor for
    European Affairs. Lot 67D271. Records Relating to the US–Canada Interna-
    tional Joint Commission and International Boundary Waters, 1948–1966.
    Alaska: Int'l Rail and Hwy Commission to Lake Ontario: Correspondence,
    1956. Box 1. NN3-059-96-010. Memorandum of Conversation. Canadian
    Desire for a Tribunal to assess damage allegedly caused by Gut Dam and to
    reimburse claimants – Supplementary statement regarding legal questions
    involved. 23 December 1952.

16 NARA II, RG 59 – General Records of the Department of State. Office of the
    Legal Advisor. Office of the Assistant Legal Advisor for European Affairs.
    Records Pertaining to the International Joint Commission, United States and
    Canada (IJC), 1950–1964. Passamaquoddy – Tidal Power Project to Effects
    on Lake Ontario Water. Box 10. 65D171. Entry A1 5470. File: Effects on Lake
    Ontario Water Levels of the Gut Dam and Channel Changes in the Galop
    Rapids Reach of the St Lawrence River, 1958 Main Report. Main Report, Ef-
    fects on Lake Ontario Water Levels of the Gut Dam and Channel Changes in
    the Galop Rapids Reach of the St Lawrence, Report to the IJC by the Interna-
    tional Lake Ontario Board of Engineers, October 1958.

17 NARA II, RG 59 – General Records of the Department of State. Bureau of
    European Affairs. Office of British Commonwealth and Northern European
    Affairs. Records Relating to Canadian Affairs, 1957–1963. 6-D-3.17 Oil Quotas
    to [7] Columbia R. Negotiations. Box 3. HM 1993. File: 6/D.8. IJC – Gut Dam.
    1959–1963. Confidential: Gut Dam Claims. 26 March 1952.

18 NARA II, RG 76 – Boundary and Claims Commissions and Arbitrations,
    Department of State/US Embassy Canada, P 97: Individual Claims Files of
    the Lake Ontario Claims Tribunal 1965–1968, Container 2.

19 NARA II, RG 0076, Boundary and Claims Commissions and Arbitrations
    Department of State/US Embassy, Canada. Entry #P 98: Chronological and
    Subject Files Relating to the Lake Ontario Claims Tribunal 1966–68. Con-
    tainer #4. File: Final Signed Copy of Rules of Procedure. Final Statement By

Tribunal dated 27 September 1968. On the Gut Dam settlement's significance from a legal perspective, see Goodman, "Canada–United States Settlement of Gut Dam Claims"; Kornfeld, *Transboundary Water Disputes*.

20 For example, geologists in the early 1980s were still unsure about the precise causes of erosion at specific places along the Lake Ontario shoreline. NYSA, Thomas Drexhage and Parker E. Calkin, "Historic Bluff Recession along the Lake Ontario Coast, New York" (Albany, NY: New York Sea Grant Institute, 1981), 574.9297479 C555 73-4284; St Lawrence–Eastern Ontario Commission, "A Proposed Coastal Management Program for the Eastern Shore Dune-Bay-Wetland Complex" (Albany, NY: New York Coastal Management Program, New York Department of State, August 1979).

21 An example of another government body beyond the state and provincial governments is the St Lawrence–Eastern Ontario Commission. This New York State executive agency, which existed from 1971 to 1995, had a wide variety of functions along the eastern edge of Lake Ontario pertaining to the approval of land use and development applications.

22 In Ontario a bill called the Great Lakes Shoreline Right of Passage Act has been repeatedly introduced into the provincial legislature for the last decade. Despite making it through first and second readings, this bill has not yet been successfully passed.

23 The Niagara River has control works near the falls, but these are not officially used to control the levels of Lake Ontario, though all the remedial works and diversions involved with Niagara power production do alter somewhat Lake Erie's levels.

24 In 1964, when water levels were very low, the federal governments asked the IJC whether it would be feasible to maintain the waters of all the Great Lakes at a more constant level. This study was completed in 1973, when lake levels had risen to record highs. The IJC concluded that nature was the primary cause of water level changes in the Great Lakes and only a limited reduction in the range of water levels was practical. The IJC then advised the governments in its landmark 1976 report *Further Regulation of the Great Lakes* that the high economic and environmental costs of further regulation of Lakes Michigan and Huron could not be justified by the benefits. The same conclusion was reached during another IJC study in 1983 on regulating outflows specifically from Lake Erie. IJC, *Further Regulation of the Great Lakes*.

25 In terms of isostatic rebound, they noted that "there has been a progressive increase in the water levels with respect to the land around Lake Ontario as a

result of the earth's crust in the Galop Rapids reach rising at a rate of about
0.55 foot per 100 years with respect to the land at Oswego and at a rate of
about one foot per 100 years with respect to the land at the west end of the
lake." NARA II, RG 0076. Boundary and Claims Commissions and Arbitrations Department of State/US Embassy, Canada. Entry #P 98: Chronological
and Subject Files Relating to the Lake Ontario Claims Tribunal 1966–68.
Container #4. Water Levels of Lake Ontario. Report to the Government of
Canada and the Government of the United States (Under the Reference of 25
June 1952) by the International Joint Commission. 5 April 1961; Tushingham,
"Postglacial Uplift Predictions"; IJC, *Levels Reference Study*.

26 The volume of water diverted from the Chicago Sanitary and Ship Canal was
effectively limited by a 1930 US Supreme Court decision to 3,200 cfs on an
annual basis. At several times in the 1950s, the Chicago Diversion was increased temporarily. In 1967, a US Supreme Court ruling put the diversions
back to 3,200 cfs. In the 1980s, the State of Illinois tried to hike up the diversion. In the 1990s, it turned out that Chicago was often exceeding the diversion limit, though mostly through accidental leakage; the diversion has of
late been kept within its legislated bounds. IJC, *Great Lakes Diversions and
Consumptive Uses*.

27 IJC, *Levels Reference Study*.

28 IJC, *Protection of the Great Lakes Report*.

29 Exceptions include communities that straddle the water basin divide that
will use the diverted water for public water supply purposes, potentially
having to return it to the basin. Macfarlane and Hall, "Transborder Water
Management."

30 Quinn, "Secular Changes in Great Lakes."

31 IJC, "History of the Lake Ontario–St. Lawrence River."

32 Wilcox and Bateman, "Photointerpretation Analysis of Plant Communities."
But there is also evidence that more natural fluctuations under Plan 2014
will mobilize mercury in wetlands: Brahmstedt et al., "Assessment of Mercury Mobilization."

33 LAC, RG 25, 5026, file 1268-D-40, 54, St Lawrence Seaway Project – General
File, 8 January 1960 to 27 February 1962, Memorandum to Deputy Minister
re: Peaking Tests at St Lawrence River Power Project, 17 September 1962.

34 Plan 1998 fell short of the expectations of Lake Ontario south shore property
owners who expected a new plan to appreciably reduce the frequency and
magnitude of high lake levels, failed to satisfy the expectations of boaters on

the upper river who wanted to maintain higher summer river levels into the fall to extend the boating season, and also drew criticism from environmentalists who wanted a more natural range of lake levels.

35 NYSL, Thomas E. Croley II, "Great Lakes Climate Change Hydrologic Impact Assessment IJC Lake Ontario–St. Lawrence River Regulation Study" (Ann Arbor, NOAA Great Lakes Environmental Research Laboratory, September 2003), I 49.44/8:BTP-R 3017-2018.

36 This discussion of Plan 2014 draws from Clamen and Macfarlane, "Plan 2014."

37 IJC, *Lake Ontario–St. Lawrence River Plan 2014*.

38 Clamen and Macfarlane, "Plan 2014."

39 Crichton, "Local Officials Demand Action on Rising Lake Ontario Water Levels."

40 Shermerhorn, "Revisiting Plan 2014."

41 McDermott and Orr, "Muddled Maps Complicate Future of Lake Ontario Shoreline."

42 Since 2020, the IJC's Great Lakes–St Lawrence River Adaptive Management (GLAM) Committee has been studying changes to the Lake Ontario outflow regulation plan. GLAM completed Phase 1 of the review in November 2021, and as of this writing was in the midst of Phase 2: https://ijc.org/sites/default/files/GLAM_Phase2_Strategy_eng.pdf.

CONCLUSION

1 Macfarlane and Watson, "Hydro Democracy."

2 Though the Second World War is a starting date for the Anthropocene preferred by many, others points to other different dates much further back in time, such as the Industrial Revolution or the beginning of agriculture.

3 McNeill and Engelke, *Great Acceleration*.

4 Busch and Lary, "Assessment of Habitat Impairments."

5 EPA-Canada, *State of the Great Lakes 2022 Report*; IJC, *Second Triennial Assessment of Progress on Great Lakes Water Quality*.

6 There are also plans to send the sewage effluent from new housing developments north of Toronto, located in the Lake Huron watershed, to Lake Ontario at the Duffin Creek Water Pollution Control Plant. Hristova, "Ontario Issues Order"; Syed, "Dereliction of Doodie."

7 DeBues et al., "Stream Nutrient and Agricultural Land-Use"; Liu et al., "Agricultural Intensification," 17–25.

8 Gateley, *Saving the Beautiful Lake*, 54. Switzerland's Nestlé company opened its first US factory in Fulton, on the Oswego River, in the late 1800s because of the local dairy industry. This facility later began to specialize in chocolate, with the Crunch bar and Nesquik invented here. The factory closed in 2003. Farfaglia, *Nestle in Fulton, New York.*

9 Lake Ontario Partnership, *Lake Ontario: Lakewide Action and Management Plan, 2018–2022*; McGoldrick and Murphy, "Concentration and Distribution of Contaminants."

10 O'Gorman, ed., "State of Lake Ontario in 2014."

11 Weidel et al, "Lake Ontario April Prey Fish."

12 Burlakova et al., "Six Decades of Lake Ontario."

13 During the 1970s, Asian carp were purposefully introduced into the American South to act as natural vacuums in fish farms. By the 1990s, the carp had escaped and have since been inexorably working their way northward up the Mississippi River and its tributaries. These fish, which grow up to a metre long, are resilient and prolific: they reproduce at astounding rates (i.e., up to a quarter-million eggs per year), live for several decades, and can daily eat 20 per cent of their weight. The main preventative measure to keep these carp from infiltrating further up the canal are electric underwater barriers installed just miles from Lake Michigan by the US Army Corps of Engineers that send out different levels of electronic shocks designed to stun fish and prevent their passage. But the effectiveness of this obstacle does not exactly instill confidence. Would a fish be protected from shock if it was swimming between two vessels? Or if a fish was pulled through in the wake of a vessel, which has been reported? What about a large school of fish, or a particularly persistent fish? Or in the event of a power outage? To help prevent such scenarios, plans are in place to add acoustic and air bubble deterrents, along with more electric barriers at additional locations in the Chicago waterway. But closing this canal, or creating some type of aquatic separation, is by far the best option.

14 Don Procter, "'Donnie' Continues Boring Massive Coxwell Bypass Tunnel," *Daily Commercial News*, 21 October 2020, https://canada.constructconnect.com/dcn/news/infrastructure/2020/10/donnie-continues-boring-massive-coxwell-bypass-tunnel.

15 Acciona's website about the Deep Lake Water Cooling System: https://www.acciona.com/projects/deep-lake-water-cooling-system.

16 Henry Regier notes that serious planning and environmental impact

discussions about this Deep Lake Water Cooling System, of which he was a part, date back to the late 1980s. Henry Regier, personal correspondence with Daniel Macfarlane, 16 June 2021.

17 Mark Mattson, interview with Daniel Macfarlane, 23 July 2021.

18 Ibid.

19 Ibid.

20 Casselman and Scott, "Fish-Community Dynamics of Lake Ontario."

21 Environmental Law and Policy Center, "Assessment of the Impacts of Climate Change."

22 Lenters, "Long Term Trends."

23 Dobiesz and Lester, "Changes in Mid-Summer Water Temperature."

24 Gilbert, "Ice on Lake Ontario at Kingston"; Hewer and Gough, "Lake Ontario Ice Coverage."

25 Hewer and Gough, "Lake Ontario Ice Coverage."

26 Mcclearn, "As Ice Cover Dwindles."

27 Liam Healy, "A New Study Is Shining a Light on How Lake Ontario Changes throughout the Year," *RochesterFirst*, accessed 26 January 2024, https://www.rochesterfirst.com/environment/a-new-study-is-shining-a-light-on-how-lake-ontario-changes-throughout-the-year/amp.

28 Boyce, *Belleville*, 160.

29 Tiro, "Sorry Tale," 1021.

30 It is worth noting that freshwater sources, including Lake Ontario, naturally emit some methane on their own.

31 Kheraj, "History of Long-Distance Oil Spills in Canada."

32 Kimmerer, *Braiding Sweetgrass*.

33 Whyte, Caldwell, and Schaefer, "Indigenous Lessons about Sustainability"; Simpson, *As We Have Always Done*; Smith, Tuck, and Yang, eds., *Indigenous and Decolonizing Studies in Education*.

34 Eric Gross, "Hello! My Name Is … Erie? Personhood for the Great Lakes," *LawSciForum* (15 October 2023): https://mjlst.lib.umn.edu/2023/10/15/hello-my-name-iserie-personhood-for-the-great-lakes.

Bibliography

ARCHIVAL AND PRIMARY SOURCES

Archives of Ontario (AO)
Hydro-Electric Power Commission of Ontario (HEPCO)
International Joint Commission (IJC)
Library and Archives Canada (LAC)
New York State Archives (NYSA)
New York State Library (NYSL)
State Reservation at Niagara, State of New York
Power Authority of the State of New York (PASNY)
President Franklin D. Roosevelt's Office Files
Royal Ontario Museum, John W. Kerr diaries
St Lawrence University Archives (SLUA)
Syracuse University Library (SUL)
US National Archives and Records Administration II (NARA II)
US Senate

INTERVIEWS AND PERSONAL CORRESPONDENCE

Steve Bertman, personal correspondence with Daniel Macfarlane, 11 November 2021.
Colin Duncan, personal correspondence with Daniel Macfarlane, 20 March 2020; 6 April 2020.
Colin Duncan, interview with Daniel Macfarlane, 22 April 2020.
Mark Mattson, interview with Daniel Macfarlane, 23 July 2021.

Shawn Micallef, interview with Daniel Macfarlane, 14 July 2021.

Henry Regier, personal correspondence with Daniel Macfarlane, 7 June 2021; 11 June 2021; 16 June 2021; 9 October 2021; 15 November 2021.

SECONDARY SOURCES AND PRINTED PRIMARY SOURCES

Adam, G. Mercer. *Toronto, Old and New: A Memorial Volume, Historical, Descriptive and Pictorial, Designed to Mark the Hundredth Anniversary of the Passing of the Constitutional Act of 1791* (1891): 168–9. Found in Joshua MacFadyen. "These Well-Wooded Towns: Supplying Fuel Wood to Canadian Urban Markets, 1868–1921." *Social History/histoire sociale* 54, no. 111 (2021): 283–310.

Agassiz, Louis, and James Eliot Cabot. *Lake Superior: Its Physical Character, Vegetation, and Animals, Compared with Those of Other and Similar Regions.* Boston: Gould, Kendall and Lincoln, 1850.

Alexander, Jeff. *Pandora's Locks: The Opening of the Great Lakes–St. Lawrence Seaway.* East Lansing: Michigan State University Press, 2009.

Alghoul, Fares. "Beauty of One of North America's Oldest Nude Beaches Highlighted in Toronto Art Exhibit." *Toronto Star*, 11 March 2023. https://www.thestar.com/life/together/2023/03/11/beauty-of-one-of-north-americas-oldest-nude-beaches-highlighted-in-toronto-art-exhibit.html.

Angus, James T. *A Respectable Ditch: A History of the Trent–Severn Waterway, 1833–1920.* Montreal and Kingston: McGill-Queen's University Press, 1988.

Annin, Peter. *Great Lakes Water Wars.* 2nd ed. Washington: Island Press, 2019.

Aquila, Richard. *The Iroquois Restoration: Iroquois Diplomacy on the Colonial Frontier, 1701–1754.* Lincoln: University of Nebraska Press, 1997.

Ashworth, William. *The Late, Great Lakes: An Environmental History.* Toronto: Collins, 1986.

Babian, Sharon A. *Setting Course: A History of Maritime Navigation in Canada.* Transformation Series No. 14. Ottawa: Canada Science and Technology Museum, 2003.

Backhouse, Constance. *Colour-Coded: A Legal History of Racism in Canada, 1900–1950.* Toronto: University of Toronto Press, 1999.

Bain, David. "Recreation on Toronto Island, the Peoples' Resort, 1793–1910." *Ontario History* 111, no. 2 (Fall 2019): 153–80.

Baldwin, Norman S., Robert W. Saalfeld, Margaret Ross Dochoda, Howard J. Buettner, and Randy L. Eshenroder. "Commercial Fish Production in the Great Lakes, 1867–2006." Ann Arbor: Great Lakes Fishery Commission, 2009. http://www.glfc.org/commercial/commerc.php.

Banks, Robert D. *Warriors and Warships: Conflict on the Great Lakes and the Legacy of Point Frederick*. Toronto: Dundurn Press, 2023.

Bannerman, Roger. "Phosphorus Uptake and Release by Lake Ontario Sediments." Corvallis: US Environmental Protection Agency, 1975. New York State Library: LEG 733.1-4 ONFPL 75-10176.

Barbour, Dale. *Undressed Toronto: From the Swimming Hole to Sunnyside, How a City Learned to Love the Beach, 1850–1935*. Winnipeg: University of Manitoba Press, 2021.

Bartram, John. *Observations on the Inhabitants, Climate, Soil, Rivers, Productions, Animals, and Other Matters Worthy of Notice, Made by Mr. John Bartram, in His Travels from Pennsylvania to Onondaga, Oswego and Lake Ontario in Canada, 1751*. London: J. Whiston and B. White, 1751.

Baskerville, Peter. *Sites of Power: A Concise History of Ontario*. Toronto: Oxford University Press, 2005.

Becker, W.H. *From the Atlantic to the Great Lakes: A History of the US Army Corps of Engineers and the St. Lawrence Seaway*. Washington, DC: United States Army Corps of Engineers, 1984.

Benidickson, Jamie. "Private Rights and Public Purposes in the Lakes, Rivers and Streams of Ontario, 1870–1930." In *Essays in Canadian Legal History*, vol. 2, edited by David H. Flaherty, 365–417. Toronto: University of Toronto Press, 1983.

– *The Culture of Flushing: A Social and Legal History of Sewage*. Vancouver: UBC Press, 2007.

– "The IJC and Water Quality in the Bacterial Age." In *The First Century of the International Joint Commission*, edited by Daniel Macfarlane and Murray Clamen, 122–25. Calgary: University of Calgary Press, 2020.

Berger, Todd R. *Lighthouses of the Great Lakes*. Minneapolis: Voyageur Press, 2002.

Biggar, Glenys. *Ontario Hydro's History And Description of Hydro-Electric Generating Stations*. Toronto: Ontario Hydro, 1991.

Blackhawk, Ned. *The Rediscovery of America: Native Peoples and the Unmaking of U.S. History*. New Haven: Yale University Press, 2023.

Blair, Peggy. *Lament for a First Nation: The Williams Treaties of Southern Ontario*. Vancouver: UBC Press, 2008.

Bobiwash, Rodney. "The History of Native People in the Toronto Area: An Overview." In *The Meeting Place: Aboriginal Life in Toronto*, edited by Frances Sanderson and Heather Howard-Bobiwash, 1–15. Toronto: Native Canadian Centre of Toronto, 1997.

Bocking, Stephen. *Ecologists and Environmental Politics: A History of Contemporary Ecology*. New Haven: Yale University Press, 1997.

– "Fishing the Inland Seas: Great Lakes Research, Fisheries Management, and Environmental Policy in Ontario." *Environmental History* 2, no. 1 (1997): 52–73.

Bockner, Louis. "On Tyendinaga Mohawk Territory, the Kenhté:ke Seed Sanctuary Preserves Not Just Plants, but Culture and Language, Too." *Narwhal* (3 January 2022). https://thenarwhal.ca/tyendinaga-mohawk-territory-seed-sanctuary.

Bohaker, Heidi. *Doodem and Council Fire: Anishinaabe Governance through Alliance*. Toronto: University of Toronto Press, 2020.

Bolduc, Denise, Mnawaate Gordon-Corbiere, Rebeka Tabobondung, and Brian Wright-McLeod, eds. *Indigenous Toronto: Stories That Carry This Place*. Toronto: Coach House Books, 2021.

Bogue, Margaret Beattie. *Fishing the Great Lakes: An Environmental History, 1783–1933*. Madison: University of Wisconsin Press, 2000.

Bonnell, Jennifer. *Reclaiming the Don: An Environmental History of Toronto's Don River Valley*. Toronto: University of Toronto Press, 2014.

Botts, Lee, and Paul Muldoon. *Evolution of the Great Lakes Water Quality Agreements*. East Lansing: Michigan State University Press, 2005.

Bouchier, Nancy, and Ken Cruikshank. *The People and the Bay: A Social and Environmental History of Hamilton Harbour*. Vancouver: UBC Press, 2016.

Boyce, Gerry. *Belleville: A Popular History*. Toronto: Dundurn, 2008.

Brahmstedt, Evie S., Hao Zhou, Erin M. Eggleston, Thomas M. Holsen, and Michael R. Twiss. "Assessment of Mercury Mobilization Potential in Upper St. Lawrence River Riparian Wetlands under New Water Level Regulation Management." *Journal of Great Lakes Research* 45 (2019): 735–41.

Brandão, José António. *"Your Fyre Shall Burn No More": Iroquois Policy Towards New France and Its Native Allies to 1701*. Lincoln: University of Nebraska Press, 1997.

Brant, Beth. *I'll Sing 'Til the Day I Die: Conversations with Tyendinaga Elders*. Toronto: McGilligan Books, 1995.

Brant, Corey. *Great Lakes Sea Lamprey: The 70 Year War on a Biological Invader*. Ann Arbor: University of Michigan Press, 2019.

Brenden, Travis O., Russell W. Brown, Mark P. Ebener, Kevin Reid, and Tammy J. Newcomb. "Great Lakes Commercial Fisheries: Historical Overview and Prognoses for the Future." In *Great Lakes Fisheries Policy and Management: A Binational Perspective*, edited by William W. Taylor, Abigail J. Lynch, and Nancy J. Leonard, 339–99. Lansing: Michigan State University Press, 2013.

Brimacombe, Philip. *The Story of Oakville Harbour*. Oakville: Oakville Historical Society, 1975.

Brown, Ron. *From Queenston to Kingston: The Hidden Heritage of Lake Ontario's Shoreline*. Toronto: Dundurn, 2010.

Brooke, John. *Climate Change and the Course of Global History: A Rough Journey*. Cambridge, UK: Cambridge University Press, 2014.

Broyld, dann J. *Borderland Blacks: Two Cities in the Niagara Region during the Final Decades of Slavery*. Baton Rouge: Louisiana State University Press, 2022.

Bryce, B. *A Hydraulic Engineering History of the St. Lawrence Power Project with Special Reference to Regulation of Water Levels and Flows*. Toronto: Ontario Hydro, 1982.

Bukowczyk, John J., Nora Faires, David R. Smith, and Randy Widdis. *Permeable Border: The Great Lakes Basin as Transnational Region, 1650–1990*. Pittsburgh: University of Pittsburgh Press, 2005.

Burd, Camden. *The Roots of Flower City: Horticulture, Empire, and the Remaking of Rochester*. Ithaca: Cornell University Press, forthcoming.

Burlakova, Lyubov, Alexander Y. Karatayev, Allison R. Hrycik, Susan E. Daniel, Knut Mehler, Lars G. Rudstam, James M. Watkins, Ronald Dermott, Jill Scharold, Ashley K. Elgin, and Thomas F. Nalepa. "Six Decades of Lake Ontario Ecological History according to Benthos." *Journal of Great Lakes Research* 48 (2022): 274–88.

Busch, Wolf-Dieter N., and Sandra J. Lary. "Assessment of habitat impairments impacting the aquatic resources of Lake Ontario." *Canadian Journal of Fisheries and Aquatic Sciences* 53, no. S1 (1996): 113–20.

Busch, Wolf-Dieter N., and David P. Braun. "A Case for Accelerated Reestablishment of American Eel in the Lake Ontario and Champlain Watersheds." *Fisheries* 39, no. 7 (July 2014): 298–304.

Campbell, Claire. *Shaped by the West Wind: Nature and History in Georgian Bay*. Vancouver: UBC Press, 2004.

Camu, Pierre. *Saint-Laurent et les grands lacs au temps de la voile, 1608–1850*. LaSalle: Hurtubise, 1996.

– *Le Saint-Laurent et les Grands Lacs au temps de la vapeur, 1850–1950*. LaSalle: Hurtubise, 1996.

Canada and the United States. "Great Lakes Water Quality Agreement," 15 April 1972. https://www.ijc.org/sites/default/files/Docket%20200%201972-04-15%20GLWQA.pdf.

Canada and the United States. "Great Lakes Water Quality Agreement of 1978," 22 November 1978. https://www.ijc.org/sites/default/files/Docket%20200%201978-11-11%20GLWQA.pdf.

Canniff, William. *History of the Settlement of Upper Canada (Ontario), with Special Reference to the Bay of Quinte.* Glasgow: Good Press, 2019 [1869].

Casselman, J.M., L.A. Marcogliese, T. Stewart, and P.V. Hodson. "Status of Upper St. Lawrence and Lake Ontario Eel Stock: 1996." In *The American Eel in Eastern Canada: Stock Status and Management Strategies,* edited by R.H. Peterson, 106–20. Proceedings of Eel Management Workshop, 13–14 January 1997, Quebec City. Canadian Technical Report of Fisheries and Aquatic Sciences No. 2196, Ottawa: Department of Fisheries and Oceans, 1997.

Casselman, J.M., and K.A. Scott, "Fish-Community Dynamics of Lake Ontario: Long-Term Trends in the Fish Populations of Eastern Lake Ontario and the Bay of Quinte." In *State of Lake Ontario: Past, Present and Future,* edited by M. Munawar, 349–83. Stuttgart, Germany: Ecovision World Monographs, 2002.

Chapman, Paul. "Agriculture in Niagara: An Overview." In *Niagara's Changing Landscapes,* edited by Hugh J. Gayler, 279–300. Montreal and Kingston: McGill-Queen's University Press, 1994.

Christie, W.J. "Review of the Changes in the Fish Species Composition of Lake Ontario." Technical Report No. 23. Ann Arbor: Great Lakes Fishery Commission, 1973.

Christie, Catherine E., and John P. Smol. "Ecological Effects of 19th Century Canal Construction and other Disturbances on the Trophic State History of Upper Rideau Lake, Ontario." *Journal of Lake and Reservoir Management* 12, no. 4 (1996): 448–54.

Clamen, Murray, and Daniel Macfarlane. "Plan 2014: The Historical Evolution of Lake Ontario–St. Lawrence River Regulation." *Canadian Water Resources Journal/Revue canadienne des ressources hydriques* 43, no. 4 (2018): 416–31.

Clark, James S. "Climate and Indian Effects on Southern Ontario Forests: A Reply to Campbell and McAndrews." *Holocene* 5 (1995): 371–9.

Coates, Colin and Dagomar Degroot. "'Les bois engendrent les frimas et les gelées': Comprendre le climat en Nouvelle-France." *Revue d'histoire de l'Amérique française* 68, nos. 3–4 (2015): 197–219.

Cochrane, Hugh. *Gateway to Oblivion: The Great Lakes Bermuda Triangle.* Toronto: Doubleday, 1980.

Colborn, Theodora E. *Great Lakes, Great Legacy?* Washington, DC: Conservation Foundation and the Institute for Research and Public Policy, 1990.

Colborn, Theo, Dianne Dumanoski, and John Peterson Myers. *Our Stolen Future: Are We Threatening Our Fertility, Intelligence, and Survival?: A Scientific Detective Story.* New York: Plume, 1997.

Conway, Tenley. "Boundaries and Connectivity: The Lower Don River and

Ashbridge's Bay." In *Reshaping Toronto's Waterfront*, edited by Gene Desfor and Jennefer Laidley, 151–74. Toronto: University of Toronto Press, 2011.

Cook, Isabella A. *Pioneer History of Sodus Point, N.Y.* Sodus Point, NY: Sodus Bay Historical Society, 1994 [1915].

Cooper, James Fenimore. *The Pathfinder.* New York: Oxford World's Classics Edition, 1999 [1840].

Corcoran, Patricia L., Todd Norris, Trevor Ceccanese, Mary Jane Walzak, Paul A. Helm, and Chris H. Marvin. "Hidden Plastics of Lake Ontario, Canada and Their Potential Preservation in the Sediment Record." *Environmental Pollution* 204 (2015): 17–25.

Carnochan, Janet. *Niagara.* Toronto: W. Briggs, 1914.

Crichton, Alex. "Local Officials Demand Action on Rising Lake Ontario Water Levels," WXXI News, 21 April 2017. https://www.wxxinews.org/government/2017-04-21/local-officials-demand-action-on-rising-lake-ontario-water-levels.

Crombie, David. "Royal Commission on the Future of the Toronto Waterfront: Interim Report." Toronto: Minister of Supply and Services Canada, 1989.

Crowder, A.A. "Rates of Natural and Anthropogenic Change in Shoreline Habitats in the Kingston Basin, Lake Ontario." *Canadian Journal of Fisheries and Aquatic Science* 53, no. S1 (1996): 121–35.

Duncan, Colin. *The Centrality of Agriculture: Between Humankind and the Rest of Nature.* Montreal and Kingston: McGill-Queen's University Press, 1996.

Duncan, Colin A.M., and Andrew Marcille. "Meditations on Ice." In *Border Flows: A Century of the Canadian-American Water Relationship*, edited by Lynne Heasley and Daniel Macfarlane, 273–6. Calgary: University of Calgary Press, 2016.

DeBues, Max J., M. Catherine Eimers, Shaun A. Watmough, Mohamed N. Mohamed, and Jessica Mueller. "Stream Nutrient and Agricultural Land-Use Trends from 1971 to 2010 in Lake Ontario Tributaries." *Journal of Great Lakes Research* 45 (2019): 752–61.

Degroot, Dagomar. *The Frigid Golden Age: Climate Change, the Little Ice Age, and the Dutch Republic, 1560–1720.* Cambridge, UK: Cambridge University Press, 2019.

Dempsey, Dave. *On the Brink: The Great Lakes in the 21st Century.* Lansing: Michigan State University Press, 2004.

Desbarats, Catherine, and Allan Greer. "North America from the Top Down: Visions of New France." *Journal of Early American History* 5 (Fall 2015): 109–36.

Dobiesz, Norine E., and Nigel P. Lester. "Changes in Mid-Summer Water Temperature and Clarity across the Great Lakes between 1968 and 2002." *Journal of Great Lakes Research* 35 (2009): 371–84.

Dorsey, Kurkpatrick. *The Dawn of Conservation Diplomacy: U.S.–Canadian Wildlife Protection Treaties in the Progressive Era*. Seattle: University of Washington Press, 1998.

Drescher, Nuala. *Engineers for the Public Good: A History of the Buffalo District, U.S. Army Corps of Engineers*. Washington, DC: United States Army Corps of Engineers, 1999.

Du Bois, Eugene E. *The City of Frederick Douglass: Rochester's African-American People and Places*. Rochester: Landmark Society of Western New York, 1994.

Durham, R.W., and B.G. Oliver. "History of Lake Ontario Contamination from the Niagara River by Sediment Radiodating and Chlorinated Hydrocarbon Analysis." *Journal of Great Lakes Research* 9, no. 2 (1983): 160–8.

Egan, Dan. *The Death and Life of the Great Lakes*. New York: Norton, 2018.

Egerton, Frank N. "History of Ecological Sciences, Part 50: Formalizing Limnology, 1870s to 1920s." *Bulletin of the Ecological Society of America*. Hoboken: Wiley Periodicals, 2016.

Egerton, Frank N. "History of Ecological Sciences, Part 57: Aspects of Limnology in America, 1930s to about 1990, Led by Hutchinson and Hasler." *Bulletin of the Ecological Society of America*. Hoboken: Wiley Periodicals, 2016.

Ellsworth, Joan E. "The Eastern Lake Ontario Commercial Fishery, 1673–1900." MA thesis, Queen's University, 1983.

Englebert, Robert, and Andrew Wegmann, eds. *French Connections: Cultural Mobility in North America and the Atlantic World, 1600–1875*. Baton Rouge: Louisiana State University Press, 2020.

Environmental Law and Policy Center. "An Assessment of the Impacts of Climate Change on the Great Lakes." Chicago: Environmental Law and Policy Center, 2020.

Environmental Protection Agency and Canada, *State of the Great Lakes 2022 Report*. Washington and Ottawa: 2022.

Environmental Protection Agency and New York Department of Environmental Conservation. "Lakewide Impacts of Critical Pollutants on United States Boundary Waters of Lake Ontario." New York and Albany: EPA and NYSEC, 1994.

Eshenroder, Randy L., and Brian F. Lantry. "Recent Changes in Successional State of the Deep-Water Fish Communities of Lakes Michigan, Huron, and Ontario and Management Implications." In *Great Lakes Fisheries Policy and Management*, edited by William W. Taylor, Abigail J. Lynch, and Nancy J. Leonard, 137–66. Lansing: Michigan State University Press, 2013.

Evenden, Matthew. *Allied Power: Mobilizing Hydro-Electricity during Canada's Second World War*. Toronto: University of Toronto Press, 2015.

Eyles, N., M. Doughty, J.I. Boyce, M. Meriano, and P. Chow Fraser. "Geophysical and Sedimentological Assessment of Urban Impacts in a Lake Ontario Watershed and Lagoon: Frenchman's Bay, Pickering, Ontario," *Geoscience Canada* 3, no. 30 (2003): 115–28.

Eyles, N., M. Meriano, and P. Chow-Fraser. "Impacts of European Settlement (1840–Present) in a Great Lake Watershed and Lagoon: Frenchman's Bay, Lake Ontario, Canada." *Environmental Earth Sciences* 68, no. 8 (2013): 2211–28.

Fairburn, Jane. *Along the Shore: Rediscovering Toronto's Waterfront Heritage*. Toronto: ECW Press, 2013.

Farfaglia, Jim. *Nestle in Fulton, New York: How Sweet It Was*. Mount Pleasant, SC: Arcadia, 2018.

Fenton, William N. *The Great Law and the Longhouse: A Political History of the Iroquois Confederacy*. Norman: University of Oklahoma Press, 2010.

Fergen, Joshua T., Ryan D. Bergstrom, Michael R. Twiss, Lucinda Johnson, Alan Steinman, and Valoree Gagnon. "Updated Census in the Laurentian Great Lakes Watershed: A Framework for Determining the Relationship between the Population and This Aquatic Resource." *Journal of Great Lakes Research* 48, no. 6 (2022): 1337–44.

Flannery, Tim. *The Eternal Frontier: An Ecological History of North America and Its Peoples*. New York: Grove Press, 2002.

Fletcher, Ron. *The Humber: Tales of a Canadian Heritage River*. Toronto: RWF Heritage Publications, 2006.

Flint, R. Warren, and Robert J.J. Stevens. *Lake Ontario: A Great Lake in Transition*. Great Lakes Monograph No. 2. Ann Arbor: Great Lakes Fishery Commission, 1989. New York State Library, SAI 050-4 INVHW 79-70229.

Ford, Ben. *The Shore Is a Bridge: The Maritime Landscape of Lake Ontario*. College Station: Texas A&M University Press, 2018.

Forkey, Neil S. "Maintaining a Great Lakes Fishery: The State, Science, and the Case of Ontario's Bay of Quinte, 1870–1920." *Ontario History* 87 (1995): 45–64.

– *Shaping the Upper Canadian Frontier: Environment, Society, and Culture in the Trent Valley*. Calgary: University of Calgary Press, 2003.

Foster, Jennifer. "Toronto's Leslie Street Spit: Aesthetics and the Ecology of Marginal Land." *Environmental Philosophy* 4 (2007): 117–33.

Foster, Jennifer, and Gail Fraser. "Predators, Prey and the Dynamics of Change at the Leslie Street Spit." In *Urban Explorations: Environmental Histories of the*

Toronto Region, edited by L. Anders Sandberg, Stephen Bocking, Colin Coates, and Ken Cruikshank. Titles on Demand, 2013.

Freeman, Bill. *A Magical Place: Toronto Island and Its People*. Toronto: Lorimer, 1999.

French, Orland. *Wind, Water, Barley and Wine: The Nature of Prince Edward Country*. Belleville: Wallbridge House Publishing, 2013.

Futter, Martyn N. "Patterns and Trends in Southern Ontario Lake ice Phenology." *Environmental Monitoring and Assessment* 88 (2003): 431–44.

Gargan, John Joseph. "The Politics of Water Pollution in New York State: The Development and Adoption of the 1965 Pure Water Program." PhD diss., Syracuse University, 1968.

Gateley, Susan Peterson. *Sweet Water Stories of Lake Ontario*. Wolcott: Whiskey Hill Press, 1998.

– *Saving The Beautiful Lake: A Quest For Hope*. Self-published, Lulu.com, 2016.

– *A Natural History of Lake Ontario*. Cheltenham, UK: History Press, 2021.

Gayler, Hugh J. "Urban Development and Planning in Niagara." In *Niagara's Changing Landscapes*, edited by Hugh J. Gayler. Montreal and Kingston: McGill-Queen's University Press, 1994.

Genesee/Finger Lakes Regional Planning Board. *The Lake Ontario Shoreline: A Regional Overview of Environmental Problems*. Rochester, NY: Genesee/Finger Lakes Regional Planning Board and US Department of Housing and Urban Development, 1971.

Gibson, Sally. *More than an Island: A History of the Toronto Island*. Toronto: Clarke Irwin, 1984.

Gifford, Jim. *Hurricane Hazel: Canada's Storm of the Century*. Toronto: Dundurn Press, 2004.

Gidgaa Migizi (Doug Williams). *Michi Saagiig Nishnaabeg: This Is Our Territory*. Winnipeg: ARP Books, 2018.

Gilbert, Robert. "Ice on Lake Ontario at Kingston." *Journal of Great Lakes Research* 17, no. 3 (1991): 403–11.

Government of Canada, Department of Marine and Fisheries. *First Annual Report*. Ottawa: Department of Marine and Fisheries, 1869.

Goodman, Carl F. "Canada–United States Settlement of Gut Dam Claims: Report of the Agent of the United States Before the Lake Ontario Claims Tribunal." *International Legal Materials* 8, no. 1 (1969): 118–43.

Grady, Wayne. *The Great Lakes: The Natural History of a Changing Region*. Toronto: Greystone Books, 2011.

Grbic, J., P. Helm, S. Athey, and C.M. Rochman. "Microplastics Entering Northwestern Lake Ontario Are Diverse and Linked to Urban Sources." *Water Research* 174 (2020): 1–10.

Great Lakes Commission. *Annual Report of the Great Lakes Regional Water Use Database: Representing 2021 Water Use Data*. Ann Arbor: Great Lakes Commission, 2022. https://waterusedata.glc.org/pdf/2021-Water-Use-Report-FINAL.pdf.

Great Lakes Fishery Commission. "Limnological Survey of Lake Ontario, 1964." Technical Report No. 14. Ann Arbor, MI: Great Lakes Fishery Commission, 1969.

Great Lakes United. *The Great Lakes Green Book: Summary of a Citizens' Action Agenda for Restoring the Great Lakes–St. Lawrence River Ecosystem*. Toronto: Great Lakes United, 2003.

Green, Walter Henry. *History, Reminiscences, Anecdotes, and Legends of Great Sodus Bay, Sodus Point, Sloop Landing, Sodus Village, Pultneyville, Maxwell*. 2nd ed. Rochester: Henderson-Mosher, 1947.

Grover, Velma I., and Gail Krantzberg, eds. *Great Lakes: Lessons in Participatory Governance*. Boca Raton: CRC Press, 2012.

Guiry, Eric J., Michael Buckley, Trevor J. Orchard, Alicia L. Hawkins, Suzanne Needs-Howarth, Erling Holm, and Paul Szpak. "Deforestation Caused Abrupt Shift in Great Lakes Nitrogen Cycle." *Limnology and Geography* 65, no. 8 (2020): 1921–35.

Haile, Clarence L., Gilman D. Veith, G. Fred Lee, and William C. Boyle. *Chlorinated Hydrocarbons in the Lake Ontario Ecosystem (IFYGL)*. Ecological Research Series. Washington, DC: EPA, 1975.

Hamalainen, Pekka. *Indigenous Continent: The Epic Conquest for North America*. New York: Liveright, 2022.

Harris, Amy Lavender. *Imagining Toronto*. Toronto: Mansfield Press, 2010.

Harris, Cole. *The Reluctant Land: Society, Space, and Environment in Canada Before Confederation*. Vancouver: UBC Press, 2008.

Hartshorn, Max. "Strange Things Out There: Inside Lake Ontario's 'Bermuda Triangle.'" *Global News*, 18 August 2021. https://globalnews.ca/news/8140913/lake-ontario-vortex-marysburgh-bermuda-triangle-zed-files.

Hartig, John. *Burning Rivers: Revival of Four Urban-Industrial Rivers That Caught Fire*. London: Multi-Science, 2010.

Hartig, John, and Michael Zarull. *Under RAPS: Toward Grassroots Ecological Democracy in the Great Lakes Basin*. Ann Arbor: University of Michigan Press, 1992.

Hartig, John, and M. Munawar. *Ecosystem-Based Management of Laurentian*

Great Lakes Areas of Concern: Three Decades of U.S.-Canadian Cleanup and Recovery. East Lansing, MI: Michigan State University Press, 2021.

Hauptman, Laurence M. *The Iroquois Struggle for Survival: World War II to Red Power*. Syracuse: Syracuse University Press, 1986.

– *Conspiracy of Interests: Iroquois Dispossession and the Rise of New York State*. Syracuse: Syracuse University Press, 2001.

– *In the Shadow of Kinzua: The Seneca Nation of Indians since World War II*. Syracuse: Syracuse University Press, 2014.

Heasley, Lynne. *The Accidental Reef and other Ecology Odysseys in the Great Lakes*. East Lansing: Michigan State University Press, 2021.

Heasley, Lynne, and Daniel Macfarlane. "Negotiating Abundance and Scarcity: Introduction to a Fluid Border." In *Border Flows: A Century of the Canadian–American Water Relationship*, edited by Lynne Heasley and Daniel Macfarlane. Calgary: University of Calgary Press, 2016.

Heasley, Lynne, and Daniel Macfarlane, eds. *Border Flows: A Century of the Canadian-American Water Relationship*. Calgary: University of Calgary Press, 2016.

Hele, Karl S., ed. *Lines Drawn upon the Water: First Nations and the Great Lakes Borders and Borderlands*. Waterloo: Wilfrid Laurier University Press, 2008.

– *The Nature of Empire and the Empires of Nature: Indigenous Peoples and the Great Lakes Environment*. Waterloo: Wilfrid Laurier University Press, 2013.

Hewer, Michah J., and William A. Gough. "Lake Ontario Ice Coverage: Past, Present and Future." *Journal of Great Lakes Research* 45 (2019): 1080–9.

Hill, A. Suzanne. "A Serpent in the Garden: Implications of Development in Canada's Niagara Fruit Belt." *Journal of Historical Sociology* 15, no. 4 (2002): 495–514.

Hill, Susan M. *The Clay We Are Made Of: Haudenosaunee Land Tenure on the Grand River*. Winnipeg: University of Manitoba Press, 2017.

Hoggarth, James. *Waashkiigmaang Nbi Wi – Nagamo: Our Curve Lake First Nation Water Song Sharing Oral History*. Community publication funded by Canadian Water Network, Createspace Independent Publishing Platform, 2017.

Hough, Jack Luin. *The Geology of the Great Lakes*. Urbana: University of Illinois Press, 1958.

Hristova, Bobby. "Ontario Issues Order for Hamilton to Improve Sewage Monitoring after Spills into Lake Ontario." CBC News, 18 January 2023. https://www.cbc.ca/news/canada/hamilton/ontario-order-sewage-hamilton-1.6718374.

International Joint Commission. *Water Levels of Lake Ontario: Report to the Government of Canada and the Government of the United States*. Ottawa and Washington: IJC, 1961.

– *Pollution of Lake Erie, Lake Ontario and the International Section of the St. Lawrence River*. Ottawa and Washington: IJC, 1970.
– *Further Regulation of the Great Lakes*. Ottawa and Washington: IJC, 1976.
– *Great Lakes Diversions and Consumptive Uses: Final Report*. Ottawa and Washington: IJC, 1985.
– "Fifth Biennial Report under the Great Lakes Water Quality Agreement of 1978." Ottawa and Washington: IJC, 1990.
– *Levels Reference Study: Great Lakes–St. Lawrence River Basin*. Ottawa and Washington: IJC, 1993.
– *Protection of the Great Lakes Report*. Ottawa and Washington: IJC, 2000.
– *Status of Restoration Activities in Great Lakes Areas of Concern: A Special Report*. Ottawa and Washington: IJC, 2003. https://www.ijc.org/sites/default/files/aoc_report-e.pdf.
– "History of the Lake Ontario–St. Lawrence River Order of Approval and the Regulation Plan and Related Studies." Ottawa and Washington: IJC Staff Paper, 2012.
– *Lake Ontario–St. Lawrence River Plan 2014: A Report to the Government of Canada and the Unites States by the International Joint Commission*. Ottawa and Washington: IJC, 2014. http://www.ijc.org/en_/Plan2014/Report.
– *Second Triennial Assessment of Progress on Great Lakes Water Quality*. Ottawa and Washington: IJC, 2020. https://ijc.org/en/2020-TAP-Report.
International Lake Erie Water Pollution Board and the International Lake Ontario–St. Lawrence River Water Pollution Board. *Pollution of Lake Erie, Lake Ontario and the International Section of the St. Lawrence River*. Ottawa and Washington: IJC, 1969. https://www.ijc.org/sites/default/files/C118.pdf.
Jackson, John N. *The Welland Canals and Their Communities: Engineering, Industrial, and Urban Transformation*. Toronto: University of Toronto Press, 1997.
Jackson, John N., with John Burtniak and Gregory P. Stein. *The Mighty Niagara: One River – Two Frontiers*. Amherst: Prometheus Books, 2003.
Jackson, Paul S.B. "From Liability to Profitability: How Disease, Fear, and Medical Science Cleaned up the Marshes of Ashbridge's Bay." In *Reshaping Toronto's Waterfront*, edited by Gene Desfor and Jennefer Laidley, 75–96. Toronto: University of Toronto Press, 2011.
Jameson, Anna. *Winter Studies and Summer Rambles in Canada*. London: Saunders and Otley, 1838.
Jenks, Andrew. "Model City USA: The Environmental Costs of Victory in World War II and the Cold War." *Environmental History* 12 (2007): 552–77.
Joan Holmes and Associates, and Victor Konrad, "Mohawks of Bay of Quinte

Resource Harvesting Activities: Final Report." Ottawa: Joan Holmes and Associates, 1999.

Joan Holmes and Associates. "Aboriginal Title Claim to Water Within the Traditional Lands of the Mississaugas of the New Credit." Ottawa: Joan Holmes and Associates, 2015. http://mncfn.ca/wp-content/uploads/2017/02/MNC-Aboriginal-Title-Report.pdf.

Johnson, Jon. "The Indigenous Environmental History of Toronto, 'The Meeting Place.'" In *Urban Explorations: Environmental Histories of the Toronto Region*, edited by L. Anders Sandberg, Stephen Bocking, Colin Coates, and Ken Cruikshank, 59–71. Titles on Demand, 2013.

Kaiser, Klaus L.E. "Mirex: An Unrecognized Contaminant of Fishes from Lake Ontario." *Science* 185, no. 4150 (1974): 523–5.

Kaminsky, Ray, Klaus L.E. Kaiser, and Ronald A. Hites. "Fates of Organic Compounds from Niagara Falls Dumpsites in Lake Ontario." *Journal of Great Lakes Research* 9, no. 2 (1983): 183–9.

Karamanski, Theodore. *Mastering the Inland Seas: How Lighthouses, Navigational Aids, and Harbors Transformed the Great Lakes and America*. Madison: University of Wisconsin Press, 2020.

Kehoe, Terence. *Cleaning Up the Great Lakes: From Cooperation to Confrontation*. Dekalb: Northern Illinois University Press, 1997.

Kehm, Walter H. *Accidental Wilderness: The Origins and Ecology of Toronto's Tommy Thompson Park*. Toronto: University of Toronto Press, 2020.

Kerr, S.J. "An Historical Review of Fish Culture, Stocking and Fish Transfers in Ontario, 1865–2004." Peterborough: Fish and Wildlife Branch, Ontario Ministry of Natural Resources, 2006.

Ketola, H. George, Paul R. Bowser, Gregory A. Wooster, Leslie R. Wedge, and Steven S. Hurst. "Effects of Thiamine on Reproduction of Atlantic Salmon and a New Hypothesis for Their Extirpation in Lake Ontario." *Transactions of the American Fisheries Society* 129 (2000): 607–12.

Kennard, Jim, with Roland Stevens and Roger Pawlowski. *Shipwrecks of Lake Ontario: A Journey of Discovery*. Toledo: National Museum of the Great Lakes, 2019.

Kennedy, Gregory, and William Kappel. "Survey of Lake Ontario Bottom Sediment off Rochester, New York, to Define the Extent of Jettisoned World War Materiel and its Potential for Sediment Contamination." Ithaca: NYSDEC and USGS, 2000. New York State Library: SAI 045-4 SURIT 219-1168.

Kheraj, Sean. "A History of Long-Distance Oil Spills in Canada," *Canadian Historical Review* 101, no. 2 (2020): 161–91.

Killan, Gerald. *Protected Places: A History of Ontario's Provincial Parks System.* Toronto: Dundurn Press, 1993.

Kimmerer, Robin Wall. *Braiding Sweetgrass: Indigenous Wisdom, Scientific Knowledge, and the Teaching of Plants.* Minneapolis: Milkweed Editions, 2013.

Knight, William. "Samuel Wilmot, Fish Culture, and Recreational Fisheries in late 19th Century Ontario." *Scientia Canadensis* 30, no. 1 (2007): 75–90.

Knight, William, and Stephen Bocking. "Fisheries, Invasive Species, and the Formation and Fracturing of the Great Lakes System." *Canadian Geographer/ Le Geographe canadien* 60, no. 4 (2016): 446–57.

Koch, Alexander, Chris Brierley, Mark M. Maslin, and Simon L. Lewis. "Earth System Impacts of the European Arrival and Great Dying in the Americas after 1492." *Quaternary Science Reviews* 207 (2019): 13–36.

Konrad, Victor. "An Iroquois Frontier: The North Shore of Lake Ontario during the Late Seventeenth Century." *Journal of History Geography* 7, no. 2 (1981): 129–44.

Kornfeld, Itzchak E. *Transboundary Water Disputes: State Conflict and the Assessment of Their Adjudication.* Cambridge, UK: Cambridge University Press, 2019.

Krantzberg, Gail. "The Great Lakes Remedial Action Plan Program: A Historical and Contemporary Description and Analysis." In *The First Century of the International Joint Commission*, edited by Daniel Macfarlane and Murray Clamen, 367–93. Calgary: University of Calgary Press, 2020.

Krantzberg, Gail, Savitri Jetoo, Velma I. Grover, and Sandhya Babel, eds. *Plastic Pollution: Nature Based Solutions and Effective Governance.* Boca Raton: CRC Press: 2023.

La Rocque, Barbara Wall. *Wolfe Island: A Legacy in Stone.* Toronto: Dundurn, 2009.

Lake Ontario Partnership. *Lake Ontario: Lakewide Action and Management Plan, 2018–2022.* Ottawa and Washington: Environment and Climate Change Canada and the US Environmental Protection Agency, 2018.

Langston, Nancy. *Toxic Bodies: Hormone Disruptors and the Legacy of DES.* New Haven: Yale University Press, 2010.

– *Sustaining Lake Superior: An Extraordinary Lake in a Changing World.* New Haven: Yale University Press, 2017.

– *Climate Ghosts: Migratory Species in the Anthropocene.* Waltham: Brandeis University Press, 2021.

Larkin, Janet Dorothy. *Overcoming Niagara: Canals, Commerce, and Tourism in the Niagara-Great Lakes Borderland Region, 1792–1837.* Albany: SUNY Press, 2018.

Lenters, John D. "Long Term Trends in the Seasonal Cycle of Great Lakes Water Levels." *Journal of Great Lakes Research* 27, no. 3 (2001): 342–53.

Leveridge, Bill. *Fair Sport: A History of Sports at the Canadian National Exhibition Since 1879.* Toronto: Canadian National Exhibition, 1978.

Liong-Ting Hang, Walter, and Joseph P. Salvo. *Ravaged River: Toxic Chemicals in the Niagara.* New York: New York Public Interest Research Group, 1981.

Litten, Simon. "Toxic Chemicals in NYS Tributaries to Lake Ontario: A Report on Sampling Undertaken in 2007 and 2008 with Special Emphasis on the Polychlorinated Dibenzodioxins and Furans." New York: EPA, 2009. https://www.dec.ny.gov/data/DecDocs/932121/Report.HW.932121.2009-03-26.ToxicsChemicalsInTributariesToLakeOntario.pdf.

Liu, F.S., B.R. Lockett, R.J. Sorichetti, S.A. Watmough, and M.C. Eimers. "Agricultural Intensification Leads to Higher Nitrate Levels in Lake Ontario." *Science of the Total Environment* 830 (2022): 154534.

Lizars, Kathleen Macfarlane. *The Valley of the Humber, 1615–1913.* Toronto: W. Briggs, 1913.

Lu, Hon Q., and Gene Desfor, "Cleaning Up the Waterfront: Development of Contaminated Sites." In *Reshaping Toronto's Waterfront,* edited by Gene Desfor and Jennefer Laidley, 245–62. Toronto: University of Toronto Press, 2011.

Lyon-Jenness, Cheryl. *For Shade and for Comfort: Democratizing Horticulture in the Nineteenth-Century Midwest.* West Lafeyette: Purdue University Press, 2003.

Lytwyn, Victor P. "Waterworld: The Aquatic Territory of the Great Lakes First Nations." In *Gin Das Winan: Documenting Aboriginal History in Ontario,* Occasional Papers No. 2, edited by Dale Standen and David McNab. Toronto: Champlain Society, 1996.

MacLeitch, Gail. *Imperial Entanglements: Iroquois Change and Perspective on the Frontiers of Empire.* Philadelphia: University of Pennsylvania Press, 2001.

Macfarlane, Daniel. "'A Completely Man-Made and Artificial Cataract': The Transnational Manipulation of Niagara Falls." *Environmental History* 18, no. 4 (2013): 759–84.

– *Negotiating a River: Canada, the US, and the Creation of the St. Lawrence Seaway.* Vancouver: UBC Press, 2014.

– "'As Nearly as May Be': Estimating Ice and Water in the Niagara and St. Lawrence Rivers." *Journal of Historical Geography* 65 (2019): 73–84.

– *Fixing Niagara Falls: Environment, Energy, and Engineers at the World's Most Famous Waterfall.* Vancouver: UBC Press, 2020.

– "Nature Empowered: Hydraulic Models and the Engineering of Niagara Falls." *Technology and Culture* 61, no. 1 (2020): 109–43.

– *Natural Allies: Environment, Energy, and the History of US–Canada Relations.*
Montreal and Kingston: McGill-Queen's University Press, 2023.

Macfarlane, Daniel, and Andrew Watson. "Hydro Democracy: Water Power and
Political Power in Ontario." *Scientia Canadensis* 40, no. 1 (2018): 1–18.

Macfarlane, Daniel, and Noah Hall. "Transborder Water Management and Governance in the Great Lakes–St. Lawrence Basin." In *Transboundary Environmental Governance Across the World's Longest Border,* edited by Stephen Brooks
and Andrea Olive, 31–50. East Lansing: Michigan State University Press, 2018.

Macfarlane, Daniel, and Lynne Heasley. "Water, Oil, and Fish: The Chicago River
as a Transnational Matrix of Place." In *City of Lake and Prairie: Chicago's Environmental History,* edited by Kathleen Brosnan, Will Barnett, and Ann Keating,
91–106. Pittsburgh: University of Pittsburgh Press, 2020.

MacGregor, Rob, Alastair Mathers, Peter Thompson, John M. Casselman, John
M. Dettmers, Steven LaPan, Thomas C. Pratt, and Bill Allen. "Declines of
American Eel in North America: Complexities Associated with Bi-national
Management." *American Fisheries Society Symposium* 62 (2008). http://glfc.org/
pubs/clc/aeel2008.pdf.

MacNaughton, Colleen. "More than a Drop in the Bucket: Public Attitudes and
the Development of Water Service in Kingston, Ontario, 1842–1894." *Historic
Kingston* 43 (1995): 55–68.

Makarewicz, Joseph C., Betsy Landre, Stephen Lewandowski, John Terninko,
and Elizabeth Thorndike. "Lake Ontario Coastal Initiative Action Agenda."
Technical Report No. 21. Rochester: Lake Ontario Coastal Initiative, 2006.

Malcomson, Robert. *Lords of the Lake: The Naval War on Lake Ontario, 1812–1814.*
Montreal: Robin Brass Studio, 2001.

Manion, N.C., L. Campbell, and A. Rutter. "Historic Brownfields and Industrial
Activity in Kingston, Ontario: Assessing Potential Contributions to Mercury
Contamination in Sediment of the Cataraqui River." *Science of the Total
Environment* 408 (2010): 2060–7.

Martin, John P. "The Oil and Gas Industry in the Empire State: Past, Present and
Future." Search and Discovery Article No. 110134. American Association of
Petroleum Geologists, 2010. https://www.searchanddiscovery.com/documents/
2010/110134martin/ndx_martin.pdf.

Martin, Roscoe C. *Water for New York: A Study in State Administration of Water
Resources.* Syracuse: Syracuse University Press, 1960.

McCalla, Douglas. *Planting the Province: The Economic History of Upper Canada
1784–1870.* Toronto: University of Toronto Press, 1993.

– *Consumers in the Bush: Shopping in Rural Upper Canada*. Montreal and Kingston: McGill-Queen's University Press, 2015.

Mcclearn, Matthew. "As Ice Cover Dwindles on the Great Lakes, Researchers Scramble to Understand the Implications." *Globe and Mail*, 12 March 2023. https://www.theglobeandmail.com/canada/article-great-lakes-ice-coverage-decline.

McCullough, A.B. *The Commercial Fishery of the Canadian Great Lakes*. Ottawa: Minister of the Environment, 1989.

McDermott, Meaghan M., and Steve Orr. Rochester. "Muddled Maps Complicate Future of Lake Ontario Shoreline." *Democrat and Chronicle*, 8 January 2018. https://www.democratandchronicle.com/story/news/2018/01/08/maps-lake-ontario-shoreline/1003068001.

McDonnell, Michael. *Masters of Empire: Great Lakes Indians and the Making of America*. New York: Hill and Wang, 2015.

McFadden, David W. *A Trip Around Lake Ontario*. Toronto: Coach House Press, 1988.

McGoldrick, Daryl J., and Elizabeth W. Murphy. "Concentration and Distribution of Contaminants in Lake Trout and Walleye from the Laurentian Great Lakes (2008–2012)." *Environmental Pollution* 217 (2016): 85–96.

McGreevy, Patrick. *Imagining Niagara: The Meaning and Making of Niagara Falls*. Amherst: University of Massachusetts Press, 1994.

McGucken, William. *Lake Erie Rehabilitated: Controlling Cultural Eutrophication, 1960s–1990s*. Akron: University of Akron Press, 2000.

McKelvey, Blake. *Rochester: The Water Power City, 1812–1854*. Cambridge, MA: Harvard University Press, 1945.

– *Rochester: The Flower City, 1855–1890*. Cambridge, MA: Harvard University Press, 1949.

– "The Port of Rochester: A History of its Lake Trade." *Rochester History* 16, no. 4 (1954): 1–24.

– *Rochester: The Quest for Quality, 1890–1925*. Cambridge, MA: Harvard University Press, 1956.

– *Rochester: An Emerging Metropolis, 1925–1961*. Cambridge, MA: Harvard University Press, 1961.

– *Snow in the Cities: A History of America's Urban Response*. Rochester: University of Rochester Press, 1995.

McMahon, Michael. "Toronto's Urban Organic Machines: The R.C. Harris Water Treatment Plant and the Ashbridge's Bay Wastewater Treatment Plant." In

Urban Explorations: Environmental Histories of the Toronto Region, edited by L. Anders Sandberg, Stephen Bocking, Colin Coates, and Ken Cruikshank, 189–209. Titles on Demand, 2013.

McNaught, Donald C., Marlene Buzzard, and Steve Levine, "Zooplankton Production in Lake Ontario as Influenced by Environmental Perturbations." Washington, DC: EPA, 1975.

McNeill, J.R., and Peter Engelke. *The Great Acceleration: An Environmental History of the Anthropocene since 1945*. Cambridge, MA: Harvard University Press, 2016.

Meach, J.H. *Illustrated Historical Atlas of the Counties of Frontenac, Lennox, Addington*. Philadelphia: Borquin, 1878.

Meehan, O.M. "The Canadian Hydrographic Service: From the Time of Its Inception in 1883 to the End of the Second World War." Edited by William Glover, with David Gray. Ottawa: Canadian Nautical Research Society, 2004.

Meisner, J.D., J.L. Goodier, H.A. Regier, B.J. Shuter, and W.J. Christie. "An Assessment of the Effects of Climate Warming on Great Lakes Basin Fishes." *Journal of Great Lakes Research* 13 (1987): 340–52.

Melosi, Martin. *The Sanitary City: Urban Infrastructure in America from Colonial Times to the Present*. Baltimore, MD: Johns Hopkins University Press, 2000.

Mika, Nick, and Helma Mika. *Mosaic of Belleville: An Illustrated History of a City*. Belleville: Mika Silk Screening, 1966.

Mills, E.L., J.M. Casselman, R. Dermott, J.D. Fitzsimons, G. Gal, K.T. Holeck, J.A. Hoyle et al. "A Synthesis of Ecological and Fish-Community Changes in Lake Ontario, 1970–2000." Technical Report No. 67. Ann Arbor: Great Lakes Fishery Commission, 2005.

Milner, J.W. "Report on the Fisheries of the Great Lakes: The Result of Inquiries Prosecuted in 1871 and 1872 (1874)." In *United States Commission of Fish and Fisheries*, "Part II, The Report of the Commissioner for 1872 and 1873," Appendix A: The Fisheries of the Great Lakes.

Minns, C.B., D.A. Hurley, and K.H. Nicholls, eds. *Project Quinte: Point Source Phosphorus Control and Ecosystem Response in the Bay of Quinte, Lake Ontario.* Ottawa: Fisheries and Oceans Canada, Canadian Special Publication of Fisheries and Aquatic Sciences, 1996.

Minns, C.K., M. Munawar, and M.A. Koops, eds. *Ecology of the Bay of Quinte: Health, Management and Global Implications*. Lansing: Michigan State University Press, 2022.

Moir, Michael. "Planning for Change: Harbour Commissions, Civil Engineers, and Large-Scale Manipulation of Nature." In *Reshaping Toronto's Waterfront*, edited by Gene Desfor and Jennefer Laidley, 23–48. Toronto: University of Toronto Press, 2011.

Monmonier, Mark. *Lake Effect: Tales of Large Lakes, Arctic Winds, and Recurrent Snows.* Syracuse: Syracuse University Press, 2012.

Moodie, Susanna. *Roughing It in the Bush; or, Forest Life in Canada.* Toronto: HarperCollins, 2011 [1852].

Moore, Jonathan. "The LaSalle Causeway." *Historic Kingston* 47 (1999): 30–61.

Morgan, Cecilia. *Creating Colonial Pasts: History, Memory, and Commemoration in Southern Ontario, 1860–1980.* Toronto: University of Toronto Press, 2015.

Morrison, Brian P. "Chronology of Lake Ontario Ecosystem and Fisheries." *Aquatic Ecosystem Health and Management* 22, no. 3 (2019): 294–305.

Neilson, Melanie A. "Trace Metals in Lake Ontario." Scientific Series No. 133. Burlington: Inland Waters Directorate, Environment Canada, 1983. New York State Library: ENV 214-4 TOXCN 215-2400.

Nelles, H.V. "The Islands." In *Urban Explorations: Environmental Histories of the Toronto Region*, edited by L. Anders Sandberg, Stephen Bocking, Colin Coates, and Ken Cruikshank, 271–90. Titles on Demand, 2013.

Nelson, Scott Reynolds. *Oceans of Grain: How American Wheat Remade the World.* New York: Basic Books, 2022.

Nriagu, Jerome O., and Henry K.T. Wong. "Historical Records of Metal Pollution in Sediments of Toronto and Hamilton Harbours." *Journal of Great Lakes Research* 9, no. 3 (1983): 365–73.

Oberg, Michael Leroy. *Peacemakers: The Iroquois, the United States, and the Treaty of Canandaigua, 1794.* New York: Oxford University Press, 2015.

O'Connor, John W. "A History of the First Fresh Water Port in the United States." Paper read before the Oswego Historical Society, 24 February 1942. http://oswegohistorian.org/wp-content/uploads/2010/08/A-History-of-the-First-Fresh-Water-Port-in-the-United-States.pdf.

O'Connor, Ryan. *The First Green Wave: Pollution Probe and the Origins of Environmental Activism in Ontario.* Vancouver: UBC Press, 2015.

O'Connor, Kristin, and Chris McLaughlin. "Economic Benefits of Remediating Contaminated Sediments at Hamilton Harbour's Randle Reef." In *Great Lakes Revival: How Restoring Polluted Waters Leads to Rebirth of Great Lakes Communities*, edited by John Hartig, Gail Krantzberg, John C. Austin, and Paula McIntyre. Ann Arbor: IAGLR, 2019.

O'Meara, Jennifer. "Port Granby Low-Level Radioactive Waste Mound Safely Closed." *Clarington This Week*, 28 October 2021. https://www.durhamregion.

com/news-story/10505253-port-granby-low-level-radioactive-waste-mound-safely-closed.

O'Reilly, Henry. *Sketches of Rochester; with Incidental Notices of Western New York.* Rochester: William Alling, 1838.

Ontario Ministry of Natural Resources and Forestry. "Lake Ontario Fish Communities and Fisheries: 2019 Annual Report of the Lake Ontario Management Unit." Picton: Ontario Ministry of Natural Resources and Forestry, 2020. http://www.glfc.org/loc_mgmt_unit/LOA%2020.01.pdf.

Osborne, Brian. "A Canadian 'Riverscape,' National 'Inscape': The St. Lawrence in the Canadian National Imagination." *Études Canadiennes/Canadian Studies: Revue Interdisciplinaire des Études Canadiennes en France* 50 (2001): 257–75.

Osborne, Brian S., and Donald Swainson. *Kingston: Building on the Past.* Westport: Butternut Press, 1988.

Parmenter, Jon. *The Edge of the Woods: Iroquoia 1534–1701.* East Lansing: Michigan State University Press, 2010.

Parsons, Christopher. *A Not-So-New-World: Empire and Environment in French Colonial North America.* Philadelphia: University of Pennsylvania Press, 2018.

Passfield, Robert. *Military Paternalism, Labour, and the Rideau Canal Project.* Bloomington: AuthorHouse, 2013.

Pasternak, Shiri, Sue Collis, and Tia Dafnos. "Criminalization at Tyendinaga: Securing Canada's Colonial Property Regime through Specific Lands Claims." *Canadian Journal of Law and Society/Revue Canadienne Droit et Societe* 28, no. 1 (2013): 65–81.

Patch, S.P., and W.D. Busch. "Fisheries in the St. Lawrence River – Past and Present: A Review of Historical Natural Resources Information and Habitat Changes in the International Section of the St. Lawrence River." Cortland: US Fish and Wildlife Service, 1984.

Patterson, Neil A. "Why Kingston Did Not Become a Major Industrial Centre." *Historic Kingston* 34 (1986): 103–17.

Pielou, E.C. *After the Ice Age: The Return of Life to Glaciated North America.* Chicago: University of Chicago Press, 1992.

Pitkanen, Laura. "A Hot Commodity: Uranium and Containment in the Nuclear State." PhD diss., University of Toronto, 2014.

Pound, Arthur. *Lake Ontario.* New York: Bobbs-Merrill, 1945.

Preston, David. *The Texture of Contact: European and Indian Settler Communities on the Frontiers of Iroquoia, 1667–1783.* Lincoln: University of Nebraska Press, 2009.

Pritchard, James. "For the Glory of God: The Quinte Mission, 1668–1680." *Ontario History* 65 (1973): 133–48.

Prudham, Scott, Gunter Gad, and Richard Anderson. "Networks of Power: Toronto's Waterfront Energy Systems from 1840 to 1970s." In *Reshaping Toronto's Waterfront*, edited by Gene Desfor and Jennefer Laidley, 175–202. Toronto: University of Toronto Press, 2011.

Quinn, Frank H. "Secular Changes in Great Lakes Water Level Seasonal Cycles." *Journal of Great Lakes Research* 28, no. 3 (2002): 451–65.

Rafuse, Ted. *Coal to Canada: A History of the Ontario Car Ferry Company*. Port Hope: Steampower Publishers, 2000.

Rang, S., J. Holmes, S. Slota, D. Bryant, E. Nieboer, and H. Regier. "The Impairment of Beneficial Uses in Lake Ontario." Ottawa: Great Lakes Environment Office, Environment Canada, 1991.

Rannie, William F. *Lincoln: The Story of an Ontario Town*. Beamsville: W.F. Rannie Publisher, 1974.

Raphael, C. Nicholas, Eugene Jaworski, Carl F. Ojala, and Daniel S. Turner. *Future Dredging Quantities in the Great Lakes*. Ecological Research Series. National Environmental Research Center, 1974.

Read, Jennifer. "Origins of the *Great Lakes Water Quality Agreements*: Concepts and Structures." In *The First Century of the International Joint Commission*, edited by Daniel Macfarlane and Murray Clamen, 347–65. Calgary: University of Calgary Press, 2020.

– "Addressing 'A Quiet Horror': The Evolution of Ontario Pollution Control Policy in the International Great Lakes, 1909–1972." PhD diss., University of Western Ontario, 1999.

Recht, Michael. "The Role of Fishing in the Iroquois Economy, 1600–1792." *New York History* 78, no. 4 (1997): 5–30.

Regier, Henry. "A Candidate Hypothesis about Ecogenic Science Applied to Fish and Fisheries within the Great Laurentian Basin during the 19th and 20th Centuries." *AEHM* 22, no. 3 (2019): 238–57.

Regier, H.A., P. Lin, K.K. Ing, and G.A. Wichert. "Likely Responses to Climate Change of Fish Associations in the Laurentian Great Lakes Basin: Concepts, Methods and Findings." *Boreal Environment Research* 1 (1996): 1–15.

Rice, Brian. *The Rotinonshonni: A Traditional Iroquoian History through the Eyes of Teharonhia:wako and Sawiskera*. Syracuse: Syracuse University Press, 2016.

Richter, Daniel. *The Ordeal of the Longhouse: The Peoples of the Iroquois League in the Era of European Colonization*. Chapel Hill: University of North Carolina Press, 1992.

Riley, John L. *The Once and Future Great Lakes Country: An Ecological History.*
Montreal and Kingston: McGill-Queen's University Press, 2013.

Ripmeester, Michael. "'It Is Scarcely to Be Believed...': The Mississauga Indians
and the Grape Island Mission, 1826–1836." *Canadian Geographer/Le Géographe
canadien* 39, no. 2 (1995): 157–68.

Robertson, J. Ross. *The Diary of Mrs. John Graves Simcoe, Wife of the First Lieu-
tenant-Governor of the Province of Upper Canada.* Toronto: W. Briggs, 1911.

Ruhland, Kathleen M., Andrew M. Paterson, and John P. Smol. "Lake Diatom
Responses to Warming: Reviewing the Evidence." *Journal of Paleolimnology* 54
(2015): 1–35.

Russell, Peter. *How Agriculture Made Canada: Farming in the Nineteenth Century.*
Montreal and Kingston: McGill-Queen's University Press, 2012.

Rustige, Rona. *Tyendinaga Tales.* Kingston and Montreal: McGill-Queen's University Press, 1998.

Sanger, Penny. *Blind Faith: The Nuclear Industry in a Small Town.* Toronto:
McGraw-Hill, 1981.

Scarpino, Philip. "Great Lakes Fisheries: International Response to the Decline of
the Fisheries and the Lamprey/Alewife Invasion." In *A History of Water, Volume
2: The Political Economy of Water,* edited by Terje Tvedt and Richard Coopey.
London: I.B. Tauris, 2006.

– "Addressing Cross-Border Pollution of the Great Lakes after World War II: The
Canada–Ontario Agreement and the Great Lakes Water Quality Agreement." In
Transnationalism: Canada–United States History into the Twenty-First Century,
edited by Michael Behiels and Reginald Stuart, 115–32. Montreal and Kingston:
McGill-Queen's University Press, 2010.

Seguin, Marc. *For Want of a Lighthouse: Building the Lighthouses of Eastern Lake
Ontario.* Bloomington: Trafford, 2015.

Shannon, Timothy. *Iroquois Diplomacy on the Early American Frontier.* New York:
Viking Penguin, 2008.

Shaw, Ronald E. *Canals for a Nation: The Canal Era in the United States, 1790–
1860.* Lexington: University of Kentucky Press, 1990.

Shermerhorn, Jacob. "Revisiting Plan 2014," *Rochester Beacon,* 21 April 2022.
https://rochesterbeacon.com/2022/04/21/revisiting-plan-2014.

Shpuniarsky, Heather. *The Village of Hiawatha: A History.* Hiawatha: Hiawatha
First Nation, 2015.

Simpson, Audra. *Mohawk Interruptus: Political Life across the Borders of Settler
States.* Durham: Duke University Press, 2014.

Simpson, Leanne Betasamosake. *As We Have Always Done: Indigenous Freedom through Radical Resistance*. Minneapolis: University of Minnesota Press, 2017.

– *A Short History of the Blockade: Giant Beavers, Diplomacy, and Regeneration in Nishnaabewin*. Edmonton: University of Alberta Press, 2022.

Slonosky, Victoria C. *Climate in the Age of Empire: Weather Observers in Colonial Canada*. Chicago: University of Chicago Press, 2018.

Sly, P.G. "Sedimentology and Geochemistry of Modern Sediments in the Kingston Basin of Lake Ontario." *Journal of Great Lakes Research* 10, no. 4 (1984): 358–74.

Smith, Stanford H. "Early Changes in the Fish Community of Lake Ontario." Great Lakes Fishery Commission Technical Report 60. Ann Arbor: Great Lakes Fishery Commission, 1995.

Smith, Donald B. "The Dispossession of the Mississauga Indians: A Missing Chapter in the Early History of Upper Canada." *Ontario History* 73, no. 2 (1981): 67–87.

– *Sacred Feathers: The Reverend Peter Jones (Kahkewaquonaby) and the Mississauga Indians*. Lincoln: University of Nebraska Press, 1987.

– *Mississauga Portraits: Ojibwe Voices from Nineteenth-Century Canada*. Toronto: University of Toronto Press, 2013.

Smith, Linda Tuhiwai, Eve Tuck, and K. Wayne Yang, eds. *Indigenous and Decolonizing Studies in Education: Mapping the Long View*. New York: Routledge, 2019.

Smithson, Gordon D. "The Coal Merchants of Kingston." *Historic Kingston* 47 (1999): 76–97.

Snider, C.H.J. *Tales From the Great Lakes*. Toronto: Dundurn, 1996.

Snyder, Charles McCool. *Oswego: From Buckskins to Bustles*. Port Washington: Ira J. Friedman, 1968.

Somerville, Kyle. "'This Is Where I Love to Go': The (Re)creation of Place at Ontario Beach Park and the Monroe County Lakeshore." *Rochester History* 75, no. 1 (2013): 1–33.

St Lawrence–Eastern Ontario Commission. "A Proposed Coastal Management Program for the Eastern Shore Dune–Bay–Wetland Complex." Albany: New York Coastal Management Program, New York Department of State, 1979.

Steeves, Paulette. *The Indigenous Paleolithic of the Western Hemisphere*. Lincoln: University of Nebraska Press, 2021.

Stewart, Emily et al. "Pond Sediments on Nesting Islands in Eastern Lake Ontario Provide Insights into the Population Dynamics and Impacts of Waterbird Colonies." *Journal of Great Lakes Research* 45, no. 2 (2019): 350–9.

Stewart, T.J., A. Todd, and S. Lepan. "Fish Community Objectives for Lake Ontario," Fishery Management Document 2017-01. Ann Arbor: Great Lakes Fishery Commission, 2017. http://www.glfc.org/pubs/FisheryMgmtDocs/Fmd17-01.pdf.

Styran, Roberta M., and Robert R. Taylor. *This Great National Object: Building the Nineteenth-Century Welland Canals*. Montreal and Kingston: McGill-Queen's University Press, 2012.

– *This Colossal Project: Building the Welland Ship Canal, 1913–1932*. Montreal and Kingston: McGill-Queen's University Press, 2016.

Stradling, David. *The Nature of New York: An Environmental History of the Empire State*. Ithaca: Cornell University Press, 2010.

Summers, John. "'The Coldest Sport in the World': Iceboating in Toronto Harbour, 1824–1941." *Material History Review* 35 (1992): 35–46.

Swan, Alison, ed. *Fresh Water: Women Writing on the Great Lakes*. Lansing: Michigan State University Press, 2006.

Syed, Fatima. "Dereliction of Doodie: Ontario's Plans for York Region's Sewage Could Hurt the Great Lakes – and US Relations." *Narwhal*, 30 January 2023. https://thenarwhal.ca/great-lakes-agreement-poop.

Szylvian, Kristin M. "Transforming Lake Michigan into the 'World's Greatest Fishing Hole': The Environmental Politics of Michigan's Great Lakes Sport Fishing, 1965–1985." *Environmental History* 9, no. 1 (2004): 102–27.

Tanner, Howard. *Something Spectacular: My Great Lakes Salmon Story*. East Lansing: Michigan State University Press, 2018.

Tarr, Joel. *The Search for the Ultimate Sink: Urban Pollution in Historical Perspective*. Akron: University of Akron Press, 1996.

Taylor, Alan. *The Civil War of 1812: American Citizens, British Subjects, Irish Rebels and Indian Allies*. New York: Penguin, 2011.

Temby, Owen, and Don Munton. "The International Joint Commission and Air Pollution: A Tale of Two Cases." In *The First Century of the International Joint Commission*, edited by Daniel Macfarlane and Murray Clamen, 313–46. Calgary: University of Calgary Press, 2020.

Thomas, Arad. *Pioneer History of Orleans County, New York*. Albion: H.A. Bruner Orleans American Steam Press Print, 1871.

Thomas, R.L. "Lake Ontario Sediments as Indicators of the Niagara River as Primary Source of Contaminants." *Journal of Great Lakes Research* 9, no. 2 (1983): 118–24.

Thompson, Carol. "Combining Algae, Plastic Has 'Scary' Implications for Great Lakes, Experts Fear." *Detroit News*, 2 April 2023. https://www.detroitnews.com/

story/news/environment/2023/04/02/microplastics-algae-great-lakes-envron
mental-problems-wayne-state-university-research/69976455007.

Thwaites, Reuben, ed. *The Jesuit Relations and Allied Documents: Travels and Ex-plorations of the Jesuit Missionaries in New France, 1610–1791* (73 vols., Cleveland, 1896–1901). Hathi Trust: https://babel.hathitrust.org/cgi/mb?a=listis&c=325 346059.

Tiro, Karim M. "A Sorry Tale: Natives, Settlers, and the Salmon of Lake Ontario, 1780–1900." *Historical Journal* 59, no. 4 (2016): 1001–26.

Tomkiewicz, Virginia, and Shirley Cox Husted. *Eight Miles Along the Shore: An Illustrated History of Greece, New York.* Rochester: Flower City Printing, 1982.

Turcotte, Dorothy. *Places and People on Bronte Creek.* Grimsby: Dorothy Turcotte, 1993.

Tushingham, A.M. "Postglacial Uplift Predictions and Historical Water Levels of the Great Lakes." *Journal of Great Lakes Research* 18, no. 3 (1992): 440–55.

US Fish and Wildlife Service. "Report to Congress: Great Lakes Fishery Resources Restoration Study." Washington, DC: Department of the Interior, Fish and Wildlife Service, 1995.

US Army Corps of Engineers. "Fort Niagara: Formerly Used Defense Sites Program Management Action Plan." US Army Corps of Engineers, Environmental Programs, Annual Report to Congress, 2019.

– "Fort Ontario: Formerly Used Defense Sites Program Management Action Plan." US Army Corps of Engineers, Environmental Programs, Annual Report to Congress, 2019.

Utley, William Edward, and Patricia Kay Scott. *Fort Niagara: The Key to the Inland Oceans and the French Movement to Dominate North America.* iUniverse: 2019.

VanNijnatten, Debora and Carolyn Johns. "The International Joint Commission and the Evolution of the Great Lakes Water Quality Agreement: Accountability, Progress Reporting, and Measuring Performance." In *The First Century of the International Joint Commission*, edited by Daniel Macfarlane and Murray Clamen, 395–430. Calgary: University of Calgary Press, 2020.

Visser, Melvin. *Cold, Clear, and Deadly: Unraveling a Toxic Legacy.* East Lansing: Michigan State University Press, 2007.

Warry, N.D., and C.H. Chan. "Organic Contaminants in the Suspended Sediments of the Niagara River." *Journal of Great Lakes Research* 7, no. 4 (1981): 394–403.

Watson, Andrew. "Coal in Canada." In *Powering Up Canada: The History of Power, Fuel, and Energy from 1600*, edited by Ruth Sandwell, 213–49. Montreal and Kingston: McGill-Queen's University Press, 2016.

Watson, Ken. *Engineered Landscapes: The Rideau Canal's Transformation of a Wilderness Waterway*. Ken Watson, 2006. http://www.rideau-info.com/canal/engineered/index.html.

Weidel, Brian C., Scott Minihkeim, Jeremy P. Holden, Jessica Goretzke, and Michael J. Connerton. "Lake Ontario April Prey Fish Survey Results and Alewife Assessment, 2021: A Report from the Lake Ontario Prey Fish Working Group to the Great Lakes Fishery Commission's Lake Ontario Committee." Great Lakes Fisheries Commission, 2021. http://www.glfc.org/pubs/lake_committees/ontario/Weideletal_April_PreyFishSurveyResults_AlewifeAssessment_year2021.pdf.

Weightman, Gavin. *The Frozen Water Trade: How Ice from New England Kept the World Cool*. New York: Harper Collins, 2002.

Wevers, Hank. "When Coal Was King: The Nineteenth Century Kingston Water Works." *Historic Kingston* 61 (2013): 122–32.

Whetung, Madeline. "(En)gendering Shoreline Law: Nishnaabeg Relations Politics Along the Trent–Severn Waterway." *Global Environmental Politics* 19, no. 3 (2019): 16–32.

Whetung-Derrick, Mae. *History of the Ojibwa of the Curve Lake Reserve and Surrounding Area*. 3 vols. Curve Lake: Curve Lake Indian Band 35, 1976.

– "Oshkigmong: The Curve in the Lake – A History of the Mississauga Community of Curve Lake: Origins of the Curve Lake Anishnabek." Peterborough: An Occasional Paper published by the Peterborough Historical Society, 2015.

Whillans, Thomas H. "Changes in Marsh Area Along the Canadian Shore of Lake Ontario." *Journal of Great Lakes Research* 8, no. 3 (1982): 570–7.

White, Richard. *The Middle Ground: Indians, Empires, and Republics in the Great Lakes Region, 1650–1815*. New York: Cambridge University Press, 1991.

White, Sam. *A Cold Welcome: The Little Ice Age and Europe's Encounter with North America*. Cambridge, MA: Harvard University Press, 2017.

Whittle, D.M., and J.D. Fitzsimons. "The Influence of the Niagara River on Contaminant Burdens of Lake Ontario Biota." *Journal of Great Lakes Research* 9, no. 2 (1983): 295–302.

Whyte, Kyle. "Settler Colonialism, Ecology, and Environmental Justice." *Environment and Society* 9, no. 1 (2018): 125–44.

Whyte, Kyle, Chris Caldwell, and Marie Schaefer. "Indigenous Lessons about Sustainability Are Not Just for 'All Humanity.'" In *Sustainability: Approaches to Environmental Justice and Social Power*, edited by Julie Sze. New York: New York University Press, 2018.

Widdis, Randy. "'Across the Boundary in a Hundred Torrents': The Changing Geography of Marine Trade within the Great Lakes Borderlands Region during the Nineteenth and Early Twentieth Centuries." *Annals of the Association of American Geographers* 101, no. 2 (2011): 356–79.

Wilcox, Douglas A., and John A. Bateman. "Photointerpretation Analysis of Plant Communities in Lake Ontario Wetlands following 65 Years of Lake-Level Regulation." *Journal of Great Lakes Research* 44 (2018): 1306–13.

Williams, Kayanesenh Paul. *Kayanerenkó:wa: The Great Law of Peace*. Winnipeg: University of Manitoba Press, 2018.

Williamson, Ronald F., and Robert von Bitter, eds. *The History and Archaeology of the Iroquois du Nord*. Ottawa: University of Ottawa Press, 2023.

Willoughby, William. *The Joint Organizations of Canada and the United States*. Toronto: University of Toronto Press, 1979.

Wong, S. Luek, John F. Wainwright, and Lynda Nakamot. "Monitoring Toxicity in Four Wastewaters in the Bay of Quinte, Lake Ontario." *Journal of Great Lakes Research* 21, no. 3 (1995): 340–52.

Wood, J. David. *Making Ontario: Agricultural Colonization and Landscape Re-Creation Before the Railway*. Montreal and Kingston: McGill-Queen's University Press, 2000.

Woodford, Arthur M. *Charting the Inland Seas: A History of the US Lake Survey*. Washington, DC: US Army Corps of Engineers, 1991.

Wooster, Margaret. *Living Waters: Reading the Rivers of the Lower Great Lakes*. Albany: SUNY Press, 2009.

Wyman, Richard L., and Robert S. Dischel. "Factors Influencing Impingement of Fish by Lake Ontario Power Plants." *Journal of Great Lakes Research* 10, no. 4 (1984): 348–57.

Young, Anna. *Great Lakes' Saga*. Toronto: Richardson, Bond and Wright, 1965.

Zeller, Suzanne. *Inventing Canada: Early Victorian Science and the Idea of a Transcontinental Nation*, 2nd ed. Montreal and Kingston: McGill-Queen's University Press, 2009.

Zhu, Bin, Dean G. Fitzgerald, Susan B. Hoskins, Lars G. Rudstam, Christine M. Mayer, and Edward L. Mills. "Quantification of Historical Changes of Submerged Aquatic Vegetation Cover in Two Bays of Lake Ontario with Three Complementary Methods." *Journal of Great Lakes Research* 33 (2007): 122–35.

Zilberstein, Anya. *A Temperate Empire: Making Climate Change in Early America*. New York: Oxford University Press, 2016.

Index